T0301093

THE WOMEN WHO WOULDN'T WHEESHT

THE WOMEN WHO WOULDN'T WHEESHT

Voices from the frontline of Scotland's
battle for women's rights

Edited by Susan Dalgety and
Lucy Hunter Blackburn

CONSTABLE

CONSTABLE

First published in Great Britain in 2024 by Constable

5 7 9 10 8 6 4

A CIP catalogue record for this book
is available from the British Library.

ISBN: 978-1-40872-070-7

Typeset in Goudy Oldstyle Pro by SX Composing DTP, Rayleigh, Essex
Printed and bound in Great Britain by Clays Ltd, Elcograf S.p.A.

Papers used by Constable are from well-managed forests
and other responsible sources.

Constable
An imprint of
Little, Brown Book Group
Carmelite House
50 Victoria Embankment
London EC4Y 0DZ

An Hachette UK Company
www.hachette.co.uk

www.littlebrown.co.uk

To every woman, past and present, who stood up and spoke out, even when her voice was shaking and her heart breaking. To every girl across the world – may you grow up to be strong, independent women, whose voice is always heard.

Contents

Introduction

wheesht (Scots) *(wiːʃt)*: a plea or demand for silence (exclamation); to silence (a person, etc.) or to be silent (verb)[*]

This book captures an important moment in contemporary political history: the five years that preceded the down-fall of Scotland's first woman first minister who, at the height of her powers, with an iron grip on her party, unexpectedly resigned, weakened in part by an unprecedented campaign by an army of Scottish women, determined to stop what they saw as a profound assault on their human rights.

Written by many of the women whose views were once dismissed by Nicola Sturgeon as 'not valid', it tells the story of a grassroots movement that took on the Scottish political establishment and its supporters in civil society, breaking down barriers between political opponents, and uniting novice campaigners, experienced activists and professional politicians in new ways. It is the story of women who were willing to risk jobs, reputations, friendships, to make their voices heard.

The opening section provides some context for the personal accounts that follow. We hope the overview of these five years

---

[*] Collins English Dictionary

in Chapter 5 and the timeline at the end will help readers less familiar with events in Scotland to put the pieces together.

As a first draft of history, most of the accounts here are from women whose experiences hit the headlines, but the battle was fought on the ground and online by women with no public profile. There is a much bigger women's history to write than this one book can contain.

If self-declaration of gender had become law in one part of the UK, women's sex-based rights and the very definition of female in language, policy and law would have been diminished across the country. Much of the detail is unique to Scotland, but it is a story which will resonate across the UK and in other countries where women face the same pressures to see themselves redefined.

The story told here is an age-old one, albeit in a contemporary setting. Above all, it is the story of the women who would not be silenced, of the women who wouldn't wheesht.

Foreword

A hashtag is born

'It's a girl.' The forty-five minutes that followed were the 'before'. Before grief. Before my mind lurched into a vision of a future I'd never have chosen for my daughter. Before the cold, grey knot of worry formed in my gut.

Three women came to break the news – two midwives and the doctor who had delivered my baby. This show of sisterhood, this rallying of female strength and compassion, still moves me. These women knew their words would change another woman's life. They set out to ensure those words would steady me as my world shifted. Being told my child had a severe learning disability was being told I had a responsibility that extended beyond my own lifetime. There was a helplessness that followed – knowing one day you'll leave your vulnerable child in a world that is too often cruel and dangerous is a harrowing, almost unbearable, realisation.

As I came to know my beautiful, funny, hard-working daughter, the pain eased, but the worry didn't. The worry could only be managed. Believing I lived in a country where safeguarding principles sat at the heart of its care system offered me some reassurance.

But that was the 'before'. Before becoming aware of how politicians in Scotland were attempting to broaden the definition of woman to include men. Before knowing there was a push to blur the line between the sexes. Before discovering my daughter's need for same-sex intimate care would be reframed as bigotry.

I became aware, in 2019, of the plans for self-ID (self-identification) to be introduced in Scotland. I found it hard to believe my country was on the verge of allowing men to self-declare their sex. It was also baffling that this proposed legislation, certain to impact the sex-based protections of women and girls, wasn't being discussed in every news broadcast and in every household. I had only found out about the plans from social media posts written by brave and knowledgeable women who had already suffered the grim consequences of daring to speak up for women and girls.

I began to speak up, convinced when I explained the very real worries I had regarding my daughter's right to same-sex intimate care, politicians would be sympathetic. For who would be callous enough to say a grown man's feelings were more important than a disabled girl's dignity and safety? Surely no one.

But that was the 'before'. Before politicians deemed my concerns for my daughter's dignity and safety not inclusive enough of adult men. Before trans activists accused me of being a pearl-clutching transphobe. Before I was told to 'wheesht' and put my concerns aside until all other issues in Scotland were put to rights.

For there were those, politicians included, who viewed a female's refusal to have a man identifying as a woman deliver her 'same-sex' intimate care as akin to racism.

There were others who believed attaining an independent Scotland was to be the only priority. Women's sex-based protections were merely a side issue, a distraction. 'Wheesht for Indy' was to be the strategy, and once an independent Scotland emerged, we might restore women's rights. Or then again, we might not.

Silencing the women who opposed self-ID was a recurring theme. If we weren't to be quiet for the purposes of independence, we were to be quiet because we were bigots whose boundaries were outdated and hateful. It was horrifying to me that politicians and organisations would think it appropriate for my daughter's dignity to be compromised to ensure a man's was not. The material reality of a man is not changed by how he perceives himself, and telling vulnerable women and girls to ignore their own discomfort to accommodate a man's perception of himself is gaslighting.

However, gaslighting and vilification would not prompt submission, it would prompt defiance. It was this defiance I hoped to articulate when I coined the slogan, 'Women Won't Wheesht'. Those three words were my message to anyone who found my speaking up for my daughter's dignity distracting or unkind. I would not shut up. I would not stand aside.

It turned out that there was a growing number of women who felt the same. The slogan seemed to capture the mood of women all over Scotland. 'Women Won't Wheesht' became our battle cry.

I hoped if the strength of women's resistance was reflected in the slogan, a slogan that would be chanted by hundreds of women outside Holyrood and written in sand on beaches across the world, it might alert more women to the changes in law that were unfolding.

It was this thought that gave me the idea of displaying ribbons in the green, white and purple of the suffragettes anywhere women might see them. In December 2020, I began tying ribbons round lampposts, pillar boxes, trees (temporarily) and anything else that stood still. I posted photographs of these displays on Twitter with the hashtag #WomenWontWheesht.

What followed was amazing. An army of women began tying their own ribbons in their own towns and cities around the world. From Orkney to Australia, from Caithness to Canada, and in so many places in between, ribbons in the suffragette colours began to appear. In a culture of no debate, the ribbons offered an opportunity for women's voices to be seen in a world that was making it almost impossible for them to be heard.

Every time I wrote the slogan 'Women Won't Wheesht', and every time I tied a ribbon, it was with this in mind: I am a mother, and I will allow no man to use my disabled daughter as his shield.

I won't lie. I won't say a man is any type of woman. I won't be forced to say women's bodies don't matter – aren't matter. I won't say woman is merely a fragile, flimsy feeling, or the wisp of a limitless thought that can be stretched as thin as a veil any man can slip on and off.

I won't pretend woman is the sum total of the traits a man can emulate. To say this would be to say a man can stand in a woman's place. And that place could be administering what should be same-sex intimate care to my vulnerable, disabled daughter.

This woman will never wheesht.

SECTION 1
Setting the Scene

Chapter 1

In the beginning there was Scotland . . .

Susan Dalgety and Lucy Hunter Blackburn

The chief executive of Stonewall could not have been more contrite. On 16 February 2015, when announcing that the world-famous campaign group for lesbian and gay rights was now going to focus on trans equality, Ruth Hunt made a heartfelt apology.

In the foreword to *Trans People and Stonewall*, Hunt acknowledged that the organisation, established in 1989, had, until now, always maintained a strict distinction between sexual orientation and gender identity.

'Historically, we thought it was the right thing to do,' she said, adding that she had now changed her mind. And she apologised on behalf of Stonewall: 'We recognise the impact of mistakes we have made in the past. We are aware that we have missed opportunities to open up this conversation far sooner. We apologise to trans people for the harm that we have caused.'

Four hundred miles away, in the Equality Network's office in central Edinburgh, it's not hard to imagine its director, Dr Tim Hopkins, smiling at the news of Stonewell's late transition to the gender identity cause.

Thanks in no small part to Hopkins, an understated computer scientist, Scotland had been at the forefront of the global campaign for trans rights for two decades. Central to Scotland's campaign was a demand for self-declaration (self-ID) – the right for anyone over sixteen years old to obtain legal recognition as a member of the opposite sex, or as being neither sex, by a simple administration process.

By the time Stonewall had announced its new focus, Hopkins, the Equality Network, and a host of other organisations such as the Scottish Trans Alliance (STA), LGBT Youth Scotland (LGBTYS), and Stonewall Scotland, had every reason to believe that their decades-long mission was about to succeed. Scotland's civil service was sympathetic to their cause, with the leadership of the Scottish Prison Service (SPS) and NHS (the National Health Service) Scotland already strong allies. Scotland's tight-knit political class was on board. Even the national feminist organisation Engender was an ally, citing intersectional feminism as proof that 'trans women are women'. And crucially, Nicola Sturgeon, Alex Salmond's deputy, had just been appointed first minister. She seemed determined to emerge from under the shadow of her former boss by proving her progressive credentials at home, and on the world stage.

But how did Scotland become home to such a powerful trans movement? One which put redefining 'woman' at the heart of its campaigning, with the enthusiastic support of civic Scotland, and so on a collision course with women's sex-based rights.

It started in Inverness, the capital of the Highlands, with trans activist Julia Gordon, who, from 1995, had incorporated a transgender support group within Reach Out Highland, an LGB charity. As James Morton, writing as head of the Scottish Trans Alliance, pointed out in *Trans Britain*, Gordon was 'ideally placed to recognise the benefits of collaborative LGBT activism and was able to convey this to other trans people across Scotland'.

When the embryonic Equality Network held its first community conference in 1997 in Edinburgh City Chambers, 'transgender people' got equal billing with lesbian, gay and bisexual people. Julia Gordon ran a 'Transgender Issues' workshop, which concluded:

> *While the overall goal for equal treatment and recognition for transgendered people is felt to be a long way off; it is tempting to draw comparisons with the struggle for 'gay' rights and how prejudices have been challenged and social attitudes changed in a relatively short time . . . it must surely follow for the transgender community in Scotland to build closer ties with the Equality Network.*

Despite concerns from some lesbian and gay activists about closer involvement, as well as from some transvestites and transsexuals, the Equality Network decided to incorporate the trans community in its work. From its inception in 1997 it was Scotland's national LGBT campaign – eighteen years before Stonewall embraced gender identity ideology.

Edinburgh University, where Tim Hopkins had taught from the 1980s, was the academic cradle for Scotland's drive towards self-ID. In 1996, the university's Lesbian and Gay Society (BLOGS) added a new right of 'self-definition' to its constitution:

> *The Society accepts its members and others attending meetings as being the gender, sexuality and sexual orientation which they choose to define themselves, regardless of birth certificate, physical appearance, usual gender role or sexual or other behaviour. They will be accepted thus for the purposes of attending regular and special meetings, and in how they are addressed and treated in the group.*

Two years later and the first elections of the Scottish Parliament gave Tim Hopkins and the Equality Network a unique opportunity to press for legal change. The devolved administration was established by the 1997 Labour government to give Scotland, which had always had a distinct legal system from England and Wales, direct power over a wide range of policy areas, including education, health, justice, rural affairs, housing, environment, transport, and crucially some aspects of equalities policy.

The newly elected members of the Scottish Parliament (MSPs) would prove keen to flex their political and legislative muscle from the outset, and the Equality Network was only too eager to help them.

In April 1999, a few weeks before the Scottish Parliament elections on 6 May, it published its manifesto, *Equality at Holyrood*, which set out policy aspirations for 'lesbian, gay, bisexual and transgender people'. As well as calling for the immediate repeal of 'Section 28' (2A in Scotland), the 1988 law that prohibited local authorities from 'promoting homosexuality by teaching or by publishing material' and for civil marriage to be available to couples 'regardless of gender', the manifesto demanded that the 'gender identity of transgender and transsexual people be recognised in law' and that all public bodies should adopt 'equal opportunities policies and practices which include sexual orientation and gender identity'.

The ill-defined term 'gender identity' had fully entered Scottish public space.

The 1999 manifesto was to provide the framework for a determined campaign by the Equality Network, its offshoot, the Scottish Trans Alliance, and other groups such as Stonewall Scotland and LGBT Youth Scotland to secure self-ID, and to embed gender identity in all aspects of public policy, from equality guidance for schools to the collection of vital data. As Lucy Hunter Blackburn told the *Herald* in December 2023:

> *We had a group of people who were very convinced that what you felt yourself to be was more important than anything else. They were active in politics for decades . . . the Equality Network . . . was set up from the very start on gender identity. It's not an add-on, unlike Stonewall, which changed course.*

Young people were a key demographic for the trans lobby. Stonewall set up an LGB youth project in Edinburgh in 1989, which by 2003 had evolved into the national organisation, LGBT Youth Scotland, and included a group for trans-identified youth. Its first chief executive was James Rennie.

LGBTYS's influence in schools and education policy grew apace. Even the conviction of Rennie in 2009, found guilty of raping a three-month-old baby and sentenced to life imprisonment for his central role in one of Scotland's worst-ever paedophile rings, did not affect the clout it had with senior politicians and civil servants or, crucially, its government funding. Nor did the quality of its work seem to matter. In 2017, it drew up transgender guidance for schools. However, the document was heavily criticised for its misunderstanding of equality law, so much so that the Scottish Government was forced to commit to replacing it. Despite this failure, LGBTYS helped shape the Scottish Government's new guidance *Supporting Transgender Pupils in Schools*, published in 2021, and almost 60 per cent of Scotland's secondary schools now participate in its Charter Award scheme which places emphasis on social transition as a response to children experiencing confusion over their sex.

Another target was the NHS. Stonewall Scotland won funding in 2002 to manage a six-year-long LGBT health equality project, which included a 'trans awareness training resource pack' for NHS staff. A key element was a thirty-minute film, which was later used to train youth workers, teachers, council staff and the police, as well as NHS personnel. And the Scottish Transgender Alliance was instrumental in shaping NHS Scotland's 2011 Gender Reassignment Protocol, ensuring that it included the most recent recommendations from an organisation called the World Professional Association for Transgender Health (WPATH). Scotland was later able to boast that it was the first country in the world to implement a protocol based on WPATH's 'best practice'. In 2013, NHS England announced it would adopt the Scottish guidance.

But perhaps the most illuminating example of the trans lobby's entryism into public policy was its capture of the SPS, as James Morton explains in *Trans Britain*: 'We strategised that by working intensively with the Scottish Prison Service to support them to include trans women as women on a self-declaration basis within very challenging circumstances, we would be able to ensure all other public services should be able to do the same.'

In 2014 SPS published its policy, giving the STA's logo equal prominence to its own on the front cover, and with James Morton's name in the document's metadata.

Feminist organisations and women-only support services were also carefully targeted for their support. Engender, Scotland's feminist membership organisation, was set up thirty years ago by second wave feminists to advocate for women's equality. A new generation of activists and staff introduced 'an intersectional lens' to Engender's work, encouraged by the Equality Network and trans activists like Jo Clifford who, according to James Morton, helpfully pointed out the 'errors in some second wave feminist theories about trans people'.

And civil servants 'warmly and cogently' argued for support services like Scottish Women's Aid and Rape Crisis Scotland to be 'trans-inclusive'. Mridul Wadhwa, who transitioned in India before moving to Scotland, was held up as a poster child for the slogan 'trans women are women', controversially holding senior roles in a range of women's support services from 2014. Today, all Scottish government-funded organisations that provide services for female victims of male violence and sexual assault must have a trans-inclusion plan as a condition of their government grant.

Tim Hopkins realised early on that to be successful in realising the Equality Network's ambitious 1999 manifesto, particularly its pledges on gender identity, he would need to secure funding for staff and other resources. At a dinner he organised in 2005, he found civil servants more than willing to listen, as James Morton describes: 'We used a combination of friendly charm together with emotive descriptions peppered through the dinner conversations to illustrate to the civil servants the need for trans-specific government equality funding.'

Little more than a year later, Hopkins had secured a one-year funding package for the Scottish Trans Alliance. The surprise election of a minority SNP (Scottish National Party) government in May 2007, under the leadership of Alex Salmond, with his protégée Nicola Sturgeon as his deputy, led to concerns that the funding would be short-lived, but the SNP was keen to be seen as a progressive government.

A commendation from the Council of Europe Commissioner for Human Rights – recognising Scotland as the first national government in Europe to fund a trans-equality project – was sufficient incentive for the new, ambitious administration. In early 2008, STA's funding was extended to a three-year package.

More funding was to follow, first from the European Union to allow Scottish trans activists to meet regularly with fellow campaigners in the Netherlands, Germany and Ireland. Even Scotland's tourism marketing agency was eager to help. In 2014 VisitScotland gave STA a six-figure sum for a weekend-long event, the 'Trans and Intersex Conference of the Isles', bringing together campaigners from the rest of the UK and Ireland. The Scottish Government and Edinburgh University also made a financial contribution to the event.

Armed with government cash, and with the ear of government ministers, leading opposition MSPs and senior civil servants, STA and its parent body, the Equality Network, was able to turn its attention to the big prize: legislative change.

It found an enthusiastic backer in the leader of the Scottish Greens, Patrick Harvie MSP who, in 2009, successfully introduced the Scottish Parliament's first piece of hate crime legislation – the Offences (Aggravation by Prejudice) (Scotland) Act. This made being motivated by prejudice towards a person's 'actual or presumed sexual orientation, transgender identity or disability' an 'aggravator' – increasing the seriousness of any crime. And lobbying by STA secured the first legal acknowledgement of 'non-binary' identities. Using insults such as, 'Oi freak, are you Pete Burns's love child' as anecdotal evidence, civil servants were persuaded to accept the line, 'any other gender identity that is not standard male or female gender identity', in the bill.

Hopkins and others now focused their energies on securing the self-identification of sex for anyone over sixteen years old, as set out in the Equality Network's 1999 manifesto: 'The Scottish Parliament should legislate to allow transgender and transsexual people to register their gender identity for legal purposes.'

The 2004 Gender Recognition Act, in force across the UK, did not go far enough for gender identity advocates.

They argued that the medical diagnosis required for a Gender Recognition Certificate (GRC) was, among other things, 'inhumane'. But first they successfully lobbied to use the 2014 Equal Marriage Bill to change the law for married people. An amendment, originally drafted by the Equality Network, which allowed a transgender person to obtain a GRC without the written consent of their spouse, was accepted by parliamentarians.

Tom French is the director of communications for the SNP group at Westminster. He worked for the Equality Network in 2014, when he wrote in *Pink News*, praising Scotland for being at the forefront of trans-inclusive laws and policies:

> *The significance of this amendment is not just that it is a key part of the package of measures that will secure genuine marriage equality for transgender and intersex people but also that it upholds the important principle that access to gender recognition is a human right, and a deeply personal matter of autonomy, that no one should be able to block . . .*
>
> *It is precisely because we have a government and parliament that are committed to equality for LGBT people that Scotland has developed a proud reputation of being at the forefront of LGBT equality in Europe, leading the way in introducing trans-inclusive policies and laws.*

Buoyed by this legislative success, the Equality Network and STA now turned their attention to securing self-ID in law. In November 2014, at the VisitScotland-funded conference, the Equality Network and STA unveiled its Equal Recognition campaign, calling for reform of the GRA to a process of self-ID. They were perfectly placed to win.

Their long-term strategy to embed gender identity and self-ID in Scotland's political and civic space had succeeded beyond expectations. Civil servants were convinced, some evangelical. Civil society – including, crucially, government-funded women's organisations such as Engender and Rape Crisis Scotland – were strong allies. Engender welcomed the Equal Recognition campaign, describing it at the time as being inspired by feminism: 'Campaigning for the right to make your own decisions about your body and the right to make your own decisions about how to live your life will no doubt be very familiar to Engender members and indeed the Equal Recognition Campaign takes much inspiration from Feminism.'

Gender identity ideology had been seeded, and taken root, across a range of public services, and senior politicians and just enough backbench MSPs were clambering over each other to show their support for their 'trans siblings'. The media, largely, were uninterested.

Even Westminster seemed on board. The 2015 Women and Equalities Committee inquiry into Transgender Equality offered Scottish gender identity ideology activists the opportunity to provide influential witness testimony, and held out the prospect of self-ID reform across the UK.

And Nicola Sturgeon, acclaimed as first minister on 22 November 2014, had reinvented herself as a social reformer, a liberal feminist in touch with contemporary society, eager to transform Scotland into a model nation, ready to take its rightful place in the pantheon of 'progressive' countries.

As the 2016 Scottish Parliament elections approached, the SNP, Scottish Greens and Liberal Democrats promised to bring the 2004 Gender Recognition Act into line with international best practice, while Scottish Labour made a pledge to remove the need for a medical diagnosis. Some politicians pointed to Ireland, where self-ID had been introduced in 2015 with little or no controversy, as proof of the policy's popularity.

The SNP won the largest number of seats – but with 63 of the 129 available failed to secure an overall majority. But with more than double the number of seats of the opposition party – the Conservatives – and Scottish Labour beaten into third place, there was no doubt that Nicola Sturgeon would form a government. She was voted in for her second term as first minister of Scotland on 17 May 2016.

Five months later, on 5 October 2016, she published her 2016–17 Programme for Government. Action 13 was to reform gender recognition law, recognising it as a 'complex area of policy'.

Unbeknown to Sturgeon, and unnoticed by a civil society that no longer challenged government but instead amplified its core messages, women across Scotland, connected by online forums and social media that brought in UK connections too, were beginning to take notice of a potential clash of rights.

Crucially, while the YES campaign to secure Scotland's exit from the UK had not convinced enough Scottish voters in the 2014 referendum, it had spawned an energetic grassroots political movement that cut across party lines and encouraged thousands of previously unengaged women to get involved in campaigning. They were not yet ready to hang up their banners.

Nicola Sturgeon, who later self-identified as 'feminist to her fingertips' was about to find out just how complex self-ID was, not just for policy-makers but for her personally.

Chapter 2

Not just a piece of paper:
why women pushed back

Lucy Hunter Blackburn, Lisa Mackenzie and Kath Murray

In 2003, the opposition health spokesperson Nicola Sturgeon led what one newspaper described as an 'outcry' after it emerged that there were still some hospital wards where 'the male and female patients are sharing sleeping, toilet, and bathing facilities'.

The future first minister was quick to condemn the practice, saying mixed-sex wards should be 'a thing of the past by now. They are yet another example of a broken pledge by Labour on health.'

While the project to substitute self-declared gender (self-ID) for sex in policy and law had already begun in Scotland by 2003, it was not yet shaping political discussion. By the time MSPs were considering changes to the law, many organisations had already been persuaded to change their policies, often to radical effect. These changes would, however, pass largely below the radar until well into the following decade.

Nearly two decades after Ms Sturgeon's condemnation of mixed-sex wards, NHS Ayrshire and Arran issued its new

Supporting Trans Service Users policy. It was developed 'through consultation with trans representatives and the Scottish Trans Alliance' (STA), and clearly stated that patients would be offered a bed on a male or female ward according to the 'gender in which they are currently living', regardless of whether they had had any physical interventions or held a Gender Recognition Certificate (GRC). To illustrate how this might work, the policy invited staff to imagine a woman patient who 'appears to be agitated. When asked what's concerning her, the woman explains she didn't expect to be sharing the ward with a man and points to the bed opposite. She states it's inappropriate to have "him" in the ward with the other women. She tells the nurse she can't relax.'

In such a scenario, hospital staff were advised to meet the patient's concerns by stressing that 'the ward is indeed female only and that there are no men present'. Noting that 'ultimately it may be the complainant who is required to be removed', the policy compared the patient's objection to racism or homophobia.

Under the Equality Act 2010, sex is a protected characteristic. The Act allows men and women to be treated differently in some circumstances. It frames arguments for single-sex provision more widely than protection from male violence and sexual offending, recognising that privacy, dignity and fairness matter, as well as safety. It states, for example, that separate facilities can be justified, simply because 'the circumstances are such that a person of one sex might reasonably object to the presence of a person of the opposite sex'. There is no equivalent provision in relation to race or sexual orientation.

The Act allows employers to restrict certain roles to people of one sex, on similar principles. The Act also provides for sports to separate men and women due to physical differences between the sexes; allows interventions to address inequalities based on sex; permits single-sex schools; and enables associations to be set up that are open only to people of the same sex. Nothing in the Act suggests that single-sex services should be rare or exceptional, only that they should always be defensible as a 'proportionate means of achieving a legitimate aim'.

Yet by the end of the last decade, many organisations had adopted policies based on the same principles as that of NHS Ayrshire and Arran – prioritising self-ID over sex, and often acknowledging the input of the STA, Stonewall, or other advocacy groups. These policies had been introduced without wider consultation or public discussion, and as became clear with little or no consideration for the impact on women and girls.

Among these was the 2014 policy of the Scottish Prison Service (SPS), developed in conjunction with the STA, which stated that for any prisoner the accommodation chosen 'should reflect the gender in which the person in custody is currently living'. No surgery or other physical change was required. The policy stated: 'A male-to-female person in custody living permanently as a woman without genital surgery . . . should not be automatically regarded as posing a high sexual offence risk to other people in custody.'

Our own research found that in developing the policy, the SPS undertook no systematic assessment of the potential impact on women prisoners or staff. Under this policy, the SPS moved men convicted of murder, torture, and serious assault, who subsequently declared themselves to be women, into women's prisons. Eventually, a convicted double rapist, Adam Graham/Isla Bryson, would be sent from court to a woman's prison in January 2023, in a remarkable flashpoint at the end of Nicola Sturgeon's leadership.

Guidance for domestic abuse support services issued in 2015, developed using Scottish Government funding by, among others, Scottish Women's Aid, and the STA, stated providers 'would work to educate' any female survivors of domestic abuse uncomfortable being around another user who was male but self-ID'd as a woman, in the same way as they would deal with racism.

Other spaces and organisations affected by replacing sex with self-ID included communal changing areas and sports, youth hostels, Girlguiding and public toilets. In 2019, a six-foot-five-inch-tall male – known as Katie Dolatowski – was convicted of sexual offences against two girls, aged ten and twelve, in women's toilets in Fife. Dolatowski was later placed in a women-only hostel and, for a subsequent offence, in a women's prison.

Self-ID also carried consequences for young people. There was controversy around schools' guidance, initially produced by LGBT Youth Scotland in 2017, which advised that toilets, changing rooms, sports and overnight accommodation should cease to be separated by sex, and self-ID used instead, or else simply become fully mixed-sex. It also encouraged schools to affirm the social transition of a pupil with no onus to work with families.

In the 2016 Holyrood elections, gender identity activists sought to build on policy changes already achieved by obtaining political backing for reform of the existing Gender Recognition Act 2004 (GRA).

The 2004 Act allows a person aged eighteen years or over to apply for a GRC. This switches a person's sex for most legal purposes (bar some limited exceptions) and allows them to apply for a new birth certificate, showing the opposite sex to their original. A GRC also gives its holder enhanced privacy rights, with limited exceptions, creating criminal penalties if these are breached. The proposed Scottish Government reforms sought to remove the requirement for a medical diagnosis of gender dysphoria under the 2004 Act and rely only on a non-falsifiable 'solemn declaration' of the person's intention to live for the rest of their life 'in their acquired gender'. This was not defined further. The reforms were expected to increase the number of GRC holders ten-fold, although the government admitted the effect on numbers was hard to predict.

As supporters of reform argued that services on the ground already operated on the basis of self-ID and not sex, policy changes that had previously escaped attention suddenly came under intense public, political and media scrutiny. The move to change the law therefore exposed both the scale of policy change to date, and changes still underway.

Many women were surprised to be told that they were now expected to accept obviously male people in women-only places and activities, without challenge. They rejected the argument that this was how things had already worked for a long time, and/or that it was problem-free. They questioned the legal basis for these policies and asked what assessments had been done to consider the impact on women and girls. They found the answers unconvincing, and often based on guidance that went further than was required by the existing protection for 'gender reassignment' in the 2010 Equality Act, in the way it embraced self-ID. They did not accept the fact that there had been no proper consideration of possible impacts on women or girls proved that there were none.

Government ministers asserted that women's concerns were misplaced, pointing to protections in the Equality Act that allowed a service, space or job to exclude all males, whatever identity they declared, and with or without a GRC. At the same time, however, advocates of self-ID were busy persuading providers this exclusion could and should be used only in the most 'exceptional circumstances'.

As the 2015 guidance for domestic abuse services quoted above put it, access would 'depend on the facts of the individual case', adding that blanket bans on all male people accessing a women-only service were 'not acceptable'. It emerged that in 2015 the STA had tried to persuade MPs at Westminster to remove even this protection.

The loss of robust data on sex, which risked undermining the ability to tackle sex discrimination or understand how sex shapes women's experiences, surfaced as a significant issue. The most high-profile battle was over the approach taken to defining sex in the 2022 census. Ahead of that, anticipating the embedding of self-ID in law, the Scottish government's chief statistician issued guidance to all public bodies encouraging the collection of data using self-ID in place of sex in most contexts.

Police Scotland's policy on recording sexual offenders came under scrutiny. This stated that a 'male [accused of such an offence] who self-identifies as a woman would be expected to be recorded as a female on relevant police systems'. Challenged on this, a Police Scotland spokesman said: 'The sex/gender identification of individuals who come into contact with the police will be based on how they present or how they self-declare, which is consistent with the values of the organisation.'

It took legal proceedings over the 2018 Gender Representation on Public Boards (Scotland) Act by the new grassroots women's organisation For Women Scotland finally to put beyond doubt that policies based on substituting self-ID for sex in settings covered by the Equality Act had run ahead of the law.

These proceedings also eventually brought out that a GRC was not simply, as often claimed, a 'piece of paper' relevant only to its holder. In 2022 the Scottish courts held that a GRC changed a person's sex for the purposes of the Equality Act.

The exclusion of males with a GRC from women-only services, spaces, jobs and sports thus threatened to be more technically complex, due to their legal status as 'female' under the Act. Additional privacy rights conferred by a GRC added to this complexity. The court ruling confirmed many women's fears that a large rise in GRC holders risked making employers and service providers even more hesitant about upholding policies that protected women, for fear of increased risk of a legal challenge to any decision to exclude all men, including those who had obtained a GRC.

The court's decision also made clear that a man holding a GRC deeming him to be female would obtain full right of access to women-only clubs and associations, schools (the Scottish Government had proposed making GRCs available from the age of sixteen) and programmes to address women's under-representation in certain fields, with no exceptions.

As well as drawing attention to changes already in place, gender recognition reform therefore introduced a significant new risk – that piecemeal policy developments would acquire a solid legal foundation, making existing policies based on self-ID harder to reverse. As the Equality Network told civil servants in 2017, the GRA was purposefully worded to help those able to obtain a GRC gain access to services based on their new legal status, rather than their sex. Further, whatever the legal effects, writing self-ID into law could also be expected to send a message about state endorsement that many service providers would think twice about ignoring.

Increasingly, women found it difficult to talk about these significant developments – and the threatened loss of their sex-based rights – using ordinary words with ordinary meanings. Everyday language was co-opted into the self-ID project, as activists sought to extend the word 'woman' to include some male people, and to frame sex as mutable. The #sixwords debate at Holyrood in 2020 provided a stark example of how language itself had become a focus of tension.

In 2019 we wrote an article for an academic journal, tracing the introduction of self-ID principles in the Scottish Prison Service and the census, and the failure to consider women. A member of staff at the publisher tried, unsuccessfully, to stop its publication, describing it as transphobic, and comparable with anti-Semitic, homophobic, Islamophobic and sexist opinion. The only evidence offered in support of this argument was that we had used the word 'women' to refer to people who share the characteristic of being born female. When Lisa Mackenzie revealed her co-authorship to her then employer, the Royal College of Nursing, she was placed under investigation.

The Scottish Government's Hate Crime and Public Order (Scotland) Bill, passed in March 2021, raised further questions about freedom of speech. The bill extended the offence of 'stirring up hate' from race to other characteristics, including 'transgender identity'. It updated and extended more limited hate crime legislation introduced by Patrick Harvie, the Scottish Green Party leader, in 2009. The bill replaced a reference to 'transvestism' previously included in the definition of transgender identity to 'a person who cross-dresses'. In 2020, emails released under the Freedom of Information Act revealed that Tim Hopkins of the Equality Network had told the government that, 'A man who is not a trans woman but wears a dress for a drag performance, or a trip to *The Rocky Horror Picture Show*, or because he feels an emotional need to cross-dress occasionally is at high risk of transphobic hate crime.'

The bill also added to the list of characteristics protected for the purposes of hate crime. But the government rejected adding 'sex', arguing that that was too complicated and not favoured by its preferred women's organisations. This meant that in Scotland, cross-dressing men would be specifically protected in law from hate, but not women. Whether women should be protected under hate crime legislation – and if so, how – was batted off into yet another review.

The government also ignored the advice of its own expert review by Lord Bracadale in 2018 on the need for specific new free speech protections in relation to gender identity. Women concerned about the impact of self-ID argued that, without clear protection, it would become easier for activists to trigger police investigations into people with whom they disagreed. Even if the courts might, in the end, throw out such cases, the process would be the punishment: several such cases had already happened under less sweeping hate crime laws in England. MSPs were alerted to the low threshold for accusations of hate and hostility. The Equality Network, for example, had described those arguing that the census should gather data on sex as a binary variable, rather than based on self-identified gender, as 'anti-trans lobbyists'. In January 2019, the principal of Edinburgh University told students he had contacted the police over 'offensive stickers' found on campus, reported to include 'Female is a biological reality' and 'Woman. Noun. Adult human female'.

At stake therefore was far more than the reform of a private administrative process. Gender recognition reform was the legislative consolidation of a larger project to replace sex with self-ID across law, policy and language.

Politicians across the parties were reluctant to address the breadth of consequences of embracing the self-ID project. They were repeatedly warned that some women would self-exclude from certain services, if they could not trust them to be free of men, for reasons of dignity and privacy, as well as their sense of safety. Women survivors of male abuse tried unsuccessfully to obtain reassurance from relevant national organisations, government ministers and MSPs that their need for unambiguously single-sex provision was understood and would be catered for. Family members asked politicians how they could ensure same-sex intimate care for vulnerable children and adults, including elderly relatives, and drew a blank or were accused of bigotry. The debate failed to acknowledge the day-to-day impact of self-ID policies on women from religious and ethnic minorities. And the shift to self-ID compromised the ability of lesbians to define themselves as exclusively same-sex attracted, and to meet and organise on that basis.

Throughout this period, no evidence was produced that adult males who are willing to declare themselves to be the opposite sex, or to change their appearance, present a lower level of risk to women than other men. Women were persistently misrepresented as being concerned about whether someone was transgender, when the issue was that they were male. Politicians appeared to forget that sexual abuse encompasses flashing and voyeurism, as well as direct assault, and that most sexual offending already goes unreported and unpunished. Meanwhile, opinion polling persistently showed that the argument for cementing self-ID into law had not been won and that policy changes affecting single-sex services on the ground did not enjoy wide public support.

The Scottish Government in addition kept a distance from the Cass Review of gender identity services for children in England and Wales, denying that the equivalent services in Scotland required similar scrutiny. Ministers simply ignored Cass's advice that the social transition of young people was not a neutral intervention but could have significant effects on a child or young person. Instead, children in Scotland were to be told that they could change sex, and that the law would be changed so that they could receive the state's confirmation of that from the age of sixteen.

Many people wondered if those politicians supporting self-ID fully understood what they were doing. On 15 March 2019, Nicola Sturgeon tweeted a picture of *Invisible Women*, a best-selling book that argued, from heart-attack treatment to seat belts, that the male body was treated as the default and that a lack of robust data based on sex harmed women. Sturgeon commented: 'Even for committed feminists like me, this by @CCriadoPerez is revelatory – it should be required reading for policy and decision makers everywhere.'

One woman spoke for many more when she responded: 'Whilst I'm delighted that this book is being read, I'm confused. The first minister said women's concerns about GRA reform are misplaced. Women in Scotland are meeting in secret to discuss how we defend our rights under the Equality Act. Govt can't define woman. So?!?.'

None of the many reactions along these lines prompted a response.

Four years later, the government's inability to understand the consequences of its own legislation was put beyond doubt by its confused response to the placement of double rapist Adam Graham/Isla Bryson in the female prison estate. As the story broke, Nicola Sturgeon dismissed critics of self-ID. The proviso that she was not referring to everyone in that group felt weak, when she went out of her way to highlight that 'there are people who have opposed this bill that cloak themselves in women's rights to make it acceptable, but just as they're transphobic you'll also find that they're deeply misogynist, often homophobic, possibly some of them racist as well'.

Yet at the core of the self-ID project, which the Gender Recognition Reform (Scotland) Bill was intended to embed into law, was the principle that 'trans women are women', with 'acceptance without exception' required of all claims to that status. It was this thinking that left a class of young women on a beauty course at Kilwinning College, stripped down to their underwear for spray tanning, in the same room as Graham/ Bryson while he was awaiting trial for two counts of rape. By his own self-declaration, he was now a woman. For Women Scotland asked the first minister on Twitter if she would have told these young women they were 'bigots' for feeling uneasy around him. 'Or will you allow them their fear and discomfort now we know he is a rapist? Would it be different if he hadn't been caught?' Once again, there was no response.

Chapter 3

How social media powered a movement

Professor Sarah Pedersen

I f the media won't cover your meetings or your opinions,
how do you communicate with like-minded women? Over
the last hundred years, women in Scotland have had to be
innovative and brave in their efforts to reach out to others
and form a supportive community. Raising their heads
above the parapet and stepping into the public sphere of
debate has drawn anger from those who oppose them, but
has also brought sisterhood and support, from across the
political spectrum.

When the suffragettes wanted to advertise their meetings to
other women, they went on to the streets. Using chalk in the
suffragette colours of purple, green and white, they chalked
messages about meetings, or just the slogan 'Votes for Women',
on walls and pavements. Glaswegian suffragette Jessie Stephen
remembered that, as she chalked, people came behind her
trying to rub out her messages or drove by to splash her with
mud. Suffragettes setting out for chalking parties were advised
to go as a group for protection.

Frustrated by the lack of coverage in mainstream newspapers,
suffrage campaigners set up their own newspapers: *The Vote*,

Common Cause, *Votes for Women* and many more. To raise the visibility of their cause – and funds – women volunteered to be newsies (newspaper vendors) and stand in the street selling these newspapers to passers-by. To be a woman newsy was to draw attention to yourself and your adherence to the cause and to put your reputation and your body on the line. What is more, newsies had to stand in the gutter rather than the pavement to avoid arrest for obstruction. Only men and boys sold newspapers on the street, not respectable women, and the suffragette newsies were subjected to misogynistic abuse and hostility.

Even attending a suffrage meeting could open a woman up to abuse. Attendees at a meeting of Aberdeen University's Women's Suffrage Association in 1908 had to be smuggled into the room by a side door because fifty male students had besieged the main entrance, in an attempt to stop the meeting from going ahead. When the men realised the meeting had started, they forced the door open with a battering ram, and ran amok, shouting, ringing bells, and setting off stink bombs. On Black Friday in November 1910, Mrs Pankhurst led a deputation of women to Parliament in Westminster to appeal directly to the prime minister. Over 100 women were arrested and many more assaulted, physically and sexually, by both police and a hostile crowd of male onlookers.

By this time, the mainstream media was covering the women's suffrage campaign, but focused more on militant actions and fights with the police than the arguments and opinions of women. Newspaper cartoonists and sketch-writers had a field day depicting suffragettes as ugly spinsters who got arrested just to feel a policeman's arms around them, neglectful mothers, or silly young girls. One way in which suffrage campaigners tried to balance newspaper coverage was to write letters to the press outlining their reasons for demanding a vote. However, to identify herself with the suffrage cause opened a woman up to derision and, potentially, violence. Little wonder then that many of the letters written to Scottish newspapers on the topic used pen names such as 'Suffragette', 'Votes for Women' or 'Justice'. Publicly outing herself as a supporter of the suffragettes in the local press could cause a woman problems with friends, family and employers. The Aberdeen journalist Caroline Phillips was warned by her editor that she was identifying herself too closely with the women's suffrage movement, and that if she did not henceforth 'mind her own affairs' she would be sacked.

Mockery and attacks in the mainstream media, violent crowds in universities trying to prevent women from speaking, women journalists threatened with the sack, worries about speaking out and losing family and friends. It is perhaps not surprising that today's gender critical women find similarities with the suffragettes. I use 'gender critical' here as a shorthand for all those women who hold the view protected by the ruling in the case of Maya Forstater in 2021. It is not a label all those women would apply to themselves, but it remains for the time being the simplest way to describe the group of women brought together in recent years by a desire to defend sex as a material, unchangeable, and sometimes salient reality in language, policy and law.

When women first started to raise questions about government plans to reform the 2004 Gender Recognition Act (GRA), the shocking rise in the number of girls presenting at gender clinics, and the definition of apparently contentious words like 'woman' and 'mother', the mainstream press was rarely interested. Attacks on journalists such as Julie Bindel and Suzanne Moore in the early 2000s made it clear that gender critical voices were not welcome in the left-wing newspapers that had long been seen as the natural home for UK feminism.

While there was a considerable rise in mainstream media stories from 2015 onwards, coverage focused on incidents of confrontation or humour, just as the suffragettes had found. At the same time, news organisations tended to dismiss gender critical women as TERFs (trans-exclusionary radical feminists) and offered limited coverage of women's arguments.

However, gender critical women had something that the suffragettes did not – social media. Low-cost communication channels that allowed the spread of information, interaction, and the formation of networks. For women, who are under-represented in the mainstream public sphere, social media allowed the creation of alternative spaces for debate. The lack of editorial gatekeeping on sites such as Facebook, Twitter, and discussion forums like Mumsnet meant that gender critical discussion could forge connections between women all over the country.

The discussion forum Mumsnet played a key role in helping gender critical women find each other, share opinions and plan further action. Established in 2000 'to make parents' lives easier', by the mid-2010s the Mumsnet discussion boards had become an influential powerhouse where women discussed all aspects of their lives, including politics. The site's influence even led the 2010 General Election to be called the 'Mumsnet election', as politicians of all parties held webchats on the site in attempts to sway key floating voters.

Unlike other parenting sites, Mumsnet operates a low-key moderation policy, usually only stepping in to delete posts or ban users in extreme circumstances. Another important factor in the development of a gender critical voice on the site is the fact that usernames are allowed. Mumsnetters do not post under their own names and are able to change their usernames as they wish. While there are gender critical women's groups on social media such as Facebook, that site's requirement for users to identify themselves means that there is always the fear of infiltration of such groups and potential outing to the wider world. While Twitter allowed the use of pseudonyms, in the 2010s some gender critical women, such as Meghan Murphy and members of Fair Play for Women, found themselves banned from the site. As women's suffrage supporters had found earlier, the anonymity of Mumsnet allowed for a more confident sharing of opinions. Usernames could also be used to signal a poster's gender critical opinion, many of which also made links to the suffragettes. Similarly, gender critical women on Twitter used suffragette names and the colours of purple, green and white to signal their views to others.

The establishment of a feminism discussion topic on Mumsnet in 2010 offered gender critical women a specific space where they could be sure of finding like-minded women. It's important to remember that, unlike today, in the early and mid-2010s gender critical opinion was much more limited in the mainstream media. Mumsnet offered a space where women could share, curate and analyse any newspaper articles, blogs and social-media posts they did find. They could also share information about the women's organisations that were forming around the gender recognition reform consultations in Holyrood and Westminster. In a way, the Mumsnet feminism discussion topic became symbiotic with organisations such as Woman's Place UK, For Women Scotland, Fair Play for Women and Transgender Trend, with posters linking to their websites, quoting their material, and supporting their events. Women in public life who were openly gender critical were applauded on Mumsnet, with posters encouraging each other to reach out to those academics, journalists and politicians who were being attacked for their beliefs, to let them know they were not alone.

Posters used Mumsnet's webchats with politicians to raise questions relating to the proposed gender recognition reforms and wider issues around self-identification. Politicians who came on the site to raise the profile of their parties' women-focused policies faced demands to define the word 'woman' before such policies could be considered. The tone of the webchats became more contentious, and they were increasingly policed by Mumsnet. Some politicians pulled out of their commitment to appear on the site, apparently because they did not want to be questioned on this issue. There was even a suggestion that Liberal Democrat candidates had been banned from appearing on Mumsnet because of members' criticisms of the party's transgender policy.

Not only was Mumsnet used by gender critical women to find like-minded others and exchange information, the site was also used as a space in which to formulate action. Concerned about the way in which organisations were already making changes to guidelines and working practices in anticipation of any changes to the GRA, in 2018 a group of Mumsnetters decided to challenge Swim England's new guidelines, which used self-identification as the basis for the use of changing rooms. Calling themselves Man Friday, Mumsnetters turned up at men-only swimming sessions, self-identified as men and demanded to be allowed to swim. The resulting media coverage and a bombardment of Swim England with queries based on a template circulated on Mumsnet led to the organisation withdrawing its guidance within two weeks of the first stunts being staged.

On social media and in certain parts of the press, Mumsnet started to be attacked for offering a safe space for the expression of gender critical opinion. An article in *Vice* described it as a 'toxic hotbed of transphobia', while the *Outline* likened its openness to gender critical debate as similar to the enablement of American fascism by 4Chan. Pressure was put on advertisers to withdraw from the site.

The feminism topic on Mumsnet had become a place where women could identify a problem, share opinions and formulate action – much as feminist consciousness-raising groups did in the 1970s. The feminist scholar Nancy Fraser argues that such groups worked as 'subaltern counterpublics', formed because of women's exclusion from the public sphere. I argue that Mumsnet worked in a similar way – as a place where women could express opinions that ran counter to those in the UK's mainstream media and social media in the 2010s, and work together to organise campaigns to raise awareness of gender critical opinion and to change the public conversation on these topics.

In Scotland, gender critical women also used social media to raise awareness and form communities of action. The majority of the women I interviewed for my study of gender critical feminism in Scotland told me that the issue had first come to their attention via social media. As in England, the lack of coverage by the mainstream press was noted by interviewees, with particular criticism of the BBC and the *Guardian* for their lack of critical engagement. All interviewees mentioned Joan McAlpine's series of tweets entitled 'Sex and the census', which won *Holyrood* magazine's Tweet of the Year award in 2019. McAlpine spoke out on Twitter after the parliamentary committee she chaired scrutinised the census bill and she realised that biological sex was being ignored in favour of gender identity.

Once women became aware of problems around the reform of the GRA, they reached out offline to women they knew and trusted. 'Awkward conversations' were described, as women carefully sounded out others to see which side of the debate they were on. A community of Scottish gender critical women quickly built up using personal contacts and social media.

I use the term cooperative constellation to describe this community. It encompasses an informal grouping of politicians, policy-makers, journalists, academics and women's interest groups who work together to raise awareness, support one another and formulate action. This Scottish constellation crosses both political parties and the unionist–independence divide, but the women involved have certain similarities, in particular a keen interest in women's issues and a background in feminist action that goes back to Reclaim the Night marches, Greenham Common and the fight for gay rights. What is also clear is that – unlike similar cooperative constellations that were established in Europe in the 1990s – no funded women's organisations are members of this constellation. In fact, my interviewees were particularly critical of organisations like Engender, Zero Tolerance and Rape Crisis Scotland, who were perceived as either running scared of the debate around GRA reform or actively working against gender critical women. Interviewees felt let down by these organisations, which they saw as resistant to representing different opinions to those sanctioned by the Scottish Government, perhaps because of fears around the security of their funding. Thus, women started their own organisations, such as For Women Scotland (FWS) or Women and Girls in Scotland.

The constellation acts by providing information, support and advice, campaigning together and providing a supportive community. Researchers and policy experts, such as the policy collective Murray Blackburn Mackenzie (MBM), provide evidence and undertake research and analysis to be used by sympathetic politicians in the Scottish Parliament. Campaigns by individual women and groups such as FWS, Sole Sisters and the Scottish Feminist Network help to demonstrate public support for these politicians when they raise questions at Holyrood, while the output of bloggers and journalists publicises the issues raised and offers statements of support to individual women politicians. For example, when Johann Lamont spoke on her motion asking for the replacement of the word 'gender' with 'sex' in reference to women's ability to ask for a medical examiner of their own sex in the Forensic Medical Services bill, the hashtag #sixwords trended on Twitter. The six words were: 'for the word gender substitute sex'. The hashtag raised the profile of the debate, but also offered supplementary evidence as women spoke out online about their own experience of enduring such examinations after being raped.

Most importantly, members of the constellation raise awareness and take action. Local groups of gender critical feminists have sprung up throughout Scotland, from the Borders to the Highlands and Islands, and are making their mark both online and on the high street.

One example of the constellation's activity was the attempt to disrupt the administration of the 2022 census in Scotland. Encouraged by FWS, gender critical women used their census returns to register a protest around guidance relating to the sex question on the census and the wider issue of the Scottish government's plans to reform the GRA. FWS recommended that protestors answer the voluntary census question on religion with 'Believer in biology'. They also suggested other ways of using the paper form and envelope to disrupt the smooth administration of the census and make gender critical opinions clear, including creative uses of ribbon and glitter in the suffragette colours of purple, green and white. Protestors shared images of their census returns online, encouraging others to follow their lead.

There is a long history of women being locked out of politics. We are used to organising on our own, working together to educate and inform and formulating actions to bring our concerns to the attention of the wider world. What the suffra-gettes did with chalk and by standing in gutters, gender critical women have achieved using online spaces. When the main-stream media would not cover their concerns, women talked to each other on Mumsnet and Twitter and formulated actions that would grab the attention of the press. Scottish women have come together organically, reaching over the barriers of party politics to identify the issues that connect sister to sister, and making themselves a very visible force to be reckoned with. One which the mainstream media and funded women's organisations can no longer ignore.

The author acknowledges funding from the Royal Society of Edinburgh which supported this research.

Chapter 4

Funding the resistance

Lucy Hunter Blackburn and Susan Dalgety

How was women's activism in these years resourced? Most of all, through the time women gave, unpaid, because they decided this issue mattered. This time was often given on top of paid employment, caring responsibilities, or both.

Experience in party politics, the trade union movement, community activism and the 2014 independence referendum, and of organising local volunteer organisations, sports clubs, school associations and fundraising, were all brought to the table. Some had professional skills, in communications, design, event management, research and more. A member of Women and Girls in Scotland built their website over two days. Skills were shared and new ones learnt.

Murray Blackburn Mackenzie (MBM) are the only women in the Scottish grassroots movement who have not simply been volunteers, having eventually decided that it was not sustainable for them to continue doing the amount of work needed to analyse developments in law and policy in Scotland, without some financial support. Through crowdfunding and other small donations, MBM raised around £50,000 in total, between late 2019 and the end of 2022, with an average crowdfunder donation of around £30. Even eked out at £15 an hour, this still left much of the work needed in this period continuing to be done unpaid.

No group here had the use of an office. Work happened at kitchen tables, in spare rooms, in cafés, very occasionally in rooms booked for a few hours' use. Almost a century after Virginia Woolf argued that every woman writer needs a room of her own, very few of the women involved here had even that.

Groups have fundraised for other costs, through crowd-funding, selling merchandise and on street stalls. Sometimes individual women, who are not well known, stepped in to cover one-off costs, making it possible to bring speakers to meetings who otherwise could not afford the cost of travel, for example. One Glasgow-based group told us how they found a woman was walking miles into the city centre to attend their meetings, because she could not afford the bus fare. Some of their fundraising is used to make sure women like her can remain involved.

Physical resources needed for running street stalls were shared between groups. Public documents could be read online for free, blogs and social media provided ways to publish for little or nothing. WhatsApp and Zoom took the costs out of organising.

By far the largest fundraisers have been for the cost of court cases, in Scotland as in the wider UK. As For Women Scotland (FWS) describe later, they raised around £200,000 over the period just to meet legal costs.

Not everything was about fundraising. The embroidered banners that appeared at demonstrations were a labour of love, as were the painted slates distributed across the country. In the intense summer of 2019, Lucy and an old friend, Vicky, struck by Claire Heuchan's phrase 'Compassion Across Difference', decided with her permission to put it on a badge, splitting the cost of having a few hundred made, and giving them to women they met as a gesture of solidarity.

It should not be remarkable that women in the twenty-first century could do all this. What should be is how determined some people were that this could not be the explanation.

Constantly women were told we were being directed and funded by shadowy sources, perhaps from the US. One cheerleader for this theory was, gallingly, an organisation that has benefited from very large transatlantic donations.

Perhaps this scale of spontaneous volunteer grassroots activity was simply inconceivable to those used to doing activism as part of their job, from an office, in well-funded organisations. But sexism and ageism undoubtedly also played their part. The capability, resources and determination of women, older ones not least, were simply underestimated. What a mistake.

Chapter 5

Women rise up: 2018–23

Lucy Hunter Blackburn and Susan Dalgety

The personal accounts in this book concentrate on the five years leading to Nicola Sturgeon's sudden resignation on 15 February 2023. Here, we provide the wider context of political events and the growth of women's campaigning in Scotland.

2018

On the evening of Wednesday 14 February 2018, around a hundred women met in a community hall in Edinburgh to discuss plans to reform the Gender Recognition Act (GRA) in Scotland. The meeting had been arranged by Women's Spaces in Scotland (WSiS), a newly formed volunteer group, and London-based Woman's Place UK (WPUK), also a new volunteer-run organisation, established by three women trade union activists in response to parallel developments in England and Wales.

A meeting in Glasgow weeks earlier on the same subject had been disrupted, as had similar meetings south of the border, so the venue was kept secret until the last minute. Despite this, a group of protesters, many masked, young and male, gathered close to the entrance of the hall, banging pots and intimidating the women attending.

Inside, a woman in her forties spoke for the first time about her childhood sexual assault. A reporter present noted afterwards, 'As she cried, and some cried with her, the din of pots, pans and chants echoed through the hall. It struck me how the reality of this quiet exchange was lost to those outside.'

The previous evening Nicola Sturgeon had attended an event held less than a mile away, as the guest of Prince Harry and Meghan Markle at a party at the Palace of Holyrood House to celebrate the Scottish Government's designation of 2018 as the Year of Young People. This was, the first minister said, 'a global first' that she hoped would 'help to foster a better under-standing, cooperation and respect between generations'.

A columnist had argued a few weeks earlier that recent polling suggested Sturgeon's time was 'beginning to run out'. In reality, five more years in office lay ahead, during which time the first minister had to contend with a grassroots political campaign the like of which she had not encountered before, as women rose up to defend their sex-based rights.

In early March, just days before the consultation on reforming the GRA closed, WSiS met civil servants. It was the first meeting between the government and women critical of self-declaration (self-ID) since the SNP had been re-elected in 2016 with a commitment to 'review and reform gender recognition law, so it's in line with international best practice for people who are Transgender or Intersex'. The meeting had taken months to obtain, but in the words of one attendee, the women were left 'shocked' at their dismissive treatment.

In the same week as the meeting in Edinburgh, Susan Sinclair published her first blog as 'Scottish Women', exposing that legal reform was only one part of a larger project to replace sex with self-declared gender identity in policy as well as law.

While trying to understand why policies around bullying in schools had shifted their emphasis to gender identity and away from sexual harassment, she had discovered guidance issued to schools by the charity, LGBT Youth Scotland. 'It wasn't the trans thing that got me on board,' she explains, 'it was women and girls.' Concerned, she dug further and found the same thinking had been introduced in other areas of public policy. 'We just need to point it out to them; someone's not thought it through,' she says she believed at the time.

She went on to publish a series of careful analyses, creating a resource for other campaigners. Susan was one of the first to spot that a late amendment to the rules for public boards, nodded through in January 2018, gave self-ID its first toehold in Scottish law. As the campaign unfolded, court challenges to this legislation were to become central to political and legal developments.

In this early phase, women still hoped that established women's organisations in Scotland, not least Engender – Scotland's 'feminist organisation' – might play a constructive, mediating role. Engender had originally been a volunteer-run body, but now had access to paid staff and substantial funding, mostly from the Scottish Government. It did advertise a public meeting on gender recognition reform in May 2018, to which many women signed up, keen for a chance to discuss the changes. The meeting was cancelled and never rearranged. Instead, Engender put out a podcast which brushed aside concerns.

June saw the formation of For Women Scotland (FWS), by some of the women involved in WSiS. Around the same time, another group came together as Women and Girls in Scotland Their first piece of work was a children's rights assessment of the schools guidance, which they submitted to the Children and Young People's Commissioner for Scotland.

Also in June, the UK government launched its separate consultation on GRA reform. Sharing details of a meeting about this at Westminster placed the then rector of Edinburgh University, Ann Henderson, at the centre of a storm.

A significant moment came in October 2018 when plans to merge sex and self-declared gender in the Scottish census came before a Holyrood committee, convened by a senior SNP MSP, Joan McAlpine. When the committee called for evidence, Lisa Mackenzie, Kath Murray and Lucy, friends who had been privately following what was happening for some time, hastily formed Murray Blackburn Mackenzie (MBM) so that they could put in evidence together.

The committee's evidence session with Professor Rosa Freedman and Susan Smith of FWS on 6 December 2018 was the first time the Scottish Parliament had heard any critical arguments about replacing sex with self-declared gender. Julie Smith, who had been at the Edinburgh meeting and the first meeting with civil servants, recalls, 'It had felt really, really lonely . . . I remember crying [watching the census hearing] . . . and I don't cry.'

The committee's questioning forced ministers to backtrack on the wording of the proposed census legislation, although they soon found other ways to pursue the same end. As for Joan McAlpine, her decision to subject the issue to conventional parliamentary scrutiny marked the beginning of the end of her political career.

2019

In January 2019, WGS published their detailed work on children's rights. The following month, one of the group became the first woman involved in the growing grassroots movement to appear on television, when STV ran a news item. Supporters of the guidance either refused to take part or cancelled. The group went on to do much more work, on self-exclusion, prisons and government transparency, with a particular emphasis on the greater vulnerability of working-class women to policies and laws that lose sight of sex. Its female only provision report was the first of its kind. It platformed testimony from women who were at last able to talk about self-exclusion and how trans inclusion in women's services, including those specifically for survivors of sexual and domestic violence, had impacted them. It exposed that two major health boards could not guarantee that what was described as female-only healthcare would be delivered by female staff. The group tried to engage with Scottish Women's Aid and Rape Crisis Scotland, but neither were willing to do so.

Meanwhile, Nicola Sturgeon went to New York in February where she told the UN that concerns about GRA reform were 'misplaced'. Back in Scotland, dissent was growing, and not just among women. In April a group of fifteen SNP politicians, mostly MSPs and MPs, including Joanna Cherry, Joan McAlpine, and government minister Ash Denham (now Regan), wrote to the *Scotsman*, urging caution in taking forward legal reform.

Yet ministers refused to listen, either to senior SNP representatives, or grassroots women. As a group who had obtained a meeting with Shirley-Anne Somerville, the minister in charge of reform, described: 'They grudged us being there,' one said. 'It felt like they were going through the motions,' said another.

In June, Somerville announced a pause on work on gender recognition and plans for a further consultation, telling the Scottish Parliament, 'I am acutely aware of how divided opinion is on this issue and I want to proceed in a way that builds maximum consensus and allows valid concerns to be properly addressed.'

It felt like a breakthrough for women campaigners, but not for long. The government continued to make no effort to reach out to them. It took Somerville over three months to tell FWS that 'due to pressures on [her] diary' she was 'unable to meet them'.

As politicians and third sector bodies continued their discussions in private, 2019 became a year of public meetings, organised by a growing network of volunteers and politicians, with stickers also becoming an important symbol of resistance.

These events did not pass without challenge. As well as facing protests, at one meeting on women's rights, at the University of Edinburgh in June, security staff had to step in to protect a visiting speaker, Julie Bindel, from a local male activist who had waited outside to catch her leaving and ran at her, agitated and shouting obscenities. The aggressive confrontation at close quarters left the feminist and experienced campaigner against male violence 'very shaken'. The activist was later charged with a breach of the peace and fined. Meanwhile, a Scottish Green MSP, Andy Wightman, was forced by his party to apologise for attending the same meeting.

Over the year, several other groups had emerged, including Frontline Feminists Scotland and Women Make Glasgow. Some groups grew out of established friendships and networks, others from online connections. One-to-one meetings over coffee – and, later, Zoom – were used to sound out new members, in a climate where many women feared the consequences of going public.

In October, assisted by Joan McAlpine MSP, a group of women survivors met the then manager of the Edinburgh Rape Crisis Centre and Sandy Brindley, the chief executive of Rape Crisis Scotland, seeking reassurance that local rape crisis services were still willing to provide female-only support for those women wanting it. HEAL Survivors, formed in 2020, later told the committee examining the Gender Recognition Reform (Scotland) Bill (GRR Bill) that the women involved left this meeting 'acutely distressed that this is not the case', having been told that the service believed male users and employees should be treated as women, if they self-identified as such. HEAL described the meeting 'as a traumatising experience'.

Crucially, women involved in mainstream politics in Scotland and across the rest of the UK began to organise publicly, with the foundation of groups inside the main parties, such as SNP Women's Pledge and Labour Women's Declaration. Campaigners in Scotland and Ireland connected. In the days before the Parliament closed for Christmas, the government issued its second consultation on gender recognition reform, conceding nothing. And at the year's end, author and Edinburgh resident J.K. Rowling tweeted her support for Maya Forstater.

2020

Shirley-Anne Somerville finally conceded a meeting to FWS in February. A few weeks later, MBM met civil servants. These meetings echoed earlier ones, with government officials obviously irritated about having to meet critics of the bill. Just as the consultation drew to a close, Covid-19 hit, and the Scottish government announced that work on gender recognition reform was suspended indefinitely. Any legislation would be put off until after the next Scottish Parliament elections in May 2021. In September, the UK government announced that it would not be taking forward any change to the law here.

Attention turned to the Hate Crime and Public Order (Scotland) Bill, published in April 2020. It was presented as too urgent to delay, despite the pandemic. Work on the bill filled much of the time until activity resumed on gender recognition reform in the autumn of the following year.

Women campaigners were not alone in their concern that the extension of 'stirring up hate' in the bill beyond race risked a chilling effect on free speech. The separate 'Free to Disagree' campaign brought together the National Secular Association, Index on Censorship, the Christian Institute, and veteran gay rights campaigner Peter Tatchell, among others. Formal hearings on the hate crime bill began in October.

In December, former Scottish Labour leader Johann Lamont succeeded in forcing the government to accept a six-word amendment to the Forensic Medical Services (Victims of Sexual Offences) (Scotland) Bill, clarifying the right of victims of sexual assault to request an examiner of the same sex, not the more ambiguous 'gender'. The #sixwords hashtag became a campaign slogan.

A week later, Andy Wightman, who had voted against Lamont's amendment after it was made clear he would face disciplinary action if he did not, quit the party. He cited its 'alienating and provocative' stance on trans rights as the main reason for his resignation

Earlier in the year, FWS had taken the major step of initiating a judicial review of the use of self-ID to define who could benefit from measures to ensure women make up half of all public board members in Scotland. They lost in March 2021, but in February 2022 won on appeal a ruling that the Scottish government had acted beyond its powers. As Susan Smith describes later, this was only the first part of a legal battle that continued beyond Nicola Sturgeon's resignation.

The pandemic did not stop women campaigning. Face-to-face meetings evolved into online activity. Then as restrictions on movement eased, #SlateWoman recalls how – 'angry and scared' at how little understanding there still was about self-ID – she took action. She recalls, 'I decided to paint slates and write mainly women's words and place them where, hopefully, the public would read them and talk about the issues.' She met women in car parks with boxes of slates to distribute to other women, and be scattered around the country, with the images shared on social media.

In December, @dis_critic sparked a global campaign of ribbon-tying in suffragette colours, spread by social media. Following her lead, the images were often tagged: #Women WontWheesht. A new wave of feminist protest art was born.

2021

Controversy about the potential effects of the hate crime bill intensified in the new year. There was high drama when, for a moment, it appeared that women's concerns were being heard. As Joanna Cherry recounts, in late January 2021, Humza Yousaf, then Justice Secretary and the government minister in charge of the bill, suggested to the Justice Committee that a statement should not be treated as stirring up hate 'solely on the basis that it involves or includes discussion or criticism of matters relating to transgender identity'.

The proposed change was decried as a 'transphobes' charter' on social media. The committee convener said he was 'disturbed' by the scale of outrage to, in his words, 'really quite modest, innocent and perfectly reasonable amendments'.

At the height of the backlash, Nicola Sturgeon posted a video on Twitter one evening, described by her as unplanned and 'from the heart', on the issue of 'transphobia' in her party, but making no mention of the bill, in what women activists came to call the 'broom cupboard' video, for its eccentrically urgent and home-produced quality.

The government amendment was swiftly withdrawn, and more generic free-speech protection eventually added instead. Debating the bill two weeks later, Humza Yousaf refused to clarify how many sexes the government thought there were.

As the bill approached its final vote in March, the late Mary Gordon, a founder member of Engender in the early

1990s and the great-niece of one of the founders of the SNP, dressed the statue of Greyfriars Bobby in Edinburgh, a tourist landmark, in a crocheted coat of green, white and purple. Copying a suffragette tactic, she also chalked, 'Women's rights are not a hate crime' and '#WomenAreWatching' on a wall outside the Scottish Government's headquarters in Edinburgh. She was visited at home by police officers and warned about a possible charge of breach of the peace if she did it again.

In the bill's final debate, conducted as news of the abduction and murder of Sarah Everard broke, MSPs Pauline McNeill, Joan McAlpine, Elaine Smith and Johann Lamont argued passionately for women to be as well protected as other groups under hate crime laws. Joan McAlpine broke the SNP whip to vote with Lamont. In the final vote, Lamont and fellow Labour MSPs Elaine Smith and Jenny Marra broke the Labour whip to vote against the bill, and McAlpine abstained. The bill received its final vote of approval days before MSPs dispersed to campaign in the 2021 Holyrood elections, during which it was held up as an achievement of the SNP in government. The Act was not brought into force until April 2024.

The hashtag #HatefulHaberdashery began to circulate on Twitter, mocking the accusations of hate already being levelled at women for using suffragette-coloured ribbons as a form of protest. A few weeks later, a woman from Airdrie, Marion Millar, was questioned by the police about posts on Twitter. Joanna Cherry describes her case, only dropped six months later, in more detail. One of the tweets contained a picture of purple, green and white ribbons tied to a fence, alleged to resemble a noose. Millar's case became a lightning rod for concerns about how women risked accusations of hate crime and subsequent police investigations, for arguing that sex matters, in language, policy and law, prompting a new wave of local groups to be established, initially brought together through Twitter. These later provided the basis for the Scottish Feminist Network. And a separate 'informal network of feminists', Women Speak Scotland, was set up.

The SNP manifesto, published in April, undertook to 'work with trans people, women, equality groups, legal and human rights experts to identify the best and most effective way to improve and simplify the process by which a trans person can obtain legal recognition', promising that any changes would not affect women's existing rights or protections. Speaking at the manifesto launch, Nicola Sturgeon described herself as 'a feminist to my fingertips'.

Sole Sisters was formed in the run-up to the elections on 6 May to draw attention to women's feeling of disenfranchisement. Unable to rally because of the social distancing rules in place at the time, the group was inspired by Mexican artist Elina Chauvet, who had assembled pairs of empty shoes to draw attention to women victims of male violence. Women from around the UK sent shoes which were tied with ribbons and arranged outside the Scottish Parliament and other landmarks. The images were shared on social media, with the hashtag #VotingWithOurFeet. In late March, a woman tweeted, 'If you won't respect my sex, don't expect my X', at a senior SNP politician, a phrase that was picked up and repeated, first in Scotland, then further afield. The SNP emerged from the election as the biggest party with sixty-four seats, but still with no overall majority.

Later in May, police tweeted that they had 'received a report of controversial stickers having been placed on lampposts' in Kirkcaldy. Pictures showed the stickers had the slogan, 'Women Won't Wheesht' with hashtags including #WomensRights AreNotAHateCrime. The police explained to the media that the stickers had been reported as a 'hate incident'. The move was mercilessly mocked on social media. Images of the classic Scottish TV detective Taggart, famous for the catchphrase: 'There's been a murder' were posted with the caption, 'There's been a sticker'.

In June, MBM lodged a petition with the Scottish Parliament calling on it 'to urge the Scottish Government to require Police Scotland, the Crown Office and the Scottish Court Service to accurately record the sex of people charged or convicted of rape or attempted rape', after Police Scotland revealed that it was recording suspects based on self-ID. The petition received over 13,000 signatures. At the time of writing, the Parliament's petitions committee is still considering how to respond to this. In July, a former Scottish Women's Aid worker, Verdi Wilson, revealed how she had left her job there, because she had found it impossible to have conversations within the service about the impact of self-ID.

It came as no surprise when, at the end of August, the minority SNP government entered into a pact with the Scottish Greens, to which gender recognition reform was central. The first minister's attitude to the women's rights campaign showed no signs of softening. When a Conservative MSP referred to a rally held by FWS outside the Parliament, on the day in September that the government announced its plans for the year ahead, Nicola Sturgeon heckled, 'Shame on them.' In the same debate, she promised to bring forward gender recognition reform within a year. Speaking to the BBC soon after, she dismissed women's concerns as 'not valid'. In response, the phrase 'Nicola Sturgeon Destroyer of Women's Rights' began to gain traction, appearing first on stickers and T-shirts.

With lockdowns ended, women's groups returned to running street stalls, leafleting, and holding meetings to raise public awareness. At least thirty-five events took place in towns and cities across Scotland in the final three months of the year.

2022

A freedom of information response at the turn of the year confirmed that, since the election, the Scottish Government had only met groups who agreed with it on gender recognition reform. Its response, 'No group that has requested a meeting about the Gender Recognition Bill has been refused' immediately prompted a deluge of meeting requests from many of the volunteer organisations that had emerged in Scotland and the wider UK over the previous four years.

The Cabinet Secretary for Social Justice, Shona Robison, who was now in charge of the legislation, had little choice but to agree to meet, offering each group half an hour. As before, attendees found the engagement desultory, and it later became clear that, by this point, the bill was already in the final stages of internal clearance, prior to being published.

The Gender Recognition Reform (Scotland) Bill was introduced into the Scottish Parliament on 3 March 2022. Alongside the early stages of the bill, the long argument over the census came to a head. UK campaign group Fair Play For Women failed in their legal campaign to prevent a self-declared definition of sex being used, as they had succeeded in doing in England and Wales the year before.

The new connections women were making began to evolve into something deeper. In March 2022, Forth Valley Feminists, part of the Scottish Feminist Network, organised a well-attended day-long conference in Alloa Town Hall. Speakers from around the UK addressed topics including porn culture, prostitution and obstetric violence.

The committee charged with detailed scrutiny of the bill held its public Stage 1 oral evidence sessions in May and June, and published its report of those in October, with Conservative MSPs Pam Gosal and Rachael Hamilton taking the unusual step of submitting a minority report, dissenting from the committee's uncritical support for self-ID. The bill was debated by all MSPs in late October, passing its Stage 1 vote, but provoking the largest rebellion on the SNP benches since it had entered government in 2007, and the resignation of a government minister, Ash Regan MSP. Detailed amending Stage 2 discussions took place back in committee over two mornings in November, before the bill returned to the main chamber in December for its final Stage 3 consideration.

Street stalls and meetings continued to take place across Scotland over the year. Further groups emerged. In 2022, Scottish Lesbians arrived, saying 'it feels like we are in the fight of our lives to retain any recognition of who we are'. The Scottish Women's Rights Network and Women's Declaration International (WDI) Scotland formed part of networks stretching into the wider UK and beyond. As the bill proceeded, Scottish groups liaised with grassroots groups that had emerged across the UK, among others Fair Play for Women, Woman's Place UK, Keep Prisons Single Sex, Sex Matters and the LGB Alliance. They wrote to MSPs and the government to highlight the poor handling of contrary views, and to emphasise the importance of understanding the interaction with the Equality Act.

On 22 December 2022, the Gender Recognition Reform (Scotland) Bill was passed, by 86 votes to 39. Two hours later, the UK government announced that it was looking at whether to block the bill, using powers available to it under the devolution settlement.

2023

On 17 January, the UK government stepped in to prevent the bill from becoming law, citing excess impact on matters outside the Scottish Parliament's control. Then on 24 January, at the High Court in Glasgow, Adam Graham/Isla Bryson was convicted of two counts of rape, committed before Graham/Bryson had declared himself to be a woman.

Graham/Bryson's move from court to a woman's prison, Cornton Vale, hit the headlines. A photograph of him, taken outside court, in burgundy leggings and blond wig, was on every front page. At First Minister's Questions on 26 January, the first minister struggled badly as she sought to avoid answering questions about whether Graham/Bryson was a woman or a man.

On Wednesday 15 February 2023, at 11.00 a.m., Nicola Sturgeon unexpectedly resigned as first minister, citing no clear reasons for her departure, beyond stating that 'in my head and in my heart', this was the right time to go.

The preceding five years had seen a volunteer women's movement, organised in a network of spontaneously created, self-organised, loosely connected cells, emerge at extraordinary speed. It did so in response to the failure of a government, supposedly led by a feminist, and of other politicians and civic institutions, to engage with women making careful, serious arguments.

Women went on doing so to the bitter end of the bill process, but the more obvious it became that their arguments were of no interest to those in charge, the more they turned to public protest to be heard. Elaine Miller's noisy intervention from the public gallery at the point the bill was passed is probably the best known, but was preceded by many other attempts to catch political and media attention.

Not all groups were active throughout this period. Women moved between them, or were sometimes involved in more than one. It was demanding to be part of this movement – to face misrepresentation and hostility, threats and defamation, often on top of the personal histories and responsibilities which had led many women to become involved with it in the first place. It was costly in time and personal expense, too.

Abandoned by the established organisations built by previous generations, women had to rebuild from the ground up, at speed. They did so knowing their involvement becoming public could carry serious social and economic penalties; breaches of anonymity were a constant, real fear for many. Echoing the stresses of earlier phases of campaigning for women's rights, unsurprisingly sometimes people disagreed on how to campaign, found their priorities within the campaign changed or simply stepped back, feeling they had done all they could for now. Not all experiences were positive. But at the same time strong and lasting bonds of trust, respect and friendship were forged, often across deep party and constitutional divides. The women involved discovered that Millicent Fawcett was right: courage calls to courage.

SECTION 2

Early skirmishes: women learn the cost of speaking out

Chapter 6

Courage calls – a case study

Susan Smith

————————

**On the evening of Wednesday 20 June 2018, a group of women
meet in an Edinburgh flat and For Women Scotland is born**

For Woman Scotland (FWS) was nearly strangled in infancy.
On a bitter January day in 2019, a small group of us sat in a
meeting room in a hotel in the heart of Edinburgh's old town,
faced with the cancellation of the first public meeting under
the FWS banner or, at the very least, a risky commitment
to a massive security bill. We had about £300 in the bank,
which was not close to covering the room-hire costs, let
alone anything else. Like most such meetings at the time, the
location had been a closely guarded secret until a few hours
before kick-off. The moment the venue was revealed, the
hotel was bombarded with calls and emails which ranged from
angry men in Colorado – who had never set foot in Europe,
let alone Scotland – claiming they would withdraw their non-
existent patronage, to downright threats of violence and
vandalism. The self-described feminist group Sisters Uncut,
and a local 'radical' bookshop, were organising a march to the

Grassmarket and a protest outside the hotel. Unsurprisingly, the staff were jittery. We could only go ahead, we were told, if we quadrupled the professional security presence.

Such dramas were familiar to those across the UK who had been in the vanguard of the resurgent women's rights movement over previous years. They had happened at meetings arranged by Women's Spaces in Scotland (WSiS) in Edinburgh and Glasgow in early 2018. In Glasgow, where seasoned campaigner Venice Allan came to Scotland to give the new group practical help, two angry, intimidating young men stood up to shout at the speakers. So upset was one attendee that she wrote to the leader of the Scottish Greens and local MSP, Patrick Harvie, to beg him to facilitate a proper two-way conversation where women's concerns could be aired and, potentially, compromises reached. Mr Harvie responded that he would no more support such a meeting than he would host 'anti-Islam campaigners'.

The catalyst for those meetings was the Scottish Government's consultation on reforming the 2004 Gender Recognition Act (GRA). Eager, as always, to position Scotland as the most progressive nation in the UK, and vulnerable to being reminded of the shamefully late decriminalisation of homosexuality in Scotland, the Scottish Government was determined to get ahead of Westminster. The Scottish consultation, therefore, closed some six months before the one conducted in the rest of the UK. Consequently, it passed almost unremarked, except by the funded lobby groups with their huge resources and contact lists. The small band of women ranged against these government-backed forces seemed to have no chance in this David and Goliath fight and, when the consultation closed, it was unsurprising that many felt dispirited.

But surrender was not an option for one of the most influential and feisty women to have emerged to date in the struggle against self-ID. Magdalen Berns was a small but mighty opponent of gender identity ideology, a bundle of bristling energy and brutal put-downs who had garnered an impressive following for her YouTube channel. Magdalen had suffered personally from the corrosive impact of gender identity ideology in gay and lesbian societies, especially at Edinburgh University, where she crossed swords with the LGBT convener at the Student Association. In 2016, student newspaper the *Tab* reported that he had insulted women, labelling them 'cuntscum', and called women who refused to have sex with 'gender-neutral people with a penis' transphobes, and had advocated for them to be expelled from the University of Edinburgh. However, it was Magdalen who was officially sanctioned by the university for standing up to him.

Magdalen, her girlfriend Nicole Jones, plus Trina Budge and Marion Calder – who had all been part of the earlier WSiS campaign – met up on 20 June 2018 in Marion's sitting room in South Edinburgh, and For Women Scotland was born, after an evening of discussing feminism and then dancing to Madonna, slightly to the bemusement of Trina.

Would-be wags in the trans activist ranks have joked that the name reflects that there are only four women in the group. This bleak pun was deliberate. The four women in the room that day had no idea whether there was the appetite to continue the fight, or, indeed, what this fight would look like. One non-negotiable part of the plan, which was risky – as well as potentially alienating – was that the campaign would be public-facing. Magdalen had often said that the greater the number of women speaking up, the harder it would be to cancel them all. Nevertheless, women were all too aware that this took courage: livelihoods and personal safety were threatened by activists, some women had been sacked or had seen their personal details, including an address or the name of their child's school, posted online.

Trina, often erroneously seen as the quiet director, has a core of steel as well as a sense of the absurd, and it was she who hit the ground running. The very first press clippings saved on the FWS website chronicle how she self-identified as a man to successfully book male accommodation in Hostelling Scotland, exposing, and forcing them to review, their ludicrous policies.

The climate of intimidation meant that we could not openly advertise for women to join us. So, the four founders reached out to old contacts from feminist groups as well as women posting on the 'radicalisation portal' that is Mumsnet. Trina had found me on social media where I wrote about witches, something that had become horribly apt given women's current experience but proved useful when we responded to a future Scottish government consultation. We felt like rank amateurs, constantly expecting that someone better prepared and more influential would come along to take on the fight.

By the end of the summer, FWS was a loose group of about thirty women in secret social media groups. It was nerve-racking but also thrilling. We stickered Edinburgh from Bute House to the Engender office. We leafleted and we started to write to newspapers and to MSPs. But we had no money, and no one knew what this upstart little organisation was. A published letter was, at this time, a cause for celebration.

A more devastating problem was to come. Magdalen had previously been treated for a brain tumour, and this now evolved into glioblastoma – one of the most aggressive and deadly cancers. As summer turned into autumn, it was clear that she would not be able to take the prominent, public role she had intended, and that Nicole's focus would, inevitably, also change.

The break for FWS came in December 2018 when we were invited to give evidence to the committee examining proposed changes to the census. To this day, I am remarkably grateful that was my first experience as a witness. Not only was I on a panel with Professor Rosa Freedman, but the committee was convened by the remarkable Joan McAlpine, who would devote much of her remaining time in Parliament to fighting self-ID. Her deputy was Claire Baker, subsequently one of the two Labour MSPs to defy the whip and vote against the Gender Recognition Reform (Scotland) Bill, while Annabelle Ewing and Kenny Gibson, two of the SNP rebels, were also members. It was the first time the arguments against self-ID had been made in the Scottish Parliament. The committee was the best informed and the most intellectually curious ever to consider the subject at Holyrood.

There was nigh-delirious delight, and incredulity, on Mumsnet, with posters praising us as witnesses and Joan for asking the team from the Equality Network the 'Philip Bunce' question: 'How would a person who claims to be a woman half the week and a man on other days answer the sex question under self-ID?' Sadly, there was also the usual abuse. Joan was moved to defend our panel after an outrageous thread from a newspaper columnist. It was a small taste of the vituperative nastiness to which she would later be subjected.

After the session, Rosa agreed to speak at our first FWS meeting, scheduled for the last day of January. The publicity from the committee had given us some press attention, and journalists expressed interest in attending. We were still a baby group, with a mere 1,000 Twitter followers, but we felt that things were moving. We were also making inroads with MSPs. Trina, based in the far north of Scotland, covered hundreds of miles in her van to see her MSPs on the Parliament's regional list.

In January, before the public meeting, we hosted a meeting in Holyrood and were pleased that MSPs from all parties attended, with the notable exception of the Liberal Democrats. As a point of principle, we never revealed the names of those who came, but later most of them would nail their colours very firmly to the mast of women's rights. We will, however, always remember fondly the first meeting with the MSP who gave us chocolates and far more time than we deserved to examine the issue in detail, and who later paid the price for supporting women.

After this, the possible cancellation of our first public event in January 2019 was a body blow. The trans activists had, however, fatally underestimated Marion, who has never yet backed down in the face of a crisis. She rallied wavering hotel staff, and we decided to go ahead and deal with the bill later. Poor Trina, the only one of us with enough credit on her card to carry the deposit, bore the financial risk. While 150 guests listened to speeches from Rosa, Maggie Mellon and me, a small, bedraggled group of protestors shivered outside. Kept well away from the entrance to which ticket-holders were directed by our newly beefed-up security presence, they lacked much opportunity to berate attendees. Rosa felt so sorry for them that she arranged a delivery of hot chocolate to keep them warm.

The next day, a comprehensive report of the meeting by Libby Brooks was in the *Guardian*. Libby quoted from my speech:

> We are concerned that the Scottish government is sleepwalking towards a significant erosion of women's rights, both in terms of proposals to reform the GRA to allow self-identification and the failure to prevent other organisations running ahead of the law and adopting policies which are in breach of the Equality Act.
>
> We're not here to quibble about toilets and we're not here to create trouble for those who have battled crippling gender dysphoria. We welcome extra provisions for other vulnerable groups that don't involve dismantling existing rights. If we cannot see sex, then we cannot see sexism, we cannot define sexuality, and it is the most vulnerable women who will suffer from this.

They were words we were to repeat over and over in the subsequent years.

Libby also interviewed the protestors, quoting one who identified as trans saying, 'If a debate is what these people want, then there needs to be mutual respect.' After publication, the same person then attacked the paper for using it and tweeted that 'mutual respect' was a general policy that did not apply to us, instead he wanted to 'make them afraid'. He would not be the last to threaten us. In March, a man was charged by the police for threatening on social media to 'throat punch' members of FWS, although in a statement to the press the police spokesperson described the person involved as 'a woman'.

The attack on the *Guardian* resulted in more attention being focused on the meeting. We had announced that the increased costs were going to cripple us and, throughout the day, we were moved when dozens – then hundreds – of donations came in. Our detractors might imagine that we are sitting on piles of 'US far-right' cash, but the reality is that we are funded in the same way now as then – by contributions which are usually around £10–£20, with the occasional £50 or £100 sending us giddy with delight. In the following days, we reckoned we could clear the security bill and bank enough for another meeting.

The opportunity for further meetings presented itself when Meghan Murphy, the Canadian feminist and editor of *Feminist Current*, announced she was visiting the UK in May. Two meetings, with Meghan and her old friend and feminist researcher Bec Wonders, studying in Scotland at the time, put paid to the notion that Canada was, as often claimed, a shining example of successful 'international best practice'. They spoke about the vandalised Rape Crisis Centre in Vancouver, which was attacked for being 'women only'. The indignities, and worse, faced by women in shelters and in prisons. The terrifying trend of medicalising gender non-conforming children. And they showed footage of men attacking the Vancouver Feminist Library, ripping and spoiling the books written by women they considered ideologically impure.

Raising awareness at last seemed to be having an impact when, on FWS's first birthday, the then Equalities Minister, Shirley-Anne Somerville, announced that draft legislation allowing people to self-identify would be delayed until later in year and would be followed by another public consultation.

Not everybody was as happy as we were about this. A few days later, the leader of the Scottish Greens, Patrick Harvie, delivered a speech at Pride, where he claimed that Joan's event with Meghan had amounted to giving a 'platform for transphobic hatred and bigotry'. A small group of lesbian women carrying a banner reported that they faced a barrage of hostility after he spoke.

Magdalen died in September 2019 at the age of thirty-six. While the women who knew and loved her mourned, trans activists openly celebrated. One tweeted, 'It's OK to be happy, even celebrate when bad people die.' We had to watch while the BBC interviewed him favourably, as a case study, in discussions on the impact of self-ID on women's sports. But the love was very genuine and much greater. Women contacted us from across the world and tributes poured in. Magdalen's death was devastating for Nicole, but also incredibly tough for Marion, who had taken on many caring responsibilities. Marion organised a memorial in London which, in keeping with Magdalen's wishes, included the full spectrum of feminist voices – not all of whom always rubbed along comfortably. But this was more important.

Almost immediately we had a new goal, one of which Magdalen would have approved. The Scottish Government issued its second consultation on gender recognition reform in December 2019, and we were determined it would be far better publicised and debated than the last. Our public meeting in January of 2020 was almost twice the size of the one the year before, and we were rapidly running out of venues with large enough rooms. This meeting featured Nic Williams of Fair Play for Women, who ran such an impressive campaign during the consultation in England and Wales. It also marked one of the first public contributions from the indomitable Rhona Hotchkiss, a former governor of Scotland's women-only prison. And Sinead Watson, one of a growing number of detransitioners, spoke out from the floor.

More voices were being heard at Holyrood too. Feminist campaigner Karen Ingala Smith spoke of the difficulties self-ID posed to frontline staff working to combat violence against women – something denied by government-funded Scottish organisations. FWS women also joined in the guerrilla tactics of ReSisters who were dressing statues across the UK in 'Adult Human Female' T-shirts. Minnie the Minx and Mary Barbour have never looked more resplendent. Marion and Trina met Shirley-Anne Somerville with pages of questions which had, to date, not been answered. It will surprise no one to learn that the government has still not managed to respond. I was undergoing cancer treatment, but I couldn't miss joining the huge demonstration jointly arranged with LGB Alliance at Holyrood on 7 March 2020, the final event before the consultation closed and, as it turned out, before the spread of Covid-19 triggered lockdown.

Inside the Parliament, a back-slapping meeting for International Women's Day was under way, while outside speakers begged the government not to steal our rights. As I took to the stage, still clutching the cushions to protect my two-week-old surgery wounds, a heavily bearded older man turned up with group of very young, confused-looking people waving baby pink and blue flags. Stuffed with industrial quantities of painkillers, my memory of that event is a little hazy, but I do recall that this man's co-option of these kids angered me, and my speech that day was fierier than intended. We thought that was it. We'd fought, we'd done our best, but the forces against us were too slick and too well-funded to resist.

Little did we know that we were only just warming up.

Chapter 7

No quarter given

Ann Henderson

> **FairPlayForWomen** ✔
> @fairplaywomen
>
> Every MP has received a formal invitation for this meeting but we need YOU to make sure they come. Please email your constituency MP today telling them that you support us and ask them to confirm that they will attend. writetothem.com @Womans_Place_UK @Transgendertrd

On Sunday 7 October 2018, the new rector of Edinburgh University retweets a post on Twitter by Fair Play for Women promoting a meeting in Westminster about proposed changes to the Gender Recognition Act (GRA)

'Congratulations! A victory for women!' – the messages flooded in on social media and by post following my election as rector at the University of Edinburgh in February 2018. Friends, family, members of the women's movement and labour movement celebrated alongside me. A motion of congratulation was even tabled in the Scottish Parliament, and my term of office started full of optimism.

My small election campaign team was particularly proud of our result, as we had made history by securing the election of only the second female rector in 150 years. Since 1869, there had been fifty-two rectors, but only one woman before me when broadcaster Muriel Gray held the post in 1988.

Scotland's older universities of Glasgow, St Andrews, Aberdeen, Dundee and Edinburgh all have rectors. It's a completely unremunerated position, and at Edinburgh comes with minimal staff support. The role carries some formal duties at graduations and other events, chairing the General Council AGM, and chairing the University Court, the university's governing body.

Our campaign had focused on the additional voice that the rector can bring, speaking up on issues raised by staff and students, and encouraging dialogue with external networks and the university community. My career to date spanned community and social work, the railways, the Scottish Parliament and the Scottish Trades Union Congress (STUC), so I was looking forward to sharing my knowledge and experience, while at the same time learning more about the university and higher education. Edinburgh was four times the size it had been in 1974–8, when I studied there, having incorporated Edinburgh Art College and Moray House College of Education in recent years.

Working with, and for, women has always been important to me. It was at Edinburgh in the early 1970s that I discovered the Women's Group and the wider women's movement, and I went on to set up or strengthen women's structures in trade unions and the Labour Party. I served briefly as the Scotland commissioner on the Women's National Commission, until the incoming Conservative government of 2010 closed it down. I had built lasting female friendships across the country – this is my life.

Angi Lamb, a recently retired Edinburgh University staff member and UCU (University and College Union) activist, had contacted me out of the blue in late 2017 to ask me to stand for the post. After my election, she was chosen as the rector's assessor on University Court, and was by my side until very unexpected ill-health made it impossible for her to continue. Sadly, she died in the summer of 2020.

My term of office ran from 1 March 2018 to the end of February 2021 and, during those three years, I carried out all official duties as requested, prepared for University Court meetings, chairing and encouraging participation, and took on other engagements too. Initially Angi and I sorted out drop-in sessions; we visited different campuses and responded to as many invitations as possible to events, both internal and external, and supported various student clubs and societies. We spent time on picket lines with the UCU which was engaged in a dispute over pensions. I was very busy, as I was also still in paid employment at the Scottish Parliament and managing various family responsibilities, as so many of us do. But I was committed and keen to carry out the role to the best of my ability, knowing that I had the support of many people. Little did I know what was about to come.

I got a foretaste in August 2018, when Edinburgh Labour Students issued a statement alleging that I held transphobic and antisemitic views and was 'not fit to hold office within the Labour Party or as Rector'. They offered no evidence to back up their assertions and they were quickly dismissed. It was the summer recess, campus was quiet, and the university was aware that these comments had been made during a contested election for National Executive seats within the Labour Party.

However, the allegations of transphobia were to reappear with a vengeance in October, while I was out of the country for a few days, less than a week after the ceremony where I was installed as rector.

Weeks before, I had discovered that a London-based Labour activist was tracking my social media accounts, where I followed various feminist organisations – including Woman's Place UK (WPUK). Edinburgh Labour Students, and others on campus, had alleged that WPUK and other feminist groups were 'transphobic hate organisations'. Again, no evidence was put forward, and they had to withdraw the defamatory statements about me. But the damage was done. An influential group of students had decreed I was 'not fit to hold office'.

At the same time, Westminster was scrutinising reforms to the 2004 Gender Recognition Act. Sabbatical officers at the Edinburgh University Students' Association (EUSA) and PrideSoc – the university's LGBTQ+ society – organised a postcard campaign to MPs in support of the reforms, asserting there would be no impact on women or the 2010 Equality Act. In October, I retweeted an advert for an open meeting for MPs hosted by Fair Play for Women and other groups. It was sent from my personal account, without comment, and I remember thinking how positive it was that MPs were being encouraged to properly discuss possible legislative change. Meanwhile EUSA was encouraging students to write to their MPs telling them not to attend the meeting.

I found myself at the centre of yet another storm. Within days of returning from my holiday, I was asked to attend a meeting with senior management and student sabbatical officers, where they discussed how to remove an elected rector. There was no recognition that the allegations were not proven, and that I was being bullied and harassed on campus, and in the press. The message from the meeting was clear – I was 'not fit to hold office'. I left in tears and was signed off work.

As I sat in a café on campus, I realised I no longer felt safe. For nearly fifty years, I had been part of the movement for progressive change in women's lives. I knew what male resistance and opposition felt like. I had not expected to find it on a university campus in 2018. It felt like an attack on women, on a movement which had achieved so much, but still had so much to do.

The university pursued a complaints procedure. To this day, I do not understand how the accusation that I was 'transphobic' was valid, as it seemed to be based on an assertion that I think differently on a public policy to some others, or indeed that I thought parliamentarians should scrutinise legislative proposals. Surely a university – especially one as well-regarded as Edinburgh – should be the last place to discourage thoughtful consideration of policies and laws. It turned out I was wrong.

I sought advice from Shereen Benjamin, who had been a local UCU branch officer and involved in my election campaign. We learned that the UCU would not help me; indeed they joined forces with those who sought to shut down debate. After so many years of active trade union membership, and having had the support of this union in my rector campaign as I stood on the picket lines alongside them, this came as a shock.

Mediation services were brought in, and after three months the university concluded there were no outstanding complaints against me. There was simply no evidence.

But the campaign to discredit me did not end there. Throughout my next two years as rector, material referring to my 'transphobic' behaviour continued to circulate on campus, unchallenged. No action was ever taken.

And it was becoming clear from correspondence that students and staff were also experiencing harassment for holding what had become known as 'gender critical' views.

THE WOMEN WHO WOULDN'T WHEESHT

Lesbian staff members felt excluded from networks. Women-only events were increasingly difficult – even impossible – to arrange, and women were concerned about losing their female private facilities. My primary concern was to ensure that any student or staff member who raised these issues with me should know that they were heard and would be supported.

By this time, however, the leadership of the UCU Edinburgh branch had changed and added their voice to the allegations against me. This affected their ability to work with me in my role as rector. Similarly, while EUSA officers took up their places on the University Court, which I chaired, they withdrew from all the meetings I had set up for regular engagement. Some would even turn their back on me at events, including when we were off campus.

The rector's role is, in part, ambassadorial, yet university management did not think it appropriate to issue me with a business card until 2020, or with any official ID at external events. I was invited to speak at the International Women's Day event in the Scottish Parliament in early March 2020, and asked for my speech to be signed off and published by the university, recognising I had been invited as rector. My request was ignored. There was even an allegation against me made to my employer at the Scottish Parliament. It was withdrawn as soon as evidence was requested.

Taken individually, these will seem small matters. Taken together, it felt as if my voluntary time was not appreciated. There was no duty of care exercised towards me. And regrettably, the full potential for only the second woman rector to do something constructive with campus trade unions and the student body, was wasted.

There were times when I thought about resigning, but on reflection I felt that would achieve nothing. It wasn't my right to give up the position. That may have been what those who hounded me wanted, but it wasn't best for the women and men who had voted for me. And I knew I was not alone; that there were others facing the same political and personal challenges. The flowers, cards and messages of support I received, the cups of coffee I enjoyed, the unadvertised evening meetings where I met women from across the city: all gave me hope.

I also had some lovely messages of thanks from staff and students for attending lectures or events and, as the UCU dispute continued, I supported staff on their picket lines, many of them unaware of my own mistreatment.

And there was the memory of my parents. My mother died in 2011, having worked in the university's Department of Hispanic Studies as a part-time lecturer until retirement. My father died in 2017, after a lifetime's career in Edinburgh's publishing industry, with periods training at Moray House and teaching in an Edinburgh secondary school.

They had met at Edinburgh University as students in 1950. It was one of the personal reasons I had accepted the invitation to run for rector, as a way of marking their memory. I was thrilled when the university's library hosted an exhibition in 2019 to mark 100 years of the Spanish degree at Edinburgh University, and it included a credit to my mother's contribution. My parents would have been so proud of my election, and completely mystified, and angry, at the way in which events unfolded.

In June 2019, Shereen Benjamin and others organised an open meeting on women's rights on campus. The meeting was well attended, including by some MSPs. This was a welcome recognition that some politicians at least understood that the Scottish Government's proposals for GRA reform would require careful scrutiny. Security arrangements were extensive as a crowd of students and staff, including members of the UCU Edinburgh branch, gathered outside to hurl abuse. At the end of the meeting one of the female speakers was threatened and her assailant – a male trans activist – later accepted a fixed penalty fine after being charged with breach of the peace. The university management remained silent.

In the Scottish Parliament, where I worked, in contrast to the university, it had been possible to arrange several meetings on gender recognition reform, so that MSPs and the staff could hear different views.

As the Covid-19 pandemic started, it became clear it would have a disproportionate impact on women's lives. I took part in support calls with staff and students, and one in particular stays in my mind. A female postgraduate student, with two children under five, described how hard it was to work on her thesis with no childcare, no workspace, and no leniency on deadlines. Female academics talked of the impact of additional care responsibilities on their careers. And female catering and cleaning staff had to provide the frontline care support for students in isolation.

There was so much to campaign on, to speak up about women's lives and experiences, yet my first two years as rector had been so dominated by unfounded allegations that my ability to work on policies and campaigns, to be that additional voice, had been restricted. The culture of 'no evidence' and 'no debate' did not serve women and the university community well.

My time as rector overlapped with my election to a position on Labour's National Executive Committee (NEC), as one of the lay members representing constituency parties. Following redundancy from the STUC in 2017, I had taken a part-time post with Labour MSP Elaine Smith, then unexpectedly found myself running in, and winning, two very different election campaigns.

Within three months of joining Labour's NEC in late 2018, I was elected to the position of chair of the NEC's

Equalities Committee. Before the meeting had even finished, the LGBT Labour representative had posted a statement online alleging transphobia and calling for me to be removed. Again, no evidence was provided, but that did not stop the online abuse against me. Eventually, the Labour Party issued a statement indicating its confidence in my role as chair of the committee.

Before I joined the NEC, the Labour Party rulebook had already changed to include the undefined term 'gender identity' as a characteristic, and earlier in 2018, in the face of considerable opposition, the NEC had decided that anyone who self-identified as a woman could run for any of the positions reserved for women, including all-women shortlists.

At the same time, the Labour Party re-established the women's organisation structures which had been dismantled under Tony Blair's leadership. Women up and down the country began setting up women's branches, but some ran into difficulties as the definition of 'woman' was no longer clear in Labour's rules. This was brought to my attention as chair of the Equalities Committee, but I found it impossible to get anyone to pay heed.

Allegations of transphobia echoed round Labour's 2019 annual conference in Brighton. Anyone who so much as asked a question about protected characteristics, definitions or discrimination against women, or sought to discuss GRA reform, was shouted down. A fringe meeting held by Woman's Place UK was picketed aggressively by mainly men – some masked – shouting about trans rights and banging on the venue's windows. There were Labour staff members and conference delegates among the protesters.

It was a frightening and intimidating evening. Many of the attendees were upset, and we walked back to our hotels in pairs or groups, too uneasy to walk on our own. Once again it felt that this behaviour was designed to set women back, not move us forward.

The following month, I went to my first FiLiA conference, which was held in Bradford that year. FiLiA is part of the women's liberation movement and has held annual feminist conferences since 2013. I knew some other women from Scotland who were attending. I was not sure what to expect but found it to be a great chance to listen, learn, and discuss with women who had common goals. Mindful of the situation at Edinburgh University, and fearful of criticism, I decided not to announce my presence at the conference on social media. In hindsight that seems a ridiculous decision, but that was the environment in which I was working.

During this FiLiA conference, I met up again with some women I had come across informally at the September 2018 Labour conference. We got together and worked out a plan to launch the Labour Women's Declaration (LWD). The group's primary aim was to raise the profile of women's sex-based rights within the Labour Party and the wider socialist movement. In Scotland, founding signatories included Labour MSPs Johann Lamont, Jenny Marra and Elaine Smith.

Since its launch, LWD has been a focal point for the campaign to ensure women's sex-based rights remain clear and strong within Labour's policies at a national and local level.

Despite harassment and intimidation, LWD supporters built up an effective network across the country. Every voice and every action was part of a movement. And when it came to the sign-off for Labour's 2019 General Election manifesto, I was able to play a part as an NEC member in ensuring the inclusion of a commitment to the provisions of the Equality Act 2010.

The work is nowhere near complete, but there has been some progress, aided by the decision of the UK government to retreat from pursuing self-ID as part of GRA reform. More

MPs, councillors and MSPs are now speaking up, and LWD fringe meetings around national and regional conferences are sold out.

In Scotland, links with the LWD network have been particularly important. The early Scottish LWD signatories played an important role in parliamentary debates and continue to speak out. And while the majority of Scottish Labour MSPs supported the Gender Recognition Reform (Scotland) Bill in December 2022, in face of strong representation against this from women, a Scotland-wide network of Labour women now meets regularly, and they clearly reflect the views of the majority of Scottish Labour women. The November 2023 Scottish Labour Women's Conference overwhelmingly supported a motion that restates the importance of women's sex-based rights.

I have found reflecting on the last five years tough. The refusal of Edinburgh University to properly support only the second female rector in its history is still hard to accept. And the Labour Party's refusal – until very recently – to listen to women's voices, was astonishing for a party which claims to be the guardian of strong policies on equality.

I look back to the early days of the Scottish Parliament, when women claimed their rightful place in the new legislature and were engaged at every level – from community groups to government – in the political rebirth of our nation. There was a quiet optimism, tempered with the knowledge that there was much to do to challenge inequality, to end violence against women, to close the pay gap.

Twenty-five years later, as I watched the final debate on the GRR Bill in the Scottish Parliament, where MSPs had lost the ability to even clearly define a woman, I cried. But my sisters and I are still fighting. There is still work to be done.

Chapter 8

Finding out women don't count

Joan McAlpine

———————

On Thursday 6 December 2018, a Scottish Parliament committee, chaired by Joan McAlpine MSP, takes evidence from Professor Rosa Freedman of Reading University and Susan Smith about proposed changes to the census in Scotland

When the dry, one-page Census Bill was put before the Culture, Tourism, Europe and External Affairs Committee of the Scottish Parliament in 2018, nobody expected it to consume much time or attention.

The Census (Amendment) (Scotland) Bill was a piece of legislative house-keeping. The sort of bill which requires scrutiny by MSPs lest there be unintended consequences – but a formality nonetheless.

The committee, which I convened (chaired), had a heavy workload – including the fallout from Brexit. We were examining the circumstances around the fires at Glasgow School of Art and had conducted major enquiries into screen sector and arts funding.

The Census Bill sought to amend the Census Act, to allow two new questions to be asked on a voluntary basis – one on sexual orientation, another on transgender identity. The 1920 Census Act made it an offence not to answer questions. Over time, new questions of a personal nature were added, such as on religion or health, so amendments were made to the original legislation to allow voluntary answers. This was no different. Parliament was not being asked to approve of the questions – only their voluntary nature.

However, the first draft of this Scottish bill proposed an amendment which went further than ensuring questions were voluntary. It proposed to insert, after the word 'sex', the phrase '(including gender identity)'. This was very different from simply adding a separate question on transgender status, as was also proposed. It appeared to change the definition of sex itself.

As part of the census development process, National Records of Scotland (NRS), which runs it, produced a Topic Report on the sex question which explained why sex statistics were so important. A question to determine male or female sex has been asked since 1801. The NRS Topic Report stated: 'It is a vital input to population, household and other demographic statistics which are used by central and local government to inform resource allocation, target investment, and carry out service planning and delivery.' It went on to note: 'Sex is a protected characteristic as set out in the Equality Act 2010 and the data are widely used to inform equality impact assessments.'

So NRS understood the importance of sex data. Women continue to suffer specific discrimination on the basis of sex – and it is crucial to monitor this accurately.

Yet despite this acknowledgement, the government proposed to include 'gender identity' in the definition of sex itself. Their approach was deeply contradictory.

Worse, the Scottish Government published a policy memorandum to accompany the bill which claimed: 'society's definition of sex has changed'. This was an untested assumption and simply reflected the assertions of trans lobby groups. It claimed the sex question in the 2011 census was a matter of 'self-identification', but this had not been publicised at the time or stated on the census itself. This change certainly wasn't debated in Parliament or wider society. The government also proposed to provide 'non-binary response options' to the 2021 mandatory sex question, meaning respondents could conceal their sex.

Reading that one-page bill in 2018 made me uneasy, because of my growing understanding of the wider context. The Scottish and UK governments were considering changes to the 2004 Gender Recognition Act (GRA) to allow anyone to change their legal sex on the basis on self-declaration, eliminating the need for scrutiny, including medical diagnosis. If the gold-standard census allowed the self-identification of sex, this would inevitably be used to legitimise and establish it in law.

I had heard a Radio Four news bulletin about an attack on a sixty-one-year-old woman, Maria MacLachlan, by a group of 'trans activists' at Hyde Park Corner in London. A person calling themselves Tara Wolf was convicted of assault and fined £150. However, Maria, the victim, was criticised by the judge for referring to her male assailant as 'he'.

I was astounded by this story, having previously thought that 'trans' referred to a tiny number of male-to-female transsexuals who had undergone extensive surgery and hormone treatment to modify their bodies. This was not a group one previously associated with violence. That said, 'sex-change' stories about middle-aged truckers who had fathered several children deciding to 'become' women, always unsettled me.

These men equated the performance of femininity – make-up, long hair, clothing, silky undies – with being female. They ascribed character traits, such as submissiveness, to women. To suggest false eyelashes, high heels and passivity maketh the woman undermines, in my view, everything feminists had fought for from the 1960s to the 1980s. It is sexist.

By 2018, a new 'trans umbrella' was being promoted by organisations such as Stonewall. It included men who had made no change whatsoever to their bodies, but demanded to be called women and get access to spaces where women were vulnerable, such as changing rooms and shelters, or jobs reserved for women because they delivered intimate care to elderly or disabled females. They would demand places in schemes designed to help women overcome sex discrimination – such as on political all-female shortlists. I had begun to follow the campaign mounted by Woman's Place UK, the Labour Party organisation formed to challenge this ideology, as well as reading the excellent online research material offered by Fair Play for Women.

I was also aware of the emergence of independent Scottish groups such as For Women Scotland (FWS). These were women working around kitchen tables, after finishing their day job and putting the kids to bed. And I noticed some academics had begun to raise concerns, only to be slapped down. The most disturbing aspect of all this was not the passionate disagreement, which is healthy in a democratic society, but the insistence of the trans lobby that any discussion of the issue constituted hate speech. There was to be 'no debate'.

Feminists with long histories as social justice warriors were branded bigots. These included Linda Bellos, the former Labour leader of Lambeth Council and founder of Black History Month, Beatrix Campbell, a communist intellectual and feminist I admired, and Julie Bindel, the journalist whose work on male violence and sexual exploitation of women is so inspiring. Dame Jenni Murray, the former presenter of BBC Radio Four's *Woman's Hour,* was pilloried, and Germaine Greer, perhaps the world's most famous feminist, was 'cancelled'.

These women, along with less famous, but equally committed individuals in the trade union and labour movement, had their reputations trashed and achievements forgotten. It was terrifying – and sexist. Noisy, masked protestors physically blocked their meetings or drowned them out by banging on the walls. Disturbingly, these aggressive, reality-denying extremists had the ear of the establishment. Women's meetings were barred by local authorities and party conferences. Venues cancelled them, citing security concerns. This was a global phenomenon – with disturbing examples from Canada of a women-only rape crisis shelter vandalised by trans activists, with dead rats pinned to its doors.

In 1859, John Stuart Mill wrote: 'When we silence an opinion, we rob the human race. We rob posterity as well as our own generation. We rob those who dissent from that silenced opinion, even more than those who hold it.'

He could have been describing No Debate. In 2018, organisations and individuals advancing gender identity politics refused to appear on platforms or in media debates with women who raised concerns. They knew that when the public heard their arguments, they would lose.

Silencing women has always been the most effective way of controlling women. For centuries we were silenced almost entirely – in the family, in the courts, in politics and the workplace. In many parts of the world, such as Iran, we still are.

Historically, women who spoke up for themselves were silenced by the threat of violence. In medieval Scotland we had the 'scold's bridle', an iron torture device placed over the tongue of particularly mouthy females. But women are silenced mostly by social control – the fear that expressing the wrong opinion will result in ostracisation and ridicule.

So, when the Culture, Tourism, Europe and External Affairs Committee of the Scottish Parliament was asked to scrutinise the Census (Amendment) (Scotland) Bill in 2018, we had an opportunity to do good. First, we could scrutinise and improve a piece of flawed legislation – one of the core purposes of the committee system at Holyrood. Second, we could challenge 'no debate' and platform feminists who until then had been prevented from freely expressing themselves. To allow concerned women to challenge self-ID in the Scottish Parliament would make it difficult for them to be 'cancelled' elsewhere.

Convenors do not decide the work programme of committee, nor the selection of witnesses, or how evidence is gathered or reports presented. Any MSP member can make a proposal, and all members must sign off on decisions. But convenors are closely involved in the day-to-day planning and the detail of meetings. They can have significant influence, if they are willing to put in the work and can bring MSPs of all parties together.

Opening up the debate required some initiative. When, during an informal briefing, I asked officials at NRS whether they had spoken to organisations who opposed their view that 'our understanding of sex has changed', they looked blank. The normally excellent Scottish Parliament Information Service (SPICe), which prepares committee briefings and research, said there was no opposition to proposals in the bill.

Witnesses to committee are normally chosen to reflect the balance of written evidence you receive – after putting out an official 'Call for Evidence'. A bill as niche as the Census (Amendment) (Scotland) Act would struggle to attract much of a response without publicity. Also, the process is weighted towards organisations with dedicated public affairs teams, whose job it is to monitor Parliament, submit evidence and brief MSPs ahead of debates or evidence sessions. There is an in-built bias against the grassroots in favour of professional lobbyists.

We needed to hear evidence that reflected the views of the public – that sex is binary and observed at birth, that data should not be corrupted by ideology and must be based on material reality. I therefore approached Kathleen Stock, then professor of philosophy at the University of Sussex and one of a few academics brave enough to speak up. She was active on Twitter with a large following. If she could highlight that this obscure Census Bill in the Scottish Parliament was really rather important, we might increase, and diversify, the quality of written evidence we received. I emailed her. Kathleen was incredibly helpful. She publicised our call for evidence and gave me the names of academics who could be approached to submit papers.

By then I was also in touch with the women who would become Murray Blackburn Mackenzie (MBM), the policy analysis collective, and FWS. Between them, they spread the word and ensured we had an excellent range of submissions. From these, the committee was persuaded to invite FWS and Rosa Freedman, professor of human rights law at Reading University, to give evidence in person to Parliament. We also took oral evidence from Lucy Hunter Blackburn of MBM, a former senior civil servant, and Professor Susan McVie, professor of quantitative criminology at the University of Edinburgh, an expert on statistics and data gathering.

We succeeded in attracting a range of evidence that challenged regressive gender identity ideology. All of this was now on the parliamentary record. This included Woman's Place UK, who were quoted in our committee report into the Bill: 'An individual's biological sex is an immutable characteristic: The inclusion of a third option to the question on sex would indicate a departure from scientifically-grounded theory of human sexual dimorphism.'

Professor Rosa Freedman told us: 'Bringing in the idea of a third category – a non-binary gender – into sex, or bringing together gender identity and sex in the one question, is bringing together two characteristics protected under the Equality Act 2010 and thus, in essence, undermining them both.' Kathleen Stock pointed out that: 'Gender identity is a contested term, with no well-established meaning.'

The committee's evidence sessions included representatives from the Equality Network and Scottish Trans Alliance, funded mainly by the Scottish Government, who supported self-identification, and representatives from supportive Scottish Government agencies. But it was the presence of alternative voices which captured the public and media attention. We had started something.

Our scrutiny exposed flaws in government consultation. We did not use the term 'policy capture', but that is what happened. NRS consulted only groups promoting the self-identification of sex. It never considered that others – such as women – might be affected and worth talking to. Nor did it occur to them to explore the implications for researchers who used the census data.

A Freedom of Information (FOI) request by a member of the public exposed how vested interests could shape policy. It revealed email correspondence between officials at NRS and the Equality Network discussing our committee's findings. They clearly had a close, indeed warm, working relationship.

Our committee persuaded the Cabinet Secretary responsible for the Bill, Fiona Hyslop, to amend it. She removed the words 'including gender identity' after the word sex. There was now no confusion between the two.

When the committee report was published, I authored a Twitter thread called *Sex and the Census* which attracted global attention. It pointed out that organisations such as Scottish Trans Alliance (STA), who are funded by the Scottish Government, had previously argued in evidence to a House of Commons Committee for an end to the protections women currently enjoy in the Equality Act. They said 'single sex exemptions' should be dropped completely. It is these groups, who do not put women first, who were exclusively consulted on the census.

As well as committee scrutiny, bills are subject to two debates on the floor of Parliament – at Stages 1 and 3. This means that MSPs were made aware of the conflict of rights which self-ID could trigger. They received briefings from FWS, Woman's Place UK and others. It was an important milestone in educating decision makers.

The Census (Amendment) (Scotland) Bill passed, and that was fine. Nobody on the committee objected to a voluntary question about transgender identity being posed.

There was still some unfinished business, however. In the course of our scrutiny, we discovered that the guidance for the sex question was based on self-identification in 2011, although this was not publicised or consulted on at the time.

The committee advised NRS to consult more widely on the guidance accompanying the 2021 census sex question. This was done, but the conclusions were weighted towards a tiny sample of respondents identifying as trans. The research revealed a statistically significant proportion of the general population were hostile to guidance which allowed sex to be self-identified. As these respondents represented potentially a far larger section of the population, even a small boycott could make an impact on data. This was ignored by NRS, which pressed ahead with the original guidance. NRS also received submissions from some of the country's leading academic data users advising against self-identification in the guidance. This was, again, completely ignored.

However, the online guidance on the sex question was not part of the Census (Amendment) (Scotland) Bill. MSPs could only have stopped it if they had taken a 'nuclear option' and blocked the entire census by voting against the Census Order, an unusual parliamentary device which activates the census itself. Nobody considered this proportionate. The important thing was that we removed 'self-ID' from the face of a bill which had tried to change the definition of sex in law.

The census scrutiny determined my path for the rest of the 2016–21 parliamentary term. I was asked to speak around the country, and connected with women across the UK, hundreds of whom sent me touching thank you cards. We began to organise: at Holyrood, in the SNP and in our communities. We ran meetings in Parliament with speakers such as Meghan Murphy, the Canadian feminist. We had a session on the medicalisation of young children with the psychotherapist David Bell, a whistle-blower at the controversial Tavistock Gender Identity Service, which was later shut down after an investigation. I also received significant online abuse, including from within the SNP, which was never addressed, despite my repeated appeals for support.

Labour and SNP women came together to oppose the first attempt to take forward gender recognition in Scotland, later dropped during the pandemic. We formed SNP Women's Pledge and Labour Women's Declaration in 2019 to campaign inside our parties, with Conservative and Liberal Democrat Women taking similar steps. Also in 2019, I persuaded several SNP MSPs, MPs and councillor colleagues, including several ministers, to sign an open letter asking the Scottish Government to think carefully before changing the definition of sex. I began asking questions in Parliament, drawing attention to the distortion of crime statistics as offenders were recorded by their chosen gender identity.

STV's *Scotland Tonight* programme ran several specials on the topic – one hilarious highlight was my head-to-head with the Greens' Maggie Chapman, who refused to deny her party believed women can have a penis. The *BBC Nine* also devoted time to the subject, as did formidable journalists such as Shona Craven in the *Herald* and Gina Davidson and Susan Dalgety of the *Scotsman*.

It is easy to feel disheartened at the way the government chose to ignore this upswelling of opposition to self-ID. It was a personal agenda of the former First Minister Nicola Sturgeon, and a special interest group comprising her loyalists. She was able to introduce the Gender Recognition Reform (Scotland) Bill in 2022, after securing a coalition with the Greens. It was unpopular in the country and the UK government successfully blocked it. The SNP has lost members, as well as support, because they chose to die on this particular hill. Back in 2018–19, those of us in the party who opposed transgender ideology predicted it would damage our movement. It's been devastating.

Despite these setbacks, what started in 2018 with an obscure piece of legislation, is a great source of pride. Women were heard, and legitimised by their own Parliament. 'No debate' was cancelled.

Chapter 9

Audacious women disrupted

Sally Wainwright

————

The fourth annual Audacious Women Festival encounters trouble as it starts on Thursday 21 February 2019 in central Edinburgh

As a lesbian feminist, the existence of women's space has always been extremely important to me. Women share experiences that are different from men's, and women's space allows us to relax in the knowledge that we have some shared understanding. We don't have to explain ourselves, or justify ourselves, or apologise for being ourselves, or try to meet male expectations. The women's spaces I have helped create reflect that – from a women's aid refuge for women who had experienced male violence, to an annual lesbian festival.

Socially, I want space without men not because I'm frightened of being assaulted if a man is in the room, but because if he's there it is no longer women's space. His presence, however 'benign', changes the atmosphere.

When I was a young dyke, I met many older lesbians happy to share their experiences, joined lesbian groups, and even lived in a lesbian housing co-op. In 1980s Edinburgh there were regular women-only events, attended by lesbian and straight women alike. But these have declined to almost zero, and those that exist are increasingly forced to meet in secret. The impact of this loss on the lesbian community is rarely appreciated, even by many women's rights campaigners. Reinstating women's and lesbian space, allowing us to exercise our freedom of association, must be a priority for women organising to support each other.

In 2016 I co-founded the Audacious Women Festival, which encouraged women to commit their own acts of audacity, with the motto *Do What You Always Wish You Dared*. This opens the festival to all women, regardless of age or ability, because what is audacious for one woman may be daily practice for another. For example, while some women have always sung, I, like many women, was told to keep quiet during school singing lessons. We'd been, literally, silenced. Our Scared to Sing workshop became one of our most popular events.

The festival started audaciously. We had no funds and no resources, yet we conjured up an astounding range of workshops, exhibitions, films, music, and theatre events. There was no question but that the festival would provide women's space. Some events are open to everyone, but the majority are small, intimate, women-only workshops and sports-taster sessions. These offer women something new and personally challenging, away from the male gaze. There, women find the support and confidence to try something difficult without being intimidated by men's larger physical presence and superior physical ability, or the fear of men's voices telling them they are incompetent. That is the fundamental purpose of the festival, and why we successfully empower women to make significant changes in their lives.

From the start, we faced pressure to include an ever-widening range of men. Then, in 2019, a male trans activist somewhere in England set about making our life difficult, using social media. I only heard of one written complaint, but the publicity put pressure on both our venues to cancel us, just days before the festival was due to start. I spent two full days, with support from For Women Scotland (FWS), reassuring our venues that we were legal. Edinburgh City Council's equalities team agreed. Nevertheless, confirmation that the council would host us only came after we'd already set up.

Meanwhile, we felt obliged to refute allegations of 'transphobia', explaining that our workshops are women-only, as one of the important aims of the Festival is to provide a safe space for women to explore their potential. Of course, we said, this includes transwomen, in line with the EHRC (Equality and Human Rights Commission) guidance.

However, this wasn't enough for the gender identity zealots. Glasgow Women's Library and Edinburgh Rape Crisis Centre both cancelled their events at extremely short notice, telling us our approach 'did not align' with their 'trans inclusive' policies. Both are based on self-ID and include a much wider range of identities than the law requires, or even recognises. Ironically, Edinburgh Rape Crisis Centre's book launch was open to everyone. The authors were rape survivors who had spent weeks preparing themselves for the event. I can only imagine their feelings when they were suddenly cancelled in the name of an ideology that centres males.

We were staggered by the vitriol and negative publicity we received, and were ill-prepared to deal with criticism and harassment for quoting and following EHRC guidance. We'd bent over backwards to stay well within the law, but this had long since become irrelevant in Scotland, where de facto self-ID had already imposed itself on a largely unsuspecting population.

I felt the policy we'd been forced to adopt was a betrayal, both of our principles and of the women we set out to provide for. In fact, no trans-identifying males were interested enough to actually attend the festival. The activists' intention seemed to be solely to prevent women meeting on our own.

In 2021, the Audacious Women Festival went online because of lockdown. After resuming real-life events we have, perhaps surprisingly, not experienced any further public attacks. Nevertheless, we have faced repeated problems securing venues because of our policy. The last few years have become a constant battle to provide women's space, however transient, and we've dealt with three cancellations this year alone.

In 2022, the Maya Forstater and Allison Bailey cases determined that the perfectly conventional belief that sex is binary and immutable, is legally protected. This, combined with the activists' behaviour and outright dismissal of our significant concessions, inspired us to be braver – and more audacious – and state explicitly that our women's spaces are just that. Saying this, rather than the constant ducking and weaving we'd previously been forced to engage in, was hugely important, although it poses significant challenges in implementation.

If the recent ruling in the FWS reclaiming motion – that men with a Gender Recognition Certificate (GRC) are to be treated as 'women' – emboldens legally female men to participate, the festival will be unable to function.

Women's space cannot include men, no matter how the law defines them. It's a binary question, incapable of compromise. A space is either single-sex or it is not. Men's physicality, energy, voices, and sense of superiority are not diminished through possession of a piece of paper. Women's space provides a brief respite from this, and also from men's belief in their own entitlement. There is no clearer example of this than their insistence that the literal or metaphorical donning of a skirt entitles men to enter women's rare and precious space.

Chapter 10

A hounding in Scottish literature

Jenny Lindsay

_____

**On the evening of Sunday 2 June 2019, a celebrated
Scottish poet objects on social media to a magazine article
justifying calls for violence against women**

It is the 2nd of June 2019. I am alone in my Edinburgh
flat. It is evening, I have had two glasses of wine, when a
friend messages me with a 'WTF' and an article from the arts
publication the *Skinny* attached. The article is entitled 'Pride
and Prejudice'. Several columnists have been asked for their
views on Pride marches in 2019. I am quickly drawn to what
has led to the 'WTF'.

One of the columnists writes that they avoid Pride due to
perceived transphobia from certain lesbian groups and adds
'I [have] received much criticism for demanding violent action
against these TERFs . . . While my comments were extreme,
I stand by what I said.' This was in reference to the columnist's
tweets, which are, indeed, 'extreme': 'Any trans allies at
#PrideLondon right now need to step the fuck up and take out

the TERF trash. Get in their faces. Make them afraid. Debate never works so fuck them up.'

Another tweet states 'Beat them up' alongside a retweet about campaign group Get The L Out, a lesbian advocacy group that argues lesbians are no longer well represented by organisations such as Stonewall and should form separate activist spaces.

Undoubtedly, the wine contributed to my next decision. I took to Twitter and addressed a tweet to the *Skinny*: 'Hello! One of your commentators here advocates violence against lesbian activists at Pride. I find it extraordinary that such views are given an airing in *The Skinny*, and, for clarity, the "I stand by what I said" refers to beating up "TERFs", i.e. women. At Pride. Just FYI.'

A lay reader might be surprised that opposing violence against women at Pride could provoke any backlash, but, of course, it did. Instantly, my messages filled up with outrage from friends in the Scottish literary world who hold gender identity beliefs. I tried to navigate this as best I could, though the resulting forty-eight hours were not pleasant. In the interim, an individual at the *Skinny* emailed me admitting editorial oversight. The article was quietly amended online, removing 'TERF' and the reference to the tweets. Unfortunately, another editor at the magazine amplified the outrage by tweeting that anyone opposed to the column was 'transphobic'. The issue was, of course, an incitement to violence being normalised in a mainstream arts publication. The trans identification of the columnist was irrelevant to me: their words were addressed to 'allies', whom I knew to be a wide demographic. So far, so Twitter.

I felt that my stance was not complex enough to be misinterpreted. However, a few days later the columnist who wrote the piece attended a protest outside an event at Edinburgh

University and, afterwards, attempted to assault one of the speakers, the feminist Julie Bindel. If a general reader now assumes that those haranguing me might have laid off a little at my pointing out that publishing – and excusing – calls for violence can lead to offline violence, they would be mistaken.

On a friend's Facebook page where this series of incidents was discussed, I was extensively grilled about my views, over the course of several days, primarily by a successful novelist whom I have known for several years. A dogmatic attempt to paint me as motivated by transphobia meant that my informed responses to her attempt to smear me were ignored. As ever, when I have these discussions, I set out clearly the three core beliefs of those of us described as 'gender critical' – none of which are 'harmful' to trans-identified people at all. Women are materially definable as a category; we are legislatively, culturally and politically important on that basis; we have a right to freedom of expression and assembly to discuss issues that affect us profoundly. Which of the trio of views did my opponents disagree with?

Answers came there none. What did come was a massive escalation in attempts to smear me as transphobic. When none of my own words could be used against me, I was told that I worked with and was friends with people with 'hateful' views and therefore was guilty or 'problematic' by association.

Some of the responses to the conversation on Facebook were surreal. A woman I have never met screenshot my comments and posted them to Twitter, alongside my name and photo, tagging in Creative Scotland to a twenty-tweet thread, saying I should never receive funding again, and was a 'colonialist'.

But behind the scenes, away from the battleground of social media, things were worse. My publisher received complaints about me from fellow poets and threatened to 'distance' himself from me if I continued to 'punch down' on trans people. He refused to divulge any more information than that, refused to tell me exactly what the 'planned protest' against my book launch was; only that one had been decided on and then called off. This was, of course, alarming. I was no stranger to the treatment of women who receive the label 'TERF'. Indeed, their treatment is part of the reason I knew the gender identity movement was not the 'civil rights campaign' it often self-identifies as. I had that label now and knew the potential for harm – psychological, social, and economic – was enormous.

In July 2019, an up-and-coming poet I had booked for a high-profile event at the Edinburgh International Book Festival messaged me frantically having heard I was a 'TERF' by their friends in the grassroots poetry community. Could I please assure them I was not? A local events organiser told a friend of mine that they were going to overlook me for a paid speaking event because they were worried they would get backlash. My friend, passing this on, also started to fret frequently to me that she was concerned about her own career and connections. This person was not to remain a friend for very long.

For seven months, my ostracisation bubbled along quietly. But in February 2020, two months after I made the decision to leave Edinburgh due to the massive loss of income I was experiencing, and the impact on my mental health, it exploded publicly once more. A young – but influential – poet I have never met lambasted a small publisher on Twitter for having booked 'a huge TERF' for a forthcoming conference at Strathclyde University. That very anxious publisher had alerted me to this via email. I decided, at first, not to respond, but seven months of pressure – and all of this happening so publicly – sparked my ire.

I attempted, politely at first, to have the young poet respond, asking for an email address so we could start a dialogue, given

I had never spoken to him and had no idea what he thought my views were. This being Twitter, of course, he simply blocked me, while colleagues and peers in the poetry sector entered the fray. I witnessed myself mocked, slandered, all my work in the sector rubbished and erased, and, even when told I had become deeply unwell a couple of months previously, saw this dismissed as 'white women's tears'. A trans-identifying poet in England said that my latest poetry stage-show, which they had not seen, had 'weaponised' my own rape to attack trans people by stealth.

I hope I do not have to explain the emotional impact of seeing such a sentiment supported by my peers for a show it took me twenty-one years to work out how to write.

It was at that point that the Scottish Poetry Library (SPL) stepped in, issuing a statement calling for an end to the harassment and no-platforming attempts by poets against other poets. I was relieved and grateful that an important institution had spoken out.

That relief was short-lived.

The backlash to the SPL was extraordinary. An 'Open Letter on Transphobia' was penned by a former friend, alongside other trans-identifying poets. Signatories to this letter included people involved with Scottish PEN, academics, my own publisher, people I had mentored, and even someone I had collaborated with creatively for four years. Over 250 people signed. Every name I recognised was an emotional stabbing. The letter claimed the SPL should not platform women with gender critical views, making use of the initial judgment against Maya Forstater that such views were not 'worthy of respect in a democratic society'. It said a great deal else and is still available online for scrutiny. It gives zero concrete examples of any poet saying or doing anything transphobic.

All of this led to huge press interest. I had to develop a sense of disassociation to cope with it. As someone who values truth – indeed, who had thought all writers might hold to such lofty notions – it was a discombobulating time. I had already cancelled my leaving do; a good thing given some of the invitees supported the open letter. I was alone, surrounded by boxes, ready to move to Ayrshire, having been assisted by my Papa and a government scheme to secure funds for a deposit on a flat.

In my final week in Edinburgh, I received a frantic message from someone who worked at the SPL saying the police wanted to speak to me as the SPL had faced a threat from local activists. The police told me not to attend events unaccompanied. I hadn't been told that since I had a stalker in 2014.

I had only one event to attend. In a delicious twist, I won an award for Critical Thinking at the inaugural John Byrne Awards in March 2020 for my film-poem *The Imagined We*, a poem a gender-identity activist once described as 'TERF-lite' for using menstruation as a metaphor. I left Edinburgh, a city I had loved and had contributed to for most of my adult life, with a battered mind, not knowing who I could trust or what on earth I was going to do, just as a global virus made its way towards us, no-platforming each and every one of us. The Strathclyde conference that so vexed the small world of Scottish poetry? Cancelled.

My Papa, who had helped me in such a timely way, died in his sleep four days after I moved. I vowed that I must, no matter what, find a way out of this, in gratitude for the big skies and new start he gifted me.

As every woman who becomes hounded over this issue knows, the only way out? It's through. Keep writing. Keep talking. Most importantly, even though individuals and institutions alike sometimes seem hell-bent on making you feel so: refuse to think of yourself or any other hounded woman as 'toxic'.

My first attempt at writing my way out was via a commission for the *Dark Horse* poetry magazine, whose editor had followed my hounding in bafflement. The above is an edited extract – the full account runs to over 8,000 words. I wrote it while locked down, alone, bereaved, watching my hounding continue. Even as Covid-19 brought challenges to everyone, including massive uncertainty to the arts world, my hounders' righteous certainty was unabated. I wrote it while watching the treatment of J.K. Rowling after she published her own account of the 'TERF Wars' a few months before my own. If I'd had any sense of self-preservation left, perhaps the smears levelled at her would have made me unwilling to face the consequences of publication.

What spurred me on was *truth*. I wanted exactly what had happened out there. Fully fact-checked. Impossible to refute. So, when fretful friends or organisations came to my inbox with their nervousness about whether my view that 2 + 2 = 4 makes me monstrous, I would be able to send them the essay and say, 'Here. Make up your own mind. Here are the issues. Here is my treatment. This is happening to hundreds of women. Now. Decide. Who is in the right here?'

That essay, 'Anatomy of a Hounding: Fear & Factionalism in Scottish Poetry', contributed to the Autumn/Winter 2021 edition of the *Dark Horse* being the bestselling edition in its twenty-five-year history.

Regardless of one's views on sex, gender, or gender identity, in a healthy literary culture writers do not harass other writers to the point of ill mental health and economic penury. Event promoters do not crap themselves for booking talented writers who comment knowledgeably on a live legislative and cultural issue. Those who work for national funding bodies do not openly decry poets and writers as TERFs. Venue staff do not harass their bosses not to accept bookings from women they dislike but whose views they cannot even articulate. Book festivals do not fail to book bestselling female writers that audiences wish to hear from because a local trans-identifying poet might take the hump. This cultural atmosphere is unsustainable and miserable. Not talking about that is more harmful than pointing it out.

I have been asked to reflect on what has happened since that essay was published. In some ways, my situation has improved remarkably. I have a solid new audience base, I got my rights back from my unsupportive publisher and republished with a new, supportive one. I continue to write and perform, largely by building my own platforms. At the time of writing, I am on commission to write my debut non-fiction book, which is an exploration of the patterns of harms experienced when speaking publicly on this issue. Public awareness of both the issue and the experiences of women being hounded is far higher than it was in 2019–20.

Most importantly: we hounded women stick together, supporting each other in a way that is the opposite to the world our hounders inhabit, where one misstep can lead to an unforgiving barracking. I do not miss that world at all.

But I cannot sugar-coat this entirely. My hounding hasn't stopped. While some hounders have gone quiet, others have taken their place. Arts institutions continue to avoid associating with any woman labelled TERF. There continues to be an unacceptable atmosphere of censorship in the arts. My economic situation is such that my profit from the arts annually is less than my rent used to be in central Edinburgh. I was – and am – no more able to speak out than those who are often in far more financially secure positions than I am who continue to message me privately saying they 'wish they could support (me) publicly'. But I continue to speak for one important reason:

Why would I reward my abusers with my silence? It took twenty-one years to address my experiences of male violence and coercive control in my last creative work. I will not be so muzzled again.

While that slightly tiddly 2019 tweet may have been my 'sliding doors' moment, I was always going to have to speak out eventually. As I said in a poem that predates my hounding, 'I will not use cutlery or wipe my face silent when judged by other criteria from men'.

There is no male equivalent to the dehumanising TERF, spat from the lips of men enjoying fragile thuggery, gifted such power by this movement to abuse, to smear, to hound. It takes a great deal of chutzpah to call that progressive.

This movement we women oppose, which brooks no dissent, and is, I truly believe, causing profound harm to all involved, has also chipped away at the things most important to me in this world, at the very reasons I get out of bed in the morning. The pursuit of truth, democracy, freedom, particularly creative freedom for artists who want to explore challenging ideas. And fun. I remember when the Scottish literary world was, above all else, fun.

It may be currently unfashionable, but I think living in truth – with plenty of time for fun – is a far superior mission than what my hounders are offering. I am pleased – and grateful to those two glasses of red – that I spoke out when I did. The costs have been high, but the alternative was never going to be a possibility.

I started being hounded for opposing an incitement to violence against women by someone with demonstrably violent tendencies. In a sane world, that would not have led to anything but support. Returning to my roots, both in terms of home and firmly outlining my core values, is never going to be something I regret.

Chapter 11

A meeting that changes everything

Claire L. Heuchan

———————

An award-winning radical feminist writer speaks at the University of Edinburgh on the evening of Wednesday 5 June 2019

I don't know it yet, but today – 5 June 2019 – is the beginning of the end for me. For four years I've been blogging, tweeting, and speaking out about the tension between women's sex-based rights and self-identification on the basis of gender identity. I entered the conversation filled with youthful certainty that, if I found the right combination of words, I could make those who read them understand that the vast majority of women aren't fighting to keep our spaces out of cruelty or prejudice. Rather, these spaces are a sanctuary – a way of escaping male violence, which blights and prematurely ends the lives of women around the world, or recovering during its aftermath.

Our participation in public life – still lagging behind men's in every sphere where decisions and money are made, even in the twenty-first century – depends on safe access to toilets, changing rooms, etc. Women enter the gender debate not as oppressors, but the oppressed; a detail often glossed over by our critics. Around the world one in three women will experience some form of sexual violence within her lifetime, the perpetrator overwhelmingly likely to be male. The stakes for preserving women-only space couldn't possibly be higher.

And so, when I am invited to appear on a panel about this very subject at Edinburgh University, I agree. I board the train to Glasgow, and another to Edinburgh, keeping tight hold of my ticket and receipt. Without the offer of travel expenses, I couldn't afford to do this. Feminists organising spaces and events are generally quite good at thinking about which factors allow women to be in a room or shut them out of it. Not always, but often.

It's impossible to concentrate on my book during the journey. Dread knots my gut tight as the train gets close to Edinburgh. And that's not because of the city's rivalry with Glasgow. Nor my feelings about the women involved – I'm looking forward to catching up with Julie Bindel, and know there will be cherished friends in the audience too. Rather, I'm afraid of the protest that has been planned – the feverish opposition to women meeting and discussing our rights.

Knowing that I'm anxious, Lisa Mackenzie (of Murray Blackburn Mackenzie) invites me over for lunch beforehand; other guests include Holly Lawford-Smith, a feminist philosopher, and Professor Rosa Freedman, a fellow speaker. This woman – who has never met me before – invites me into her house, serves home-made soup, fresh bread, and delicious cheeses. And though this day is on the cusp of turning nightmarish, Lisa's kindness will stay with me for years to come.

Yet on the taxi ride to the university, I'm too anxious to participate much in conversation, a hair's breadth from a full-blown panic attack. Part of me wonders what the ever-loving fuck I'm doing here. I wasn't on the original line-up.

And when the invitation first came, I didn't know whether or not I'd accept. Meetings like this one – a discussion titled 'Women's Sex-Based Rights' – have been subject to bomb threats, had projectiles thrown at mostly female speakers, seen mostly female audience members attacked, followed from the venue, and threatened by men in balaclavas.

But I agreed for two reasons. The first is that on principle I refuse to be intimidated into silence. The second is that I have a lot of time for feminist organisers who look at what they've planned, realise certain women's perspectives are missing, and make a sincere effort to redress the imbalance.

As the streets of Edinburgh flit past, Rosa tells me how she appreciates that being a young Black lesbian publicly speaking up in favour of single-sex spaces for women has put me in an even more precarious position; that she admires my courage for doing it anyway. By the time Rosa finishes speaking, I'm nearly in tears.

In the run-up to our event, Jess Brough – a local Black feminist – had tweeted her disappointment over my participation. 'Just goes to show', she said, 'that not all skinfolk are kinfolk.' For Jess to accuse me of somehow betraying Black politics by endorsing women-only space hurts.

My Blackness as much as my girlhood made me an easy target for victimisation, being groomed and abused by a white male teacher nearly three times my age. Race and sex both played a part in shaping my support of single-sex services devoted to women who have survived sexual and domestic violence; for single-sex toilets and changing rooms as a way of circumventing that violence in the first place.

As a Black woman in a very white country, my opportunities to connect with other women of colour are rare and precious as water in a desert. It's profoundly lonely, being Black and Scottish. No part of me wants to lose links to the Black feminist community. But if that's what it takes to preserve women's right to single-sex facilities and services then so be it. It's not easy, though. And white radical feminists don't always realise that. So, Rosa's words make me feel not only seen but valued in a way that makes me want to weep.

When we pull up outside the university, it's still hours before the event is due to begin. The sun is just about breaking through the sky's uniform grey, and the cobbled streets are mercifully free from protestors.

I have no beef with protest, and can more typically be found on the side of the protestors than the protested. But the violence and intimidation tactics weaponised in the hope of scaring feminists out of advocating single-sex spaces, it gives me the fear. Female union reps have been attacked on picket lines. Protestors banged on the windows of the Labour Party's Woman's Place UK (WPUK) fringe meeting while a woman on stage disclosed experiences of sexual violence. There was even a bomb threat made against a WPUK meeting in Hastings.

None of this is liberation politics, especially when you consider that millions of women across Britain are subject to male violence every year. And it's revealing that this behaviour is reserved for feminists, as opposed to right-wing men with institutional power whose regressive views on gender have material consequences for women and trans-identifying people both.

Being able to analyse the sexual politics of feminist meetings being attacked doesn't make it any easier to live through, though. As soon as we're all gathered, a member of the university staff whisks us inside. We wait in a meeting room. There, for over an hour, Edinburgh University's Head of Security talks us through what will happen in various scenarios where one or more of us are attacked or threatened. Fists, knives and projectiles run through my mind on a sick loop. Julie senses my panic through her own, and makes a point of including me in jokes and conversation. I love her for that. But the security team's warnings are ringing in my ears.

Midway through the session, I excuse myself and stumble from the room. The snakes writhing in the pit of my stomach are trying to make their escape. I just make it to the toilet, where I vomit profusely. Sweetcorn from Lisa's soup swims in the bowl. I am consumed by an animal sort of panic, shaking and sweating in that little cubicle. I couldn't go home now even if I wanted to, with protestors swarming the building.

Gathering myself together, repairing the damage with a breath mint and lipstick, I wonder at this situation. How have we, members of a liberal democracy, reached a point where the threat of violence is being used to discourage women from having meetings to talk about our rights? All kinds of misogyny become freshly permissible if you call the woman in question a TERF.

I know a number of women booked to attend this event, and I know quite a few women planning to protest it too. There's not a world of difference between their politics. All of us believe women and trans-identifying people deserve to live full, free lives, safe from men's violence. We all want to live in a society where the trajectory of a baby's life isn't largely determined by whether they have a vagina or a penis. And we all want an end to the inequalities propping up patriarchy.

There's a lot of common ground, whether or not either 'side' wants to walk on it. And I think it's the defining tragedy of contemporary feminism that any chance of coalition, of a collaborative approach to doing feminist politics, gets trampled when there are differences in how women conceptualise gender.

If the people protesting outside had come in and listened to what we said, I don't believe there's anything they could class as hateful. Julie Bindel speaks about ending male violence against women. Rosa Freedman talks about meeting the human rights of women and trans people. Lucy Hunter Blackburn considers the problems with androcentric policy-making. Louise Moody reflects on the complicated relationship between postmodernism and material reality. And I speak from the heart about how painful this schism over gender has become for everyone involved.

I also question why violence against women is being conflated with liberation politics. Women of colour don't bring baseball bats wrapped in barbed wire to anti-racist marches and talk about fucking up white supremacist women. Disabled women don't send images of guns and nooses captioned 'shut the fuck up' to enabled women. Working-class women don't send messages to middle-class women saying they hope we get raped or better yet killed, which is exactly what one self-proclaimed trans rights activist said to me when I defined lesbianism as same-sex attraction between women. But all of this behaviour has become standard practice in gender discourse.

The event mercifully passes without a hitch. Or so I think. Julie and Rosa duck out early, taking a piece of my heart with them, to fly down south. When our meeting finishes, I go out to celebrate with the remaining speakers and friends. A security guard lets us out the back door so that we won't be followed. I have a veggie burger with chips, a crisp gin & tonic, and female company – in short, everything it takes to make me happy. Buoyed by endorphins and Edinburgh-brewed spirits, I saunter back to the train station. I feel proud of all these women for showing up, of myself for speaking the truth even though my voice shook, and ready for home.

As the carriage pulls out of Waverley, I do as every self-respected millennial does and whip out my phone. The event had a hashtag, and I want to see what the verdict is. MSPs were in the audience. But the first tweet I read makes my blood run cold. Julie had been attacked as she was leaving the venue. A young male lunged at her, calling Julie a bitch and a TERF. It took at least two security guards to get him away from Julie long enough for her to escape into a taxi. Before the event, he had tweeted about his intention to 'fuck up some TERFs'. He had also written in the *Skinny*, a popular Scottish arts magazine, calling for 'meaningful action' to be taken against 'TERFs' – which, apparently, was euphemism for fists.

I spend the next day wrapped in my dressing gown, glued to social media, though it only compounds my anxiety. Our nation's capital has a broad selection of feminist organisations – perhaps the highest concentration in Scotland. Funded by our government and with close ties to our politicians, these are the feminists closest to institutional power. Those best positioned to speak out, and – arguably – with the greatest responsibility to condemn a veteran feminist campaigner being attacked on their doorstep. But none of them release a statement challenging the attack on Julie, nor do they reach out to her privately. Their silence is unanimous. And it is deafening.

Edinburgh's feminist organisations would sooner risk being complicit through silence than stand by a woman who has devoted her adult life to eradicating every form of male violence against women and girls. This is where the gender debate has brought us. Organisations founded with the goal of challenging male violence against women are either afraid or unwilling to confront said violence when the perpetrator identifies as female.

That day at Edinburgh University robbed me of something vital; the hope necessary to keep fighting this thankless battle. But it wasn't the only factor in my stepping back from the gender debate. I've been subjected to appalling abuse for raising questions within the movement that some have found uncomfortable. I have been attacked with racialised tropes;

accused of being a traitor or a plant; scapegoated, dehuman-
ised, and othered – even women from the local Scottish gender
critical community piled on. Online abuse – particularly that
which is motivated by my race, sex, or sexuality – is always
demoralising, but there's something particularly bleak about
looking at the perpetrator's profile and seeing that she's from
a town or city near your own; that she shares mutual feminist
followers; that your paths have crossed in community spaces.

And this took a toll. Even knowing abuse is intended to
silence, I've basically stopped tweeting and blogging. Whatever joy I once found in that online space – the first where
I found radical feminist community – has long since been
outstripped by anxiety, strain, and other less-than-fun man-
ifestations that are part of what has since been diagnosed
as CPTSD. Is it the only source of trauma? Absolutely not.
Complex trauma is, as the name suggests, layered; the result of
multiple experiences spread over a prolonged period. But what
I've experienced within the gender debate, from both 'sides',
has been a significant factor.

As a consequence I've largely withdrawn from feminist
events and spaces purely gender critical in focus for fear of
that digital ugliness bleeding into the analogue. My presence
– already marginal as a Black woman – became impossible to
sustain.

On top of this I lost friends, dear ones – women I'd expected
to know and love for the rest of my life. I lost access to anti-
racist community, shunned for arguing that groups like the
Lesbian Immigration Support Group have the absolute right
to single-sex spaces. I lost connections with Glasgow Women's
Library, where I volunteered for five years.

I lost literary representation; though I was the first client
signed by Nikesh Shukla's Good Literary Agency, they dropped
me on the basis of 'perceived transphobia' – I asked the team to

provide evidence of my wrongdoing, and they combed through thousands upon thousands of my words, finding not a shred of hate. Perception trumped reality. I lost out on a book deal with Verso too – when my agent expected to receive a contract, what she got instead was stony condemnation of my support for single-sex spaces.

I lost more than I could ever have imagined possible before the age of thirty. And if you're wondering where Sister Outrider went, I burned out. I stopped writing, stopped tweeting, stopped speaking on this issue. The gender debate drained me of energy and hope. So, I turned my efforts towards other things.

In February 2021 I founded Labrys Lit, an international lesbian book group run via Zoom, in partnership with FiLiA. Every month we read a book by a lesbian author, accessing a rich and varied culture. There are now over 300 women signed up. At the beginning of 2023 I became a FiLiA Trustee, proud to serve as Director of Anti-Racism and Lesbian Community Engagement. It is the greatest joy in my life as a feminist, to be part of this extraordinary collective of left-wing women. And where the bulk of my political energies go.

As for my writing . . . I no longer write much about feminism or sex and gender. But what I do write, it makes me happy. It nourishes the spirit rather than draining it. And that will have to be enough. Perhaps I'll return to this subject, to this particular strain of feminist politics, in the future. But, for now, I'm simply glad to have been part of it; this extraordinary period of women's political engagement.

SECTION 3

The battle intensifies: women refuse to be silenced

Chapter 12

Standing up and speaking out

Rhona Hotchkiss

———————

On Sunday 13 October 2019, a newly retired prison governor speaks at the launch of the SNP Women's Pledge at the party's national conference in Aberdeen

In 2014, I fulfilled what had been an ambition since joining the prison service five years previously and moved to HMP Cornton Vale – Scotland's only all-women prison – as governor in charge. I also took charge of the project to design new prison provision for women.

It was just two years after the Angiolini Commission on Women Offenders had reported. The report brought to a wider audience what those of us in the system already knew: that women in prison are one of the most vulnerable groups in Scotland. The commission found that under 2 per cent of convicted women were in prison because they had been involved in serious violence, while 80 per cent of women in Cornton Vale were reported to have mental health difficulties. Women were five times more likely to self-harm than male prisoners. Many were repeat victims of sexual and physical violence, including domestic abuse, experienced both as adults and children. They were typically drawn from backgrounds of extreme deprivation. Caring for these women in a prison setting can be challenging, but it is very rewarding.

Working for five years with these women evoked in me a mixture of sadness, anger, pride, humility, and a reconnection with my own sense of shared humanity. It also left me determined to speak out for them whenever I could. But it was only after I retired in 2019 that I was free to publicly express my concern about the plight of women forced to share close-living spaces with 'trans-identified' men.

In 2010, when I was deputy governor of HMP Barlinnie, a male-only prison in Glasgow, we took a call from the Sheriff Court, letting us know a 'trans woman' was being transferred to us. Back then, it was still an unusual enough situation to warrant warning us and we prepared for his* arrival by clearing a private space in reception where we could deal with him. We struggled to find a staff member willing to carry out routine searching of the new prisoner until two female staff stepped up; another female manager and I had been prepared to do so if no one else would. I then turned my focus on trying to arrange for him to be transferred to HMP Cornton Vale, because, at the time, I believed that's where he should be held.

My thinking in 2010 was such that if we lived in a different society where everyone could make choices about all aspects of their lives, free from societal mores around sex roles, there would be no transgenderism because it wouldn't be necessary. I understood that there were a few – a very few – men whose hatred of their male bodies was so extreme as to drive them to seek surgery to excise their offending body parts and replace them with a simulacrum of something more acceptable. I regarded it as being akin to any other apotemnophilia, whose sufferers I was equally sympathetic to, and saw medical interventions as the lesser of two evils and crucially, having no significant impact on anyone else.

I am a lesbian and was out from the time I joined the prison service in 2009. As a governor in charge, I was the most senior out gay person the service had ever had, and I took seriously my responsibility to be visible to other staff – both LGB and heterosexual. I felt that I would be relatively difficult to intimidate or discriminate against, whereas staff of other grades might not find that so easy. Oddly enough, LGB people in Scotland's prison service generally have a relatively smooth time at work, and outright discrimination is now rare. It hasn't always been that way, of course, and I was told by other staff – mostly gay men – that jokes and comments about not wanting to work in close contact with them had been rife in the latter stages of the AIDS crisis of the 1980s.

But the only time I ever felt intimidated was in 2018, when I informed headquarters that I would not force female staff to search any male-bodied person, regardless of how they identified. Nor would I discipline them if they refused. I was warned that would be 'unhelpful' and 'not good for you'.

When I joined PRISM, the staff LGB network, at the start of my career, it represented lesbian, gay and bisexual colleagues. But in 2013, by which time I was governor of HMP Dumfries, there was a proposal to change the network to an LGBT group (Q+ wasn't on anyone's mind at that time). Three years on from my first encounter with a trans prisoner, I had done a lot of thinking and reading, and I was in the process of moving from 'be kind and non-judgemental, they're not doing any harm' to 'what on earth does gender identity have to do with being gay'? I set out my misgivings in what I hoped was a very supportive email to the group, and when the majority decision was to change our name – despite there being no trans-identified staff working in the service at that time – I wished them well and left.

In 2014 I moved to Cornton Vale. In my two years there, I encountered several trans-identified male prisoners and became implacably convinced that they should not be in a women's jail. I listened to all the arguments: they are women; they live as women; they are particularly vulnerable. But not one of those claims stood up to close examination. Trans-identified males pose the same challenges to women as all men – everyone knows fine well what those are and that's why men as a group are not permitted unfettered access to women's spaces, services and sports. Trans-identified males are not excluded from these spaces because they are trans, but because they are male, and that should hold as true for prisons.

There is another dimension that needs to be considered. I wish people would remember that women in jails have no choice: they cannot get away. They cannot avoid sharing intimate spaces, as gender identity activists are fond of suggesting to women who don't want to share public toilets with men. They cannot 'reframe their trauma', as one prominent Scottish activist outrageously suggested to rape survivors, uncomfortable with males in single-sex spaces.

Women prisoners must live in close, sometimes very close, proximity to whoever the prison service decides. They must say nothing while a man with an erection, visible through his tight leggings, enjoys their obvious discomfort. They must say nothing while an aggressive man punches walls, triggering adrenaline rushes of fear as women relive the male violence and abuse that they have suffered in the past. They must say nothing while a man, masquerading as a woman, describes in detail what he plans to do to his girlfriend with his penis when he gets out. And they must remain silent when a 'trans woman' tells them he has no intention of living as a woman in the community.

These all-too-common incidents, all ones I have witnessed or had reported to me, are compounded by the fact that in the UK, but not only the UK, a disproportionately high number of trans-identified males in prison are convicted sex offenders. Knowing all this, no one should pretend it is ever acceptable to subject women prisoners to this level of discomfort and threat day in, day out. In fact, I can think of no other vulnerable group whose safeguarding is ignored in favour of another group – trans-identified males held in the prison system – whose self-expressed and largely unexamined demands pose such an obvious risk.

Of course, not every trans-identified male I met in prison posed an overt physical threat to women. However, I came to realise that, although less obvious, emotional and psychological threats matter just as much, and that prisons have no effective way of assessing or eliminating such risk. It is not about nice men versus dastardly men, it is about men. Not all men by a long way, but just as in every other place where it matters, women in prison must be protected from those men whose presence may harm them.

The final element of my growing discomfort came from knowing that there was absolutely no need to hold men, even those most at risk, with women. The Scottish Prison Service (SPS) has an excellent track record in protecting vulnerable men: gay men; former politicians; former police and prison officers; informers and, yes, child killers and rapists. They are held, in considerable numbers, routinely and generally in safety. No one has ever suggested that the only safe place for these vulnerable males is in a women's prison. Yet, in my last few months in charge of Cornton Vale, it was mooted that a man – one of the most notorious, violent, manipulative and dangerous prisoners of the 8,500 held in Scotland – might be transferred to the women's prison, as he had started identifying as female. 'Not on my watch', I remember telling my deputy. Any plans here were dropped, although such a move was rumoured to be under consideration again, just before Adam Graham (also known as Isla Bryson) burst on the scene.

In the summer of 2017, I reluctantly moved from Cornton Vale, which I loved, as my daily commute had become impossible. I was now the governor in charge of HMP Greenock – a majority male prison, but with a women's unit making up around one-fifth of the population. It was the behaviour of trans-identified males there that finally prompted me to raise the issue internally, wherever I could, bolstered by the experience of my staff, many of whom told me that they did not agree with the policy. Not one ever said that they did.

As a governor who witnessed the situation first-hand and several times over, I raised my concerns internally at the highest levels in the SPS and associated agencies, to no effect whatsoever. Those I spoke to either agreed with me or looked blank at the idea that this might be an issue for women in prison or staff. They heard what I said but didn't understand how big this was going to become. Or they listened to me but believed that what the SPS does is driven by government policy and it's not the place of civil servants to naysay the direction provided by ministers. That last group are correct – it is politicians who decide policy.

When the Scottish government decided to introduce the Gender Recognition Reform (Scotland) Bill, I decided more people needed to know what was happening to women in prison. I spoke at length and often to Kenneth Gibson, my local MSP. He has been consistently thoughtful on this complex issue and has never failed to be a strong advocate for women and children. He was one of nine SNP MSPs who voted with their conscience and against the bill when it was passed in the Scottish Parliament.

Crucially for my future involvement in activism, I started to share information with Women and Girls in Scotland, one of the very early groups organising in opposition to gender recognition reform. It was they who introduced me to Joan McAlpine MSP, and it was Joan who encouraged and inspired me to speak in public for the first time, which I did at the launch of the SNP Women's Pledge in October 2019, a few months after I had retired from the prison service at fifty-seven years old.

From the moment I felt able at last to speak out, invitations to talk about the plight of women in prison rolled in. I quickly had more than I could reasonably fulfil – although I did try. I also became involved very early on with a new advocacy group, LGB Alliance. And I was proud to offer an LGB, and a specifically lesbian, voice at rallies outside the Scottish Parliament organised by For Women Scotland (FWS), and to speak to the media across the UK.

I also noticed a very welcome change in attitude. People, women in particular, were waking up, not just to the terrible situation facing women in prison, but to wider issues around this vulnerable group. If nothing else, this recharged interest in women and justice has been welcome. Two people in particular deserve tremendous credit for furthering this agenda. Maggie Mellon, a long-time, outspoken advocate for women in prison who, when I was governor of Cornton Vale, I used to call 'that effing Maggie Mellon'. And Kate Coleman, from Keep Prisons Single Sex, who has arguably done more than anyone else in the UK to fight for an end to the discredited policy of housing trans-identified males in women's prisons.

My activism continues to this day and will continue as long as I still feel rage and am able to speak up. It reached a frenzied zenith in the first few weeks of 2023, with the jailing of a violent male sex offender, Adam Graham/Isla Bryson, in Cornton Vale. On 24 January, after being found guilty of raping two women, he was sent to a women's prison to await sentencing. It later emerged that the SPS had overruled an initial decision by the court service to take Graham/Bryson to Barlinnie.

For three or four days it seemed that I was the only voice the media wanted to hear. Perhaps because I managed to speak in complete sentences, unlike the then first minister, Nicola Sturgeon, whose normally composed manner seemed to desert her. Her firm 'no debate' stance about the impact of her gender recognition reforms on women's rights failed in face of this most rigorous of tests: reality. Her sidekick, Shona Robison – who regularly parroted the 'no evidence of harm' mantra – was unusually silent on the matter. And the future first minister, Humza Yousaf, managed to splutter that Graham/Bryson was 'at it', while thousands of Scottish women screamed 'we warned you'. I gave up counting after fifty media requests in less than a week. I even lost any sense of which TV or radio station I was on. And I struggled to remember what clothes I'd worn last time I had been interviewed.

Since I started to speak out, I haven't suffered the more heinous attacks and threats that some of my now friends and fellow activists have endured. I haven't been threatened with rape and death, but I have been called variously a 'witch', 'bitch', 'TERF'; 'cunt', 'Nazi' and, interestingly, both a 'fascist' and a 'communist'.

I have had the standard catcall of 'no one would want to fuck you anyway' when speaking out about lesbians being dubbed transphobic for refusing to consider be-penised 'lesbians' as partners. And, rather worryingly, I was the subject of an investigation by the public standards commissioner in Scotland, when controversial private online clinic Gender

STANDING UP AND SPEAKING OUT

GP – and various trans activists – complained about my membership of Health Improvement Scotland (HIS) – an organisation whose job is to provide guidance on evidence-based practice to NHS Scotland. My 'crime' had been to object on social media to children being given clinically unevidenced courses of treatment such as puberty blockers, and to suggest that gender reassignment surgery, like all other cosmetic surgery with neither a clinical need nor benefit, should not be performed on the NHS. Perhaps the hardest of all was that the staff Pride network of HIS tried to get rid of me – the only out LGB board member they had.

Neither action was successful, and I am grateful to all of those who stood firm, not because they necessarily agreed with me, but because they understood and valued the need for free speech and diversity of thought to be protected.

I have only been able to do what I've done over the past five-plus years because of the support of my partner Linda, my family and friends. They have stood beside me when I felt that the exhaustion that comes from fighting the resolute madness that is gender identity ideology would overwhelm me. Their love and friendship continue to sustain me, along with the solidarity and sisterhood of a feminism reborn. This is embodied by my fellow activists and by the people I work with locally in the Women's Aid movement, on the Board of LGB Alliance and most recently, and most delightfully, on the board of Beira's Place, the female-only sexual violence support service set up in Edinburgh in December 2022 by J.K. Rowling. Their intelligence, humour, determination and continued decency in the face of horrendous provocation inspires and sustains me every day. I owe my sanity to them.

*I am using male pronouns to describe males who identify as women for two reasons: firstly, because it's correct; secondly, because for as long as women are under threat of sanction

– up to and including imprisonment if some self-identified progressives get their way – I will continue to make a public stand on the issue, where some others may feel they cannot.

Chapter 13

Wheesht for the witch burners

J.K. Rowling

'Don't' is the consensus in the arts and among the famous.
'Just don't.'

Don't say anything to antagonise the trans activists if you value your reputation and your career. Don't express misgivings about the brave new ideology that says 'gender identity' rather than biology determines who is a man or a woman. The debate is toxic and the safest place is well out of it, so stay silent, or speak only to repeat the slogan that functions as an indemnification from harm: Trans Women Are Women.

Some of those speaking the magic words don't believe them. I remember a private conversation with a well-known writer who described the activities of the gender ideologues as 'cultural terrorism', but in the next breath admitted that if asked a direct question, they took the 'cowardly position' (their words). They told me they'd lose work in academia if they didn't.

That doesn't, of course, mean all famous people or all writers are secret TERFs (the name given by gender activists to those women who disagree with their ideology. The term features heavily on placards and T-shirts proclaiming that these are people it's OK to punch or kill). There are plenty who sincerely subscribe to the idea that men and women are defined by our inner feelings rather than biology, and who can't see any downside to adopting this belief as a basis for safeguarding, or categorising human beings for sport or incarceration. These true believers aren't shy about telling the rest of us that their views are not only kinder and more tolerant than a body-based understanding of the sexes, but also far more sophisticated.

Never, ever underestimate how far fear of being unsophisticated will take some people in the arts.

So, by the standards of my world, I was a heretic. I'd come to believe that the socio-political movement insisting 'trans women are women' was neither kind nor tolerant, but in fact profoundly misogynistic, regressive, dangerous in some of its objectives and nakedly authoritarian in its tactics. However, I kept my thoughts to myself in public, because people around me, including some I love, were begging me not to speak. So I watched from the sidelines as women with everything to lose rallied, in Scotland and across the UK, to defend their rights. My guilt that I wasn't standing with them was with me daily, like a chronic pain.

What ultimately drove me to break cover were two separate legal events, both of which were happening in the UK.

In 2019, a researcher in England called Maya Forstater, who worked at a think tank, took her bosses to an employment tribunal. Forstater alleged that she'd been discriminated against for her belief that human beings cannot literally change sex. On the one hand, it seemed inconceivable that the tribunal would rule against Maya for holding and expressing a rational and factual belief, yet I had a dark, persistent feeling that she was going to lose, in which case the implications of such a loss for freedom of speech and belief in the UK, especially for women, would be far-reaching.

On the day in December 2019 that Maya lost her discrimination case (she'd go on to win on appeal, and gain substantial damages) I called a member of my management team to warn them what I was about to tweet, and tell them that I couldn't be talked out of it. I said the following:

> *Dress however you please. Call yourself whatever you like. Sleep with any consenting adult who'll have you. Live your best life in peace and security. But force women out of their jobs for stating that sex is real?* #IStandWithMaya.

I then posted an essay on my website, elaborating on my concerns about gender identity ideology. I've been struck, since, by how many of the people who claim to know what I believe on this issue freely admit to never reading that essay. They don't need to, they say, because their favourite trans influencers have already explained what I *really* meant. This peculiar stance seems to me to sum up the lack of critical thinking surrounding this issue, and the aversion of gender activists to exposing themselves to ideas that might shake their faith in their beloved slogans.

The following summer, in Scotland, where I've lived for three decades, the SNP government, led by First Minister Nicola Sturgeon, was gearing up to pass the Gender Recognition Reform Bill, which would remove all medical safeguarding from the transition process. A person would be able to change their legal gender as long as they'd lived in their 'acquired gender' for three months, and made a statutory declaration that they intended to keep doing so. There was no definition of what 'living in an acquired gender' meant and no requirement for psychological assessment, surgery or hormones. If the bill passed, it would mean that more male-bodied individuals could assert more strongly their right to enter spaces previously reserved for women, including abuse shelters, rape crisis centres, public changing rooms and prison cells.

Polling showed that the public strongly disagreed with what the SNP-Greens coalition was planning to do. I was so angry that the Scottish Parliament looked set to push through the Gender Recognition Reform (Scotland) Bill over public opposition that on 6 October 2022, the day of a women's protest outside Holyrood, I posted a picture of myself online wearing a T-shirt bearing the slogan: Nicola Sturgeon, Destroyer of Women's Rights.

The bill passed in December 2022. Incredibly, an amendment to prevent those convicted of sexual crimes such as rape from obtaining a Gender Recognition Certificate was voted down, a stain on the Scottish Parliament that will take a very long time to fade. (The bill was subsequently blocked by the UK government, because it was in conflict with the Equality Act.)

Sturgeon, who has described herself as 'feminist to my fingertips', spoke out in 2023 about the 'real' motivations of those who had objections to the ideology being enforced by her government, on which the public had never been offered a vote, but which, during her nine years in power, had gained a stranglehold on virtually all state institutions: 'There are some people that I think have decided to use women's rights as a sort of cloak of acceptability to cover up what is transphobia . . . just as they're transphobic you'll also find they are deeply misogynist, often homophobic, possibly some of them racist as well.'

Many were outraged by Sturgeon's words – a friend of mine ripped up her SNP membership card because of them – but I wasn't surprised. In the run-up to the Gender Recognition Reform (Scotland) Bill vote the first minister had argued exclusively along standard trans activist lines, and one of the gender ideologues' favourite talking points is that unless you buy into their philosophy, you're a homophobic white supremacist.

The backlash towards me for speaking out about Maya, about gender ideology in general and about the situation in Scotland, has been vicious. Nobody who's been through an online monstering or a tsunami of death and rape threats will claim it's fun, and I'm not going to pretend it's anything other than disturbing and frightening, but I had a good idea of what was coming, because I'd seen the same thing happen to other women, many of whom were risking careers and, sometimes, their physical safety. Very few high-profile women – with honourable exceptions, especially in sport, Martina Navratilova and Sharron Davies foremost among them – seemed prepared to stand up and give these women cover and support. I felt it was well past time that I stepped up, too.

In what might be loosely described as my professional community, there was bewilderment that I'd abandoned the safe, generally approved position to support Maya and campaign against the Scottish Gender Recognition Reform Bill. What was I playing at? This attitude was best summed up by writer Honor Cargill-Martin: 'I don't understand why [J.K. Rowling] cares so much. She has so much money – why isn't she off buying couture in Paris, rather than fighting with people on Twitter?'

People who'd worked with me rushed to distance themselves from me, or to add their public condemnation of my blasphemous views (though I should add that many former and current colleagues have been staunchly supportive). In truth, the condemnation of certain individuals was far less surprising to me than the fact that some of them then emailed me, or sent messages through third parties, to check that we were still friends. My very favourite was a handwritten note saying 'I'm so sorry for what you're going through,' which was sent by a young woman who was doing her absolute best in public to ensure that I kept going through it. That gave me one of my few laughs during a particularly tough week.

The thing is, those appalled by my position often fail to grasp how truly despicable I find theirs. I've watched 'no debate' become the slogan of those who'd once been defenders of free speech. I've witnessed supposedly progressive men arguing that women don't exist as an observable biological class, that they don't suffer biology-specific harms, or deserve biology-based rights. I've listened as certain female celebrities insist that there isn't the slightest risk to women and girls in allowing any man who self-identifies as a woman to enter single-sex spaces reserved for women, including changing rooms, bathrooms or rape shelters. I know some of these female celebrities well enough to know exactly how protected their lives are. Some have barely any experience of life without private security. Their 'public' bathrooms have stars on the door and guards outside.

I've asked people who consider themselves socialists and egalitarians what might be the practical consequences of erasing easily understood words like 'woman' and 'mother', and replacing them with 'cervix-haver', 'menstruator' and 'birthing parent', especially for those for whom English is a second language, or women whose understanding of their own bodies is limited. They seem confused and irritated by this question. Better that a hundred women who aren't up to speed with the latest gender jargon miss public health information than that one trans-identified individual feels invalidated, seems to be the view.

When I've asked what the lack of female-only spaces would mean for women of certain faith groups, or survivors of sexual violence, the response is an almighty shrug. Over and again I've heard 'no trans person has ever harmed a woman or a girl in a female space', the speakers' consciences apparently untroubled by the fact that they are parroting an easily disprovable lie, because there's ample evidence that men claiming a female identity have committed sexual offences, acts of violence and voyeurism, both inside women's spaces and without. Indeed, the Ministry of Justice's own figures show that there are proportionately more trans-identified males currently in jail in the UK for sexual offences than among male prisoners as a whole. When this inconvenient fact is raised, I'm sometimes told trans-identified sex offenders 'aren't really trans, they're just gaming the system'. Well, yes. If a system says an unfalsifiable sense of self determines who's a woman, it is impossible to keep bad faith actors out. Of course, some trans activists don't bother to argue this point at all, because they see it as irrelevant. As American trans researcher and gender activist Zinnia Jones said on Twitter: 'Literally 100% of trans people could be convicted rapists and that still doesn't actually justify excluding us from the proper restroom.'

One of the things that has most shocked me throughout this debacle has been the determined deafness of so many opinion-makers to whistle-blowers at the UK's now-discredited Tavistock Gender Identity Clinic in England. In 2017, a pair of clinicians I've since met in person tried to alert the *Guardian* newspaper to what they believed was severe malpractice at the Tavistock. The *Guardian* didn't print their letter. Medics who were resigning from the service in unusually high numbers asserted that autistic and same-sex-attracted young people, and those who'd experienced abuse – groups that were over-represented among those seeking to transition – were being fast-tracked towards irreversible medical interventions of questionable benefit by activist groups and ideologue medics.

None of this seemed to register on the celebrities who were cheerleading for the transition of young people. Their reaction to the whistle-blowers' accounts was airy dismissal. 'The doctors know best' was the stock response, ignoring the fact that a significant number of doctors disagreed profoundly with what some of their colleagues were doing. Carl Heneghan, director of the Centre of Evidence-Based Medicine at Oxford and fellow of Kellogg College, has said: 'Given paucity of evidence, the off-label use of [puberty blockers]... in gender dysphoria treatment largely means an unregulated live experiment on children.' (Whistle-blowers at the Tavistock have since been completely vindicated: after an independent investigation, it's to be closed. The Scottish equivalent, the Sandyford Gender Service, though, remains open for business.)

Looking back now, and notwithstanding how unpleasant it's been at times, I see that outing myself as gender critical brought far more positives than negatives. The most important benefit of speaking out was that I was free to act.

For twenty-five years, I've funded services for rape survivors through my charitable trust, which was set up to alleviate social deprivation, with a particular emphasis on women's and children's issues. Appalled by the fact that there was no longer any women-only rape crisis centre in my home city, I decided to set up such a service, Beira's Place, which has now been running for over a year. I've also helped fund legal action by women who'd been defamed on the basis of their gender critical beliefs, or discriminated against by their employers for believing that men cannot, literally, become women.

In Scotland, one of the consequences of Nicola Sturgeon's complete dismissal of women's well-founded concerns has been that women from the SNP, Scottish Labour and the Scottish Tories have reached out to each other and forged alliances and grassroots coalitions. I couldn't be prouder to know many of these women, and I believe the friendships that have resulted will last the rest of my life.

I've also been deeply moved by the kindness and solidarity expressed in letters and emails that arrived at my office in their thousands, at least ninety per cent of which were supportive of my position. Not one of those communications expressed the slightest dislike for trans people, and many spoke of their deep compassion for those who feel that they 'should have been' the opposite sex. Among the letter-writers were teachers, social workers, people from all corners of the medical profession, trans people who disavow a strain of activism that claims to represent them, and gay people who consider gender ideology homophobic (same-sex attraction often being described as 'genital fetishism' by the hard-line gender ideologues, who are critical of lesbians in particular for rejecting the penis-ed from their potential dating pool).

A young woman working in the arts wrote, 'What you're saying is just plain common sense. It's hard enough for me in this profession as a woman of colour; if I speak my mind on this issue, I'll never be commissioned again.' She said she hoped I didn't think she was a coward. I replied that I didn't: that I was speaking for women like her, who couldn't speak without losing their livelihoods.

A gay male social worker wrote to tell me 'we're watching safeguarding being dismantled in front of our eyes'. A female teacher told me she'd resigned because she wouldn't preach what she believed was sexist, regressive nonsense. *I will not teach young girls that if they like playing with toy cars, they're really boys*, she said. I heard from nurses, doctors and psychologists, all alarmed by what they see as the abandonment of evidence-based medicine and the repudiation of the profession's most sacred tenet: First, do no harm.

One email that will be forever branded on my memory was from a young American woman who'd had both her breasts removed and taken testosterone for several years before coming to believe she'd made a terrible mistake. She'd been 'affirmed' at every step of her medical journey. Nobody had questioned her history of poor mental health or suggested that there might be another solution for her distress than radical surgery and cross-sex hormones. That email was the first, though it hasn't been the last, that made me cry, face down, on my kitchen table. I've since had contact with many more detransitioned people, mostly but not exclusively female, all of whom believe they were egregiously failed by medical professionals.

One of my favourite writers, Colette, wrote in her book *My Apprenticeships*, 'Among all the forms of absurd courage, the courage of girls is outstanding.' For too long, I'd watched in silence as girls and women with everything to lose had stood up in the face of a modern-day witch hunt, braving threats and intimidation, not only from activists in black balaclavas holding placards promising to beat and murder them, but from institutions and employers telling them they must accept and espouse an ideology in which they don't believe, and surrender their rights.

In a sense, of course, all courage is absurd. Humans are hardwired to survive, to seek safety and comfort. Isn't it more sensible to keep your head down, to hope somebody else sorts it out, to serve our self-interest, to court approval? Possibly.

But I believe that what is being done to troubled young people in the name of gender identity ideology is, indeed, a terrible medical scandal. I believe we're witnessing the greatest assault of my lifetime on the rights our foremothers thought they'd guaranteed for all women. Ultimately, I spoke up because I'd have felt ashamed for the rest of my days if I hadn't. If I feel any regret at all, it's certainly not for all that couture I missed buying in Paris. It's that I didn't speak far sooner.

Chapter 14

Sacked for a hashtag

Gillian Philip

On Friday 26 June 2020, a Morayshire author, who specialises in Young Adult fiction, is sacked by her publisher for tweeting in support of J.K. Rowling

'A clenching feeling of unease in my belly . . .'
I put those words in the narrative mouth of Eddie Doolan, the thuggish antihero of my 2019 novel *Click Bait*. It's what he senses when he realises that something he's posted

online is coming back to haunt him in a big way. I put that boy through fictional hell, so it's perhaps justice for author-tormented characters everywhere that I was going to feel the exact same sinking sensation one year later.

That 'clenching feeling of unease' visited me on the morning of 25 June 2020. Ten days earlier, I'd posted on Twitter in support of J.K. Rowling, and added the hashtag #IStandWith-JKRowling to my profile. My timeline had been eerily quiet since, but I woke that June morning to a couple of abusive tweets. I blocked and carried on as normal, but like Eddie, I felt that coiled belly-snake of a premonition that – this time – something was different.

I hate woman's intuition and its gosh-darned reliability.

It escalated scarily quickly. Abuse and threats came thick and fast over the next twenty-four hours, increasingly relentless and in unblockable quantities. 'Transphobe' and 'TERF' were the least-worst names I was given by a horde of anonymous and coordinated accounts, and the fates they wanted me to suffer were almost admirable in their horrific inventiveness.

The next morning I was fired from my work as a jobbing writer, and my successful career in publishing was over.

This had not started with J.K. Rowling. In around 2017, I had peaked – the handy TERF-terminology for finally losing patience with the unreasonable demands made in the name of gender identity – and had been tweeting about the trans issue ever since. Maria MacLachlan's treatment at the hands of a British judge, when she was scolded for not referring to the male thug who had assaulted her by his 'preferred pronouns', had first convinced me that my unease with transgender ideology was well founded, and that kindness was not going to cut it. I'd been positively enraged by the hounding of Rachel Rooney – author of a beautiful body-positive picture book

My Body Is Me – by a vicious clique of children's authors. And while I'd always been opinionated on Twitter, and I am extremely bad at shutting up when I'm angry, my employers had never complained. Not during the Scottish independence referendum, not in the Corbyn years, not in any geopolitical situation or domestic election that wound me up to my usual mouthiness. I suspect they valued my work too much.

That's not an unjustified assumption. At this point, I'm going to rewind just a few months: to February 2020.

The phone call came bang in the middle of a two-part event in a private school auditorium in New Orleans. One audience of excited children had just filed out, following my usual successful presentation on the Erin Hunter animal fantasy series I'd been writing, for the book packager Working Partners, since 2011. Erin Hunter is a marketing invention, a fictional author whose books are in fact the work of a committee and assorted copywriters. The school staff and my media escort milled around in the empty hall, chatting about the event, waiting for round two.

When I'd first been employed on the Erin Hunter brand, expanding the company's detailed storylines and characters into full-length books, I'd also been chosen as the face of Erin on tour. It was an unnerving prospect at the time; the fan forums were notoriously outspoken and, encouraged by a few previous Erin writers, had condemned me as an impudent and unworthy interloper.

But my fears were unfounded. The tours I undertook in the States, once or twice a year for the next ten years, turned out to be wildly successful. I gave endless time to excited young fans at signings; often, I fear, to the frustration of exhausted staff. Reports were fed back, by my escorts, by school and library and bookshop employees, to Working Partners and their client, the books' publishers, HarperCollins in New York. Executives and editors at both companies were not shy about expressing their delight at my performance. I worked hard at both books and tours, and I was excellent at both. Not my verdict, but theirs, in many a thrilled email.

What a rewarding professional relationship it was. I knew my loyalty was reciprocated. I'd completed unpaid tours in the toughest of circumstances: an attack of severe depression in the Pacific Northwest; the sudden illness of my husband back home while I was in Denver, Colorado. On the latter occasion I'd completed the tour despite my fears. I paid for taxis to get my kids to and from school, and called them every day to check on them and their dad. I wanted badly to be back home, but the thing was, I didn't want to let down many hundreds of excited American children. I didn't want to let down Working Partners or HarperCollins. I had great personal relationships with them. I knew they'd be every bit as steadfast in protecting me if they had to.

I think naive is a bit of an understatement.

So, back to that call in the temporarily empty auditorium. It was my neighbours in Scotland, who'd been keeping an eye on my mother, recently diagnosed with Alzheimer's. She'd escaped their supervision and set off to walk eighty miles 'home' to Aberdeen. They'd caught her, got her hospitalised, but she'd talked her way out. It was a crisis.

I should have called off the tour, I should have gone home. I didn't. The next audience of thrilled pupils was arriving in the auditorium; how could I let them or the future scheduled schools down? My neighbour and I made ad hoc arrangements and I promised to be back as soon as I could. 'Please, please, stay in my house with Mum, put your lives on hold, use my food and wine.' I climbed back onstage for round two, game face on, and performed.

My neighbours are great guys. I'd fix everything when I got home, I knew it. What's more, Working Partners and HarperCollins would appreciate my dedication. After all, they knew I had left my husband, too – also suffering from dementia – in a care home during my absence. Ian and I had both been distressed at a two-week separation, but he'd always been proud of my work. He'd have wanted me to honour my work obligations, take no risks with my career. So, I left him.

By 11 May, he was dead.

I was wrecked and, far more importantly, so were the kids. Working Partners sent me a beautiful bouquet, my agent a kind sympathy card. Of course, I'd been right to trust them, to be as loyal and reliable as they were.

That's why, as the abuse thundered in a torrent onto my Twitter timeline and into my email inbox on 25 June, five weeks after Ian's death, I suppressed that roiling sense of foreboding. Perhaps the packager, their client and my own agent hadn't seen the abuse; not everyone is terminally online, unlike me, and they'd surely have contacted me if they had seen it. I got to sleep at five a.m. on 26 June and was woken at nine by – finally – a call from my agent.

The calls I took that morning from Julia and from Working Partners were a wake-up in ever so many ways. Indeed, there's not a person on Earth who could sleep through that deafening crowing of cocks. HarperCollins, on the other hand, never contacted me again, and when approached by the British press, denied all personal knowledge of me. No one wanted to hear about or examine the abuse and threats I'd received. The mob was the thing, and the mob had to be appeased. The final word belonged to the client, HarperCollins.

At two p.m. UK time – with the office barely open in New York – I was fired.

My wide-eyed innocence about company loyalty was, in distant hindsight, quite funny. The managing director of Working Partners told me sadly that I was 'a brilliant writer', who would never write for them again. My agent – who scrubbed me from her partnership's website with undignified haste – offered me 'a shoulder if you need one'. To be honest, I hadn't been paying her in excess of 15 per cent commission on my earnings for a go on her shoulder. And her rapid abandonment effectively ensured that I would never again write for any other major publishers. Working Partners sent letters of feigned horror to many still-anonymous complainants, as if they'd had no idea about the TERFy snake in their midst. The letters were, of course, promptly shared on social media to rub in my humiliation, and many of my most enchanting correspondents got back in touch to share their glee. I'd lost a career, but I'd gained a whole new cadre of demonic pen pals.

I don't pretend any more – though at the time I did, out of deadly pride – that the craven betrayal of friends and colleagues wasn't devastating. But unlike my fictional Eddie Doolan, what I can say with absolute sincerity is that I don't regret what I did.

I lost friends – but gained many, many more. What kept me going in the days after 26 June were the multiple messages from strangers – young, old, male, female, gay, straight – thanking me for standing up and speaking. I amassed a huge number of new allies and friends, many of whom have strikingly different political views, and that's been both reassuring and humbling. We have each other's backs in a way that I hope, but doubt, would shame former publishing colleagues. My children and their partners have been rock-steady. But I will never forgive those who made it necessary for them to hold me together, so soon after the death of their father, when our supportive positions should have been reversed.

Above all, life's more honest now. I'm more honest. My new employers in the haulage industry – I retrained as an HGV driver – recently reported that 'Gill has a mouth on her, but only when somebody else starts it', and I rather feel that'll do for my tombstone.

Perhaps most importantly, my writing will be more honest. It will be from, and for, the heart, not the pay-cheque. It's been far too long since I had time to write books I was truly proud of, books that I actually authored – books like *Click Bait*, *Bad Faith* and *The Opposite of Amber*.

What is not going to happen again is publication of any novel of mine by a large mainstream publisher. I don't regret that either. With a few honorable exceptions, the industry has been subject to the most wholesale, the most aggressive institutional capture by a freshly minted ideology. The publishing world has been overwhelmed by a belief system that denies reality, a postmodern creed that savages, without mercy, any and all heresy against its frankly ludicrous canon law: that humans can change sex on a whim, that biology means nothing, that children must be taught to believe in a brutal, impossible chimera. I'm a great believer in fantasy fiction for children, but I draw the line at telling them it's reality – especially when it threatens to do them actual physical harm.

Some senior publishing executives confess privately that they're afraid to confront their activist juniors – the very staff who tend to be the gatekeepers of the industry at the point of submissions. The capture is so total that I watch, awestruck, and not in a good way, as books are published for the youngest of readers that contravene every safeguarding principle. Books that lie to children about far more important matters than the genesis of a packaged book series. Books are published for children who cannot yet read independently. Books that tell them they can change their sex. Books that introduce them to the possibility of lifelong medical horrors. Colourful, jolly books prime them for the option of drugs that will block their perfect, natural puberty and ruin their bone and brain development, for hormones that will poison their natural sexed bodies, even for eventual surgical mutilation. Sweet picture books – shiny with rainbows and rampant with glittery unicorns – promote queer theory, and its inherent destruction of boundaries, to pre-schoolers, encouraging them to ignore their instincts, telling them to believe everything but the evidence of their own eyes and ears, instructing them above all else to 'be kind'.

There's a multitude of reasons why we got here, but I keep coming back to what first raised my hackles about gender identity ideology: its inherent, unavoidable, undeniable sexism. The entire edifice is built on gender stereotypes; it can't exist without them. I mourn for the little girls who, as I did at their age, love trucks and toy guns and camo T-shirts, but are forcefully steered either back to pink and glitter, or to 'therapeutic' intervention that will persuade them they were always meant to be boys, that their very bodies are a mistake.

I fear for the boys who, like my son, love music and dance, who can't wait to leave school and grow their hair to reach their waists. I often remember the sparky teenager who drove his sister to tears of laughter as she filmed him dressing up in her crop-top to mime a stellar performance as Baby in *Dirty Dancing*. They both had a whale of a time, recorded a video I treasure and that still makes me laugh, and then he got back in his jeans and T-shirt and sauntered out happily to drive quadbikes in the mud with his mates. It's normal. It's experimenting. It's having fun. And it's being denied to children on the whim of captured teachers, some click-hungry parents, and the creators of dead-eyed, proselytising books.

Not that it's only publishers, agents and authors who are culpable. Book trusts and literary festivals reject and ignore believers in biological reality and basic safeguarding, when they're not insisting that their more obedient authors and poets sign queer theory-compliant codes of conduct or lose what, for many, is a crucial part of their income. The Society of Authors, of all institutions, is wholly at the mercy of the gender discourse and its adherents, to the point that at its 2022 AGM, despite the efforts of a few brave souls who endured the mockery and abuse of a hostile online quorum, voted against the defence of free speech and expression by 593 to 161.

I watch it all unfold in awe because I know where it will end – and I know that it will end. Fashion, especially among the young, is infamously fickle.

Far more crucially, reality itself is impossible to deny for ever. The collective madness will come to its horrible, inevitable end, and those chickens I heard crowing on 26 June 2020 will finally come home to roost.

The book industry will at last be forced to answer for what too many people in it have enabled and encouraged: the greatest medical scandal in modern history, and their betrayal of those who fought to stop it.

Chapter 15

The battle moves to the court room

Susan Smith

———

On Friday 31 July 2020, For Women Scotland (FWS) sends a pre-action letter to the Scottish Government for a judicial review of the Gender Representation on Public Boards (Scotland) Act 2018

'When I use a word,' Humpty Dumpty said in rather a scornful tone, 'it means just what I choose it to mean – neither more nor less.'

'The question is,' said Alice, 'whether you can make words mean so many different things.'

'The question is,' said Humpty Dumpty, 'which is to be master – that's all.'

Lewis Carroll, *Through the Looking Glass*

'This Act precedes forthcoming gender recognition legislation. Parliamentary drafters and lawyers chose this language in anticipation of definitions as they are being drafted for the future Bill which should make everything clear in statute.'

Scottish Liberal Democrat leader Alex Cole-Hamilton MSP, explaining what 'becoming female' and 'living as a woman' mean during the passage of the Gender Representation on Public Boards (Scotland) Act 2018

Who is to be master and whether you can make words mean different things, has been at the heart of much of the discussion over women's rights in recent years. One hundred and fifty years after Lewis Carroll wrote his glorious nonsense exchange in *Through the Looking-Glass*, I wish this chapter were a piece of Carollian whimsical nonsense. Sadly, it is all true.

As the lockdown restrictions eased in the summer of 2020, For Women Scotland (FWS) decided to have another outdoor meeting. Venice Allan was coming up to Edinburgh and we planned a joint event with invited speakers and an open mic session. Kellie-Jay Keen, the activist also known as Posie Parker, had arranged for a digital advert in Waverley Station to celebrate J.K. Rowling's birthday. The poster was a simple black, white and red design in the style of the classic NYC promotion placards, bearing the legend: 'I ♥ J.K. Rowling'. It made no reference to any of the ongoing debates around women's rights. Predictably, however, when the sign was revealed, activists flooded Network Rail with complaints that it was political material and thus subject to restriction on railway property.

Wiser heads in LGBT organisations might have cautioned that this was, at best, tenuous and could rebound on their future campaigns. After all, if birthday wishes to a beloved children's author were now political, then the same complaint could, and would, be made against their own adverts. Also, an unremarked poster on a station platform would garner little interest, but cancelling it would shoot the story on to the pages of the national press and, of course, this was exactly what happened.

A pop-up version of the poster was also there a few days later when the socially distanced event at the bottom of the Mound, Edinburgh's traditional Speakers' Corner, took place. Speakers included some of the cancelled writers featured elsewhere in this book, but, while there was anger at the injustices, there was also a celebratory, determined atmosphere. The strength and sisterhood we have all drawn from those events matters, and we ended with a socially distanced picnic in Princes Street Gardens. We did, however, have another important reason for arranging a gathering. Two days previously, on 31 July, we had sent a Pre-Action letter to the Scottish Government signalling our intention to take them to court over the definition of 'woman' in the Gender Representation on Public Boards Act (GRPBA).

This Act was a little noticed piece of legislation, introduced without fanfare in 2017, and slipping by the Parliament in January 2018 without a single MSP noticing the sting in the detail. One person who did spot it was FWS director Trina Budge, and, although the nascent women's groups were unable to challenge it at the time, it continued to rankle. The purpose of the bill – a measure to combat institutional sexism and ensure 50:50 representation of women on public boards – had seemed perfectly reasonable. But right from the start, there were arguments about who would qualify. A hundred years after women won the right to vote, deciding what and who was a woman had suddenly become the most complicated philosophical question of the day.

For those who wonder how we arrived in 'Looking-Glass land', where Alice-like common sense is deemed heretical and Humpty's Butlerian disdain for social or linguistic norms is embedded in the establishment, the progress of the GRPBA is a cautionary tale.

The Scottish Government initially proposed that its 50 per cent objective would be for those who are 'female or who identify as female' but, after a public consultation, this was changed to 'women' when the bill was introduced to Parliament in June 2017. According to the Policy Memorandum, 'this step was taken to ensure that the Bill reflects the protected characteristic of sex in the Equality Act 2010'. In any event, the initial attempt at trans inclusion had failed to satisfy the Scottish Government-funded lobby groups which fretted about making a distinction between those who were female and those who merely identified as female. However, James Morton of the Scottish Trans Alliance (STA) had a suggestion and said in evidence to the committee:

> We would like a bit of extra information to be included for the avoidance of doubt. We propose that the bill should say that the definition of 'woman' includes a person with the protected characteristic of gender reassignment who is living in the female gender and does not include a person with the protected characteristic of gender reassignment who is not living in the female gender.

Freedom of Information (FOI) requests have revealed the extent to which civil servants relied on the Equality Network and STA for steers on policy. The Equality Network and other LGBT groups promoting self-ID also enjoyed cosy relationships with the three biggest government-funded women's groups that lobby at national level: Engender, Scottish Women's Aid, and Rape Crisis Scotland. It was odd enough that there never seemed any differences of opinion between these groups, but stranger still that there was uniformity of thought in the area of gender recognition reform, where fundamental questions were being raised about access to women's spaces. Tellingly, when the Scottish Women's Convention, which is not part of this charmed circle, eventually produced a strongly worded report in 2022 stressing the need for single-sex services, it was ignored by the three other national women's organisations, and swept under the carpet by the government.

It was therefore not surprising that no voices were raised in opposition to Morton's definition. It found favour with all six members of the committee, many of whom saw it as a precursor to gender recognition reform. This amended definition of woman was based on self-ID, and it offered precious little guidance on what constituted a woman, beyond pronouns and a name on a driving licence. To add insult to injury, people making appointments did not even have to check or ask for evidence. Soothing noises were made about how the definition was only applicable to this specific piece of legislation, but that, of course, did not prevent Tim Hopkins of the Equality Network later arguing that it set a precedent when making the case that sex in the census should also be based on identity.

Once the Act was passed, our only real hope was to take the Scottish Government to court. The Holyrood rally held before lockdown, and the extraordinary response to the second consultation on gender recognition reform, had shown us that we could mobilise huge numbers, but a judicial review was incredibly risky and not just for financial reasons. If we lost, we risked cementing the absurdity of this definition in law.

In October 2020, shortly before we went to court, Gail Ross MSP, one of the committee members who had waved through the definition, took to Twitter in support of a post opining, 'Pronouns: it costs us nothing.' Ross wrote, 'If you want to pile on or "other" this tweet – feel_free, bitches!' Of course, what Ross neglected to say was that, because of the GRPBA, pronouns could cost women. A woman could now find herself passed over for a space on a board reserved for a member of her sex, possibly in favour of a man who had reached middle age with a successful career unburdened by childbirth, caring responsibilities or sex discrimination.

There was no choice: the law was wrong, the law was bad, and if we couldn't rely on MSPs, it would have to be the court. We crowdfunded our expected costs, raising £200,000 in total from 5,278 donors, with the average donation just over £37.

At first, the court let us down. In March 2021, Lady Wise of the Outer House of the Court of Session rejected our case. We had argued that by confusing gender reassignment with sex, the Scottish Government had breached the provisions of the Equality Act, which was reserved to Westminster, and so had acted beyond its competence. Lady Wise ruled that the Act fell within an exception to the reservation of equality law that permitted the Scottish Parliament to legislate for equal opportunities to public boards. It was an unbearably disappointing decision.

I cannot recall exactly how we arrived at the decision to fight on. Our lawyers' belief that the ruling was very wrong certainly helped, but I was fretting about the mounting costs. The support from the public had been incredible, and the comments on the Crowd Justice page were uplifting, but were we asking people to help us throw good money after bad? The financial injustice rankled. The Scottish Government were, not for the first time, set on making bad laws, and the only recourse was a costly legal case, funded on our side by donations and on theirs from public funds. The public, in other words, were paying twice.

STA, almost wholly funded by the taxpayer, had intervened in our case with pro bono legal representation from a legal charity, Just Right Scotland, which also received Scottish Government grants. STA insisted no government income was used to fund its intervention. Yet, how could we allow the ruling to stand?

Unlike the civil servants or the lobby groups lined up against us, this was a part-time fight that we slotted in between jobs, businesses, children and elderly parents. We talked to lawyers on the school run and the dog walk, wrote to MSPs in a lunchbreak or, in my case during 2020, while hooked up to an IV line in chemo sessions.

I got the all-clear just before Lady Wise's ruling, and had celebrated with a walk to Cramond Island with Lisa Mackenzie of Murray Blackburn Mackenzie (MBM), a near-contemporary at school, brought back into my life by the Scottish Government's madness. We sat on camping stools clutching coffee and prosecco on a bitterly cold January morning, looking out across a millpond-still Forth towards the bridges. It was wonderful. Moments like this made everything brighter. We had purpose and we had each other.

This feeling was cemented by our first proper post-lockdown event, another demonstration at Holyrood during FMQs in September 2021. This time MSPs came out to talk and posted support on social media. We were later told that the cheers, and jeers for the first minister, and cries of 'Women Won't Wheesht' were so loud that they could be heard in the chamber. My fellow director of FWS, Marion Calder, was especially scathing about Sturgeon's record that day:

> It will be to Ms Sturgeon's shame and to Scotland's detriment if poorly conceived, dangerous, regressive assumptions about women are codified into law. Scotland is the land of the Enlightenment but also the witch-craze. This Parliament has to decide if it stands in the tradition of the former and for evidence and science or whether women are, once again, to be persecuted in Scotland. We call upon MSPs to stand up now for what is right because, believe us, women will not wheesht now or ever.

After that, how could we back down?

And so, we found ourselves in the Inner Court for round two and some barnstorming stuff from our QC, Aidan O'Neill, on the necessity of protecting women's rights, thus earning his honorary feminist stripes. He pointed out the absurdity of a law which was supposed to mitigate for structural discrimination but, nevertheless, included some men and excluded some women.

Almost exactly a year after the first decision, in February 2022, the Inner Court of Session ruled that the Scottish Government exceeded its powers by extending the definition of woman. Most gratifying was this paragraph:

> *Thus an exception which allows the Scottish Parliament to take steps relating to the inclusion of women, as having a protected characteristic of sex, is limited to allowing provision to be made in respect of a 'female of any age'. Provisions in favour of women, in this context, by definition exclude those who are biologically male.*

We were thrilled, but we also suspected, correctly as it turned out, that this was not the final chapter in the tale. A hint of what was to come came in court when Ruth Crawford QC argued for the government that 'the Equality Act did not say as my learned friend does in his note that female means biological female, it means female'. In law, it never used to be necessary to define commonly understood words, but now, the Humpty Dumpties in politics and lobby groups were making hay with definitions and retrospectively applying them to legislation. One might think that this way would lie madness and legal chaos – not usually considered winning political manifesto pledges.

One of the original Stonewall founders had told us that, sometimes, whether you won or lost in court was of less importance than what the ruling revealed about the state of the law and where amendments were needed. Following its loss, the Scottish Government was supposed to strike out the faulty definition. Instead, it added a new one. This time 'woman' was to include any male with a Gender Recognition Certificate (GRC) who had thereby been able to change his birth certificate to 'female'. If we wanted to challenge this, we had to head back to court.

Since 2018, we had frequently tried to establish from Scottish ministers and civil servants what additional rights they thought were conferred by a GRC. In public, the excuse for extending access to GRCs had been that it was a simple administrative change, important only for documents like marriage certificates. The government, and others, argued a GRC made no material difference to rights under the 2010 Equality Act, whether that was access to a single-sex service or taking advantage of a female-only positive action scheme.

But now that the Inner Court had exploded the idea that provisions based on sex could extend to any member of the opposite sex, based simply on identity, the government was suddenly prepared to make the case that a GRC did in fact confer advantages and additional rights.

If we wanted to force this contradictory position into the open, we would have to return to court, and do so just as the Gender Recognition Reform (Scotland) Bill was completing its journey through the Scottish Parliament. Win or lose, we wanted to expose the inconsistency and the obfuscation. After years of skirting the issue, the Scottish Government would finally have to set out what they believed were the legal implications of gaining a GRC. They would have to argue in court that a GRC meant a material change in a person's legal rights, even as the minister in charge, Shona Robison, made a different case in Parliament. Like the White Queen in Looking-Glass land, Ms Robison might be prepared to believe six impossible things before breakfast, but for women in Scotland this was more of a nightmare than a dream.

We hoped by going to court we might be able to wake up our politicians before it was too late. On 13 December 2022 Lady Haldane agreed with the Scottish Government's argument to the court, that GRCs were far more than just a bit of paper. Barely a week later, most MSPs agreed with the Government's opposite argument in Holyrood, that GRCs were no more than that. And whether they were down a rabbit hole or through the looking glass, at that point we knew that most of our parliamentarians were still fast asleep.

Chapter 16

Six words and a lifetime of lessons learned

Johann Lamont

————

On Thursday 10 December 2020, Johann Lamont MSP successfully moves an amendment to the Forensic Medical Services (Victims of Sexual Offences) (Scotland) Bill, which guarantees a survivor's right to choose the sex – not gender – of their examiner

Retiring is quite the thing. A time to reflect on your working life. To consider whether anything has in truth changed and whether anything you did helped.

One thing is sure, you acquire a lot of labels in life. Daughter. Wife. Mother. Teacher. Socialist. Cook. Grump. And these are just the ones worthy of quoting.

My favourite label is lifelong feminist. Not because the others do not matter – even grump – but because my commitment to women's equality has come to inform and underpin every other aspect of my political beliefs.

It was not always thus. As a young girl, for all my anxieties which would have filled the problem pages of *Jackie* magazine many times over, I knew I was at least as smart as the boys around me, and I had no doubt about my ability to beat them in an argument. But I soon realised that men ran the world, that women were paid less, had fewer opportunities, and invariably looked after the children. Men were in charge, whether in the boardroom, on the trade union picket line, at the council chamber or in the House of Commons, no matter the brilliance of the women who had bucked the trend and found a way to speak up.

I saw clearly that free collective bargaining and a Labour government were not enough if you did not address the inequality which was rooted in the differing roles and expectations of men and women. Yet the labour movement seemed reluctant to address the fundamental roots of inequality. I recall one section on the left of the party arguing that the injustice of women carrying the burden of childcare and running a home could be overcome by twenty-four-hour nurseries and twenty-four-hour restaurants. Never for a moment did they reflect that, unless the fundamental basis of the division of labour between women and men was addressed, these facilities would still be run by women, leaving men's sense of entitlement and privilege unscathed.

It is also worth noting that the idea of a minimum wage was resisted by many trade unionists, particularly those with industrial strength, despite the fact that it would disproportionately benefit women, arguing instead that the exercise of industrial power was the best way to secure better conditions. They chose to ignore the impact of job segregation and the lack of value placed on the work where women were the majority. It is to the credit of those female-dominated trade unions which took on this argument and proved, in its eventual implementation, its value to all trade union members.

Young as I was, I learned a simple lesson. Look at the world. Challenge your own ideas. Think. Change.

The campaign for equal pay, arguments for better birth control, and the bra-burning heroines who disrupted the 1970 Miss World contest, were already having an influence on me. However, the biggest impact on my political education was when I started to understand the pervasive nature of male violence, the impact of domestic abuse and the constraints on a woman tied to a husband who was 'bad to her', as my mother would say.

The emergence of rape crisis centres and women's aid refuges, the public debate about rape in marriage and the evidence of my own eyes of male violence, drew me to understand that the injustice wrought by poverty, economic inequality and unfairness in work should also allow for the reality that economic security and class were no protection from male abuse. Male violence was no respecter of class, and neither were male perpetrators confined to one social or economic grouping.

And how women organised changed over time. As a Labour member, I saw the debate shift and sometimes shift back. It moved away from women organising on their own through women's sections and conference, a move which had been prompted by the refrain of 'we don't want to be making tea while men make policy', only to move back to the recognition that women's voices and experience could be indeed be drowned out and there was a need for women's separate organisation to shape mainstream thinking and to encourage women to participate more fully at every level, including standing for election.

Over time, there were moves to create women's seats on the party's governing executive, to secure at least one woman on every shortlist, all-women's shortlists and quotas. There were rigorous debates at every stage. Arguments within party groupings about whether you should support a left candidate before a woman, or a woman before an ethnic minority candidate, or a middle-class woman before a working-class man.

When Labour established women's conferences in the 1980s, it was decreed that they should be delegate-based gatherings – women chosen by their constituency parties, socialist societies and trade unions. The idea was that the 'sensible' trade union women would keep the 'excitable' constituency women under control. Indeed, in the early meetings, the trade union delegations were often headed by a man. These attempts at control failed, as women recognised in each other – regardless of background – their common experience of discrimination, and resolved to work together, despite men's best efforts to divide them. In truth, bonds of sisterhood were forged then that have been a source of great strength and remain unbroken now. Women coming together across perceived divisions can achieve significant and lasting change.

And men were so reluctant to cede power, that all those excluded, whether on the basis of sex, class or ethnicity, were left to battle among each other for a bit of representation. Challenged for the umpteenth time on what I thought of Maggie Thatcher, I did reflect that those self-same men were never to be held to account for every ne'er do well, bigot or despot who happened to be male.

There were those, uncomfortable with the truth of the role of male entitlement and the reality of male violence, who took comfort in arguing that not all men were to blame and that not all women agreed with us – rather unhinged, possibly a little obsessive and certainly just a bit unreasonable – feminists. Our recourse then, as it must be always, was to focus on the evidence, the patterns of access, opportunity and exclusion. As we highlighted at the time, sending one woman amongst fifty Labour MPs to Westminster in 1987 was stretching the notion of a provable Labour meritocracy beyond any credibility. And the most cursory glance at the statistics on violence, sexual offending and domestic abuse uncovered a pattern of behaviour – of male behaviour – that needed to be addressed.

I outline the changes we fought for in the Labour Party and the labour movement, to make a serious point. Our starting point was equality and understanding the barriers faced by women. The debate was then about how politically you organise to change women's lives. At no point – at no point ever – did anyone argue or debate or cast doubt on the efficacy of any option based on uncertainty of how to define a woman.

And never did any man – left or right, sceptic or enthusiast for change, old or young – feel the need to lecture me, or any of the other women demanding change, about how we should 'do' our feminism. Dyed-in-the-wool traditionalists understood then what seems to have gone over the heads of many young, emboldened male activists – women have the absolute right to speak up and challenge, drawing on their own experience as women.

For what it is worth, I learned to live a long time ago with young men's disappointment at my curmudgeonly ways, but I still, on occasion, shake my head at where we have arrived. I am now lectured about biological essentialism, when my experience is that my biology has had a profound impact on my life. I find myself arguing about what women are, rather than how we change women's lives. And I am forced to watch as the reality of women's lives is stripped out of our language, our health care, our personal safety. The young me was sufficiently cynical to recognise that sexism and male violence might remain prevalent. It would never have occurred to me that I would need to find new language to describe the world that shaped my life as a woman – in the name of inclusivity.

* * *

The young me would have been surprised at my ending up in the, as then unrealised, Scottish Parliament. But there are no words to describe how my younger self might have reacted to how I had to spend my last few years as an elected member there. I would have found it tough to accept the state of political debate today and, more importantly, the lack of seriousness about the role of politics in changing lives.

The Forensic Medical Services (Victims of Sexual Offences) (Scotland) Bill was a small, but significant piece of legislation, rooted in a recognition of the trauma faced by rape survivors. It acknowledged that the process of evidence gathering could be a source of further trauma, and that while survivors might not be ready to pursue a complaint, the timeous and sensitive gathering and retention of forensic evidence might allow for a prosecution when the survivor was ready.

The Scottish Parliament committee considering the bill was supportive in its report and placed its considerations in the context of the evidence given to committee members at a meeting of women rape survivors, brought together by Rape Crisis Scotland. Amongst their demands was the right to be examined, and have forensic evidence, taken by a female. Indeed, this was highlighted as their key request.

The committee gave voice to this recommendation, asking that the policy supporting survivors be explicit in saying that survivors should be able to choose the sex of their examiner, given that the word gender was no longer being used interchangeably with sex.

I remember noting in the debate on the committee's report how speakers, from across the parties, were keen to put on record their support for the courage of the survivors who had spoken to the committee, and their wish to give survivors a voice in ensuring this legislation met their hopes. And I noted the specific recommendation – use sex not gender – recognised the need for clarity to ensure the demands of survivors were realised.

I kept an eye on the amendment stage, confident that the Scottish Government would lodge the relevant wording to give effect to the recommendation. No such amendment was lodged. I looked then to see which committee member would take action to realise the recommendation they had agreed unanimously. None did.

It became clear to me that, for some, their performance showing concern for survivors had been sufficient, while others hoped it would all just go away. What seemed like a simple request – that survivors could chose the sex of their examiner – was in conflict with a wish to assert that 'trans women are women' and that trans women should not therefore be excluded from any circumstance open to biological women. Far easier to hope that no one would notice that the recommendation had not been given force in the legislation. And far better not to have to explain why what women survivors had explicitly asked for had not been delivered.

And so, I lodged a six-word amendment at the final consideration of the bill, determined that, if the Parliament wanted to resist this recommendation, they should be seen to be doing so and explain why.

Those six words 'for the word gender substitute sex' generated their own hashtag, and when the bill was passed into law on 10 December 2020, so did the amendment after the overwhelming majority of MSPs – including government ministers – voted to accept the change. Common sense prevailed. And survivors were treated with the respect they deserved.

This process, frustrating as it was at times, is illuminating, and I believe there are important lessons to draw from it.

The desire for no debate around the issue of trans rights, where the assertion that 'trans women are women' should be accepted without question, could not be further from the debating, persuading, challenging and, yes in my case often argumentative, environment in which women's rights were secured and improved over time.

Women argued with each other, ideas developed and were tested and amended. No one simply dug their heels in. The truth remains as it always was. You cannot make real gains, you cannot win an argument, without making an argument.

It was remarkable that in debating the 'six words' amendment, little effort was made to argue against it. As a great believer in having the courage of your convictions, I found it astounding that those content to denounce the amendment as a transphobic 'dog whistle', to impugn my motives and those who supported me, who were vocal elsewhere about my behaviour, could not do the simple thing that women learned a long time ago. Say what you think. Make your case.

The pattern of behaviour I learned to expect as a young woman was also clearly on show, as I was told, 'It is not all women. You are an unreasonable woman. Look, here are women's organisations who disagree.'

And my young self would be birling were I to be told that Rape Crisis Scotland, funded to challenge and inform government action on male violence, would be the very 'other women, more reasonable women, more acceptable women' wheeled out to oppose the amendment. And this was the same organisation that, in my youth, emerged out of women's determination not just to get society to confront the reality of male sexual violence, but through their voluntary efforts, offered women survivors of rape a chance to heal. And this opposition to the 'six words' amendment was done in direct contradiction to everything rape survivors have said, throughout the generations, about the process of seeking justice reinforcing trauma, rather than being a liberation from it.

It became clear to me too that the link between understanding inequality, the political performance of showing you care about it and seeking credit for caring, is in danger of becoming entirely divorced from making a real, tangible difference in people's lives.

This is what I hope we can learn, particularly in our desire to improve women's lives, but also if we are serious about politics being more than one long pledge-card-holding, emoting, self-regarding, living-in-the-moment, performative self-indulgence. And this holds true for the trade union movement and civil society, as much as it is for those elected to Parliament or the council chamber.

It is with a particular dismay I must say that I see trade unions and their representative bodies displaying a lack of support – if not outright hostility – to women raising concerns. And in the name of inclusion, denying women the support of a movement which so often played a part in changing women's lives.

So. Debate. Consider the evidence. Stop parroting slogans and start thinking about how arguments might be resolved rather than dismissed. Stop shooting the messenger. Have some curiosity. After five years, I remain bemused at those who are happier to accept that lifelong feminists with a lifetime of supporting all those excluded and suffering injustice have, in short order, become unthinking bigots funded by shady far-right religious organisations, rather than contemplating that there might be something to think about here.

And my final point? As a young woman, and throughout my life, I have understood the power of women supporting women, of being encouraged, challenged and heartened by sisterhood. Friendships forged in early arguments about women's representation allowed political differences to be respected and challenged without our common commitment to women being lost. In the 'six words' debate, I experienced that solidarity renewed. Women spoke up. They sent messages of support, emphasising time and again that it mattered. I am forever grateful for every kind gesture of solidarity. I am grateful too for my sisters in the Parliament, Jenny Marra, Elaine Smith and Pauline McNeill, who made the case in our party grouping and publicly. And to the brave women in the SNP who chose to challenge their party leadership.

I do not resile from the reality of my own politically tribal instincts. But in the last months of my time in the Scottish Parliament, it is the cross-party, non-party and extra-parliamentary energy, resolve and determination that burns most brightly still in my mind as I look back on the privilege I was given to speak up and speak out in the hope that our daughters' lives might be fairer and safer than those of our mothers. Just as generations of women have done and will continue to do.

Politics matter. And serious politics matters most to those who have least power. Women's lives change when we understand what creates the barriers to women's equality. And are determined not just to understand but dismantle those barriers. It is time we all remembered that.

Chapter 17

Frozen out

Joanna Cherry KC MP

On Monday 1 February 2021, I was sacked from my position as the SNP's front bench spokesperson on Justice and Home Affairs at Westminster. There was no advance warning, no thanks, and no acknowledgement of the role I had played on the SNP front bench for nearly six years.

Ian Blackford MP, the then-leader of the SNP Westminster group, let it be known that I had been sacked for 'unacceptable behaviour', but he never actually spelt out what he meant by that. It was left to others, including Kirsty Blackman MP and Nicola Sturgeon in her now infamous 'broom cupboard' broadcast, to make it clear that I was being sacked for 'transphobia'. That same evening, I received threats of sexual violence from a party member who was later charged and convicted. No one in a leadership position in the SNP has ever publicly condemned his actions.

In the years leading up to and including the passage of the Gender Recognition Reform (Scotland) Bill (GRR Bill) through the Scottish Parliament, allegations of transphobia were weaponised within the SNP against those seen as a threat to Sturgeon's leadership. There was a strong correlation between those who had the guts to resist self-ID and those who had the gumption to question Sturgeon's other policy choices and management style. Our concerns have been proven right, but it has been a rocky road.

Joan McAlpine MSP was the first to come under attack for daring to suggest there was a problem with replacing the legal category of 'sex' with 'gender' in the census. In April 2019 I co-signed a letter to the *Scotsman* organised by SNP MPs, MSPs and councillors urging caution in the rush to legislate for self-ID. This fired the starting gun on a witch-hunt in which Joan and I were the main targets, but many other SNP women and some men, including the MP Neale Hanvey, were also targeted.

I decided to wait for the right moment to make what I hoped would be an effective political intervention. This came in May 2019 when Westminster's Joint Committee on Human Rights, of which I was a member, were questioning a Twitter executive about online abuse. I spent ten minutes grilling her on why Twitter's hateful conduct policy did not cover the protected characteristic of 'sex', and why tweets containing threats of extreme violence to gender critical women were allowed to remain online, while women who tweeted out facts such as 'women don't have penises' had their accounts removed. The live feed of my cross-examination went viral, and all hell broke loose.

Fraser, my chief of staff, had warned me of the likely backlash and, on his advice, I took care to preface my questions with a statement in favour of equal rights for trans people, but of course that made no difference. Hysterical accusations of transphobia rained down from all quarters, including from SNP members. Those making such allegations on social media against a sitting MP were in breach of the party's code of conduct, yet no action was ever taken against them. I received an onslaught of abuse on social media, including death threats, one of which the police considered sufficiently serious to warrant a police escort at my constituency surgery in the douce Edinburgh suburb of Colinton.

Allegations of bullying mysteriously surfaced against me and were widely covered by the press. My total exoneration, after an independent investigation by the Parliamentary Standards Commissioner, received rather less coverage. *Pink News* published a grossly defamatory story claiming I was being investigated for 'homophobia'. Like much of their output concerning gender critical lesbians, the story was wholly without foundation and, after instructing solicitors, I was successful in obtaining a public apology with costs and damages which I donated to an LGB immigration rights charity.

As a lesbian who came out in the 1980s and campaigned against section 28 (2A in Scotland) when my own party was still on the fence about LGB rights, it was particularly galling to be attacked by the gay press, gay politicians who had been in their prams or in the closet in the 1980s, and gay charities such as Stonewall and the Equality Network. After equality was won for LGB people, some campaign organisations adopted gender identity ideology to keep themselves in a job. I take consolation in my conviction that history will not judge their attacks on LGB politicians like myself kindly. However, what hurt the most was what took place within the SNP.

No SNP conference has ever voted to support self-ID, and no SNP manifesto has ever committed to anything beyond reform of the Gender Recognition Act (GRA). As in other countries, including Ireland, the intention was to introduce the policy with a degree of stealth. When we saw which way the wind was blowing, gender critical women began to organise within the SNP. But the leadership could not risk the public knowing what was at stake. Critics were discredited as 'bigots and traitors', a tactic sanctioned, I believe, by people close to the top.

At the SNP conference in October 2019, we launched the SNP Women's Pledge group. The packed meeting had to take place off the conference fringe and with security because of the hostility whipped up against us.

A few months before, a trans woman constituent had come to my constituency surgery to take issue with my interventions. When we talked, we realised that we were not actually that far apart, and we decided to write jointly to Shirley-Anne Somerville suggesting a pause on the self-ID legislation and remitting the issue to a Citizens' Assembly. So much hostility could have been avoided if our suggestion had been accepted, but we were given short shrift.

During this period, I was very busy with the parliamentary debate on Brexit, the campaign for a People's Vote, and my successful legal action to stop the unlawful prorogation of Parliament, as well as the December 2019 General Election. All the while, I was fighting a rear-guard action against attempts to have me deselected as an MP and expelled from the SNP.

As the pandemic took hold in spring 2020, the debate largely moved online, where prominent SNP activists and elected parliamentarians and councillors led attacks on me – all in breach of the party's code of conduct. No action was ever taken by SNP officials, in contrast to the treatment meted out to gender critical women, some of whom were suspended from the party on the most spurious grounds. One long-standing member told me she had her membership suspended for retweeting my newspaper column.

At the SNP National Executive Committee (NEC) elections, held during the party's online conference in November 2020, the left-wing Common Weal group and the Women's Pledge group organised a slate of candidates. These were people who wanted change in the strategic direction of the party, with more accountability – the state of the party's finances was by now an issue – and a halt to self-ID. Despite vicious attacks on our motives, we did well in the elections in which thousands of delegates voted.

In a clear effort to prevent my election, and in another flagrant breach of the party's code of conduct, SNP activists organised a cross-party public letter, accusing me of transphobia. They even went so far as to include the signatures of Stewart McDonald MP and leader of the Scottish Liberal Democrats Alex Cole-Hamilton MSP without their permission. After I instructed solicitors, the letter was toned down, but no steps were taken by the SNP to address what had occurred. Nevertheless, and perhaps because of this unpleasantness, I got more votes in the NEC elections than all the other parliamentary candidates put together, and prominent gender critical feminists Lynne Anderson and Caroline McAllister were elected as the party's equalities and women's convenors respectively.

Many took a dim view of this outbreak of democracy, and the attacks upon us escalated. Various ruses were employed to undermine our democratic mandate and NEC meetings held online were conducted in an atmosphere so vicious it is hard to describe. One by one, most of us left the NEC and many left the party. Not all of this was to do with our opposition to self-ID, but it played a large part.

Around this time, I became very concerned about the hate crime bill which Humza Yousaf as Justice Secretary was piloting through the Scottish Parliament. I thought it would breach the freedom of belief and freedom of speech protections in Articles 9 and 10 of the European Convention on Human Rights (ECHR) and that it would be weaponised against gender critical women.

I raised my concerns with Humza, suggesting he amend the bill to make it ECHR compliant and to protect those with gender critical beliefs. I was successful in convincing him that such defences were necessary, but when the government amendments were published and I tweeted in their support, I was again accused of transphobia and Nicola Sturgeon recorded her 'broom cupboard' broadcast, begging trans rights activists not to leave the SNP. This proved to be the catalyst for my sacking a few days later. The amendments were withdrawn.

Dealing with the aftermath of my sacking, the constant internal attacks within the SNP, the vicious atmosphere in the SNP Westminster group and at NEC meetings, took its toll on my health. I really struggled with the unfairness of the attacks upon me and the attempts to trash my reputation, given my long history as a human rights lawyer, an LGB activist and a feminist with experience of prosecuting sex crimes and an expert on safeguarding.

In March 2021, I took time off because of the impact on my physical and mental health. I seriously thought about leaving politics and going back to my career at the Bar. However, I came to the conclusion that I should stay in the SNP and fight.

The SNP was founded by intellectuals, artists, poets and thinkers. The lack of debate and the Stalinist adherence to the leadership line which was expected under the Sturgeon leadership would have been anathema to them. Time has shown this approach to have been a disaster for the party,

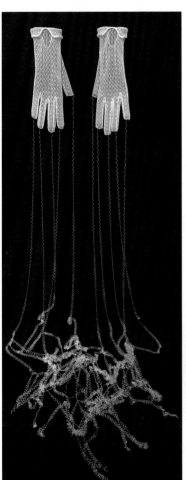

Feminist to her fingertips. Original artwork by Mr Mann, May 2022. Lace gloves, thread, wire. *(Mr Mann)*

Lessons from Canada, University of Strathclyde, Glasgow, 24 May 2019: *(left to right)* Trina Budge (FWS), Susan Smith (FWS), Bec Wonders (speaker), Meghan Murphy (speaker), Marion Calder (FWS). *(J. Hunter)*

Launch of the SNP Women's Pledge at fringe event at the SNP Conference, Aberdeen, 13 October 2019. *(left to right)* Margaret Lynch, Joanna Cherry MP, Caroline McAllister, Rhona Hotchkiss, Joan McAlpine MSP. *(Linda Semple)*

Gillian Philip at Speaker's Corner event, The Mound, Edinburgh, 2 August 2020. *(J. Hunter)*

The first picture of ribbons, accompanying the first use of #WomenWontWheesht, December 2020. *(@Dis_critic)*

Painted slate, Little Glas Maol, Cairngorms, August 2020.
(Maggie Murphy)

Greyfriars Bobby, Edinburgh, dressed by activist Mary Gordon for International Women's Day, 8 March 2021. *(PA/Jane Barlow)*

Sole Sisters protest under Covid-19 restrictions outside the Scottish Parliament, Edinburgh, April 2021. *(Rob Hoon)*

Lisa Mackenzie at Women's Rights Demonstration outside the Scottish Parliament, 2 September 2021. *(Susan Dalgety)*

Census form envelope decorated with stickers, April 2022. *(Jenny Reilly)*

Selfie tweeted by J.K. Rowling on day of the Scottish Women's Rally outside the Scottish Parliament, 6 October 2022. *(J.K. Rowling)*

Banner at the Scottish Women's Rally, 6 October 2022. *(@obsolesence)*

Nicola Sturgeon fingertips, the Scottish Women's Rally, 6 October 2022. (*Iain Masterton*)

Embroidered banner with selkie at the Scottish Women's Rally, 6 October 2022. (*Jenny Lupton*)

Johann Lamont speaks at the Scottish Women's Rally, 6 October 2022. (*J. Hunter*)

Nicole Jones, with Heather Ritchie, channelling the suffragettes, while listening to speakers at the Scottish Women's Rally, 6 October 2022. (*J. Hunter*)

The seditious scarf, the Scottish Parliament, Edinburgh, 15 November 2022. (*@obsolesence*)

Protester outside Cornton Vale women's prison, with cardboard cut-out showing actual height of a male sexual offender who had been held there, compared to average for women, 26 November 2022. (*Jenny Reilly*)

Marion Calder (FWS) at the Women Won't Wheesht candlelit Vigil for Women's Rights outside the Scottish Parliament, 20 December 2022. (J. Hunter)

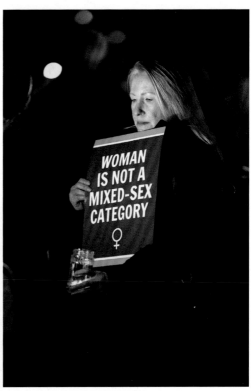

Ash Regan MSP speaking at the No to Self-ID demonstration outside the Scottish Parliament, 21 December 2022. (CDF Images)

No to Self-ID demonstration outside the Scottish Parliament, 21 December 2022. (Iain Masterton)

Pam Gosal MSP speaking to women at the No Males in Female Jails demonstration outside the Scottish Parliament, 9 February 2023.
(Pam Gosal)

Guerilla installation outside the first minister's official residence, Bute House, Edinburgh, 12 February 2023. Sticker, cardboard, metal rod, curtains.
(@Dis_critic)

Panel at FiLiA Conference in Glasgow, 15 October 2023: *(left to right)* Julie Bindel, J.K. Rowling, and Claire L. Heuchan.
(Pauline Makoveitchoux)

both in the size of our membership and our electoral fortunes. I feel vindicated, but back in 2021 it was difficult to make the decision to stay.

What helped me most was the support I received from family and friends, particularly my then-partner, Victoria. I also got backing from the gender critical feminist movement, the emerging new LGB rights movement, my colleagues at the Bar and a handful of political colleagues in the SNP and other parties. Supportive messages from J.K. Rowling and Martina Navratilova helped buoy my spirits. The camaraderie that grew up between many SNP and Labour women was heart-warming, and I made new friends with the founders of For Women Scotland (FWS) and the Murray Blackburn Mackenzie (MBM) collective, as well as with many gender critical feminists and LGB rights campaigners across Scotland and the UK. It also helped that I could not, and still cannot, walk up a street, go into a coffee shop, pub, or supermarket anywhere in Scotland without someone coming up to thank me for the stand I have taken for women's and LGB rights.

In 2021 I returned briefly to my legal practice at the Bar to defend Marion Millar, who was charged with threatening and abusive behaviour, aggravated by transphobia and homophobia. She had posted a number of tweets expressing her opposition to self-ID and gender identity theory in robust terms. I was convinced her prosecution fell foul of the right to free speech, and that it was important to take a stand.

Her case became a cause célèbre. Her several court appearances at Glasgow Sheriff Court were attended by crowds of women dressed as handmaidens chanting, 'Women Won't Wheesht'. And in July 2021, a rally was held in her support at Glasgow Green and addressed by – among others – Kate Harris from LGB Alliance.

LGB Alliance had launched in London in October 2019, and in Glasgow in January 2020, but I was afraid to go to those meetings because I felt it would lead to my expulsion from the SNP, which now seems rather ridiculous. However, by the autumn of 2021, I felt emboldened enough to accept an invitation to speak at their first annual conference in London.

The conference took place amidst significant security, but was a huge success despite delegates having to cross a picket line of trans rights activists including an SNP MP. To this day I consider it shameful that a straight politician should have seen fit to protest the right of lesbians to attend a conference organised by other lesbians to discuss their rights.

Around this time the gender critical movement began to flourish in a more public way. Sex Matters launched in London, and I joined their advisory board. Gender critical MPs and peers at Westminster were beginning to connect.

At the very end of October 2021, the Crown Office dropped proceedings against Marion Millar, having accepted the strength of her free speech defence. Both civil and criminal legal action has played an important role in advancing the gender critical cause by ensuring women and men could speak up without being criminalised or losing their livelihoods. When Maya Forstater won her appeal in July 2022, it became clear that gender critical women couldn't lose their jobs, nor be discriminated against or harassed, simply because of their gender critical beliefs. Other cases, like barrister Allison Bailey's successful case against her chambers, and the LGB Alliance's successful defence of its right to exist as a charity, have also been pivotal.

I was able to use Maya's case to defend myself against the attempts to have me deselected or expelled from the SNP. I was also able to call upon it in the summer of 2023, when the Stand comedy club, having invited me to appear as part of their Edinburgh Festival fringe programme, cancelled my interview because of the discriminatory views of some of their staff. The opinion I commissioned from senior counsel which convinced the Stand to climb down and host the event is published on my website, and has already been used by others facing cancellation, including FiLiA, whose huge international feminist conference in Glasgow in October 2023 was the subject of an unsuccessful attempt by trans rights activists to bully the venue into backing out the day before the conference was due to start.

When the new SNP leader and first minister, Humza Yousaf, felt able to condemn trans rights activists who greeted women arriving at the Glasgow FiLiA conference with abuse, led by a man shouting 'fuck you' through a microphone, I realised how much progress we had made. Double rapist Adam Graham/ Isla Bryson had peaked Scotland. The GRR Bill had been blocked because of its adverse impact on the Equality Act, and Nicola Sturgeon had resigned.

In February 2022, FWS organised a meeting of gender critical women from across the United Kingdom in Edinburgh to discuss how we should fight the bill. At the time, it felt like a done deal, but Kate Harris of LGB Alliance predicted that the legislation would never get on to the statute book. She was right. Thanks to Scotland's Court of Session upholding the basis of the Scottish Secretary's Section 35 intervention, the women who had long argued that the bill interfered with rights and safeguarding under the Equality Act were vindicated.

Many of the women involved in the campaign have paid a heavy price. I require to have security now at all my constituency surgeries. The toll on the SNP has also been high. The story of this flawed bill is a microcosm of everything that was wrong with the SNP under its previous leadership. A controversial, ill-thought-through policy that was never debated on the floor of conference, a refusal to listen to those with legitimate concerns, the demonisation of dissenters and, above all, as the opinion polls show, a failure to take the public with us. Humza Yousaf is to be commended for doing the right thing by not pursuing an appeal that could never be won. Lessons must be learned, not just by my party, but by all the political parties in Scotland who preferred shallow virtue-signalling to evidence-based policy-making.

And the manner in which the GRR Bill was passed does not reflect well on the Scottish Parliament. The one-sided scrutiny by a cross-party committee which wholly failed to acknowledge or tackle the conflict of rights issue, and which refused to meet with female sex abuse survivors, was nothing short of disgraceful. MSPs like Alex Cole-Hamilton lionised pro-self-ID activists, some of whom later turned out to have a rather unsavoury history, while turning a deaf ear to feminists with years of experience in women's rights and safeguarding. In the words of my former SNP colleague, Caroline McAllister:

> While women were targeted and abused predominantly by men, many of our political representatives looked away. Those who were directly approached dismissed women's concerns using the disingenuous excuse that both sides were as bad as each other. They seemed to think this gave them immunity from their responsibilities to women and permission to ignore safeguarding. Politicians owe women a massive apology.

She is right. Scotland needs to do politics better in future.

Chapter 18

The right to examine ideas

Shereen Benjamin

On Wednesday 13 October 2021, senior lecturer in education Shereen Benjamin realises that it has become impossible for her to host a discussion on the impact of self-ID in schools at the University of Edinburgh

It is a dark November evening in 2023. I'm standing in the lobby area of one of the University of Edinburgh's iconic buildings. Outside, a noisy protest is gathering, with the aim of sabotaging the public screening and discussion of a film. Posters around the university have declared: 'Student protesters have prevented this screening from happening twice before, and we can do it again.'

Previous attempts to run this event have, indeed, been shut down by protestors twice: first in December 2022, and again in April 2023. After the first sabotage, one of the instigators was interviewed on YouTube, likening the screening of the film to *The Birth of a Nation*, a racist American film made in 1915 and credited with being the inspiration for the reinvigoration of the Ku Klux Klan. At that first sabotage, a student activist was charged with assaulting a member of the public. At the second, protestors barred the entrances to the building, and guests were subjected to electronically amplified misogynist and ageist abuse, and to jeers and boos from crowds of protestors. In the run-up to this third attempt, a letter denouncing the film as bigotry and calling for the university to withdraw permission for the event has been sent to management and distributed by the University and College Union (UCU) Edinburgh branch to over 3,000 colleagues on its university-hosted mailing list. It was the latest in a string of electronic denunciations.

The focus of this moral outrage is the film *Adult Human Female*, described by its creators as 'the first UK documentary feature to look at the clash between women's rights and trans ideology'. I stand inside the lobby, surrounded by riot fencing, looking out at the dozens of security personnel. Police officers in high-viz and an outside security firm are providing back-up to the university's own security team. As guests arrive, they are ushered through multiple layers of security, their ID is checked, and their bags are searched. This is by far the biggest security operation I've seen at this or any other university. I know I won't breathe easily until the evening is safely over. This is the new normal for screening a feminist film at the University of Edinburgh.

How did we get here? How has the climate for public discussion of women's rights at a university become so febrile? We need to go back.

At the start of 2018, I was largely unaware of what I've come to call gender identity theory and its implications. I'd been involved in feminist politics for decades. As a young feminist I'd experienced the divisions amongst feminists becoming increasingly bitter as the women's movement of the 1970s and early 1980s lost its momentum. Divisions between materialist feminists, who, like me, considered themselves to be firmly on the political left and worked for women's rights within the labour and trade union movement; radical feminists, who focused on addressing male violence against women and girls in its many forms and who tended to work outside of what they considered patriarchal institutions; and liberal feminists, who sought incremental reform based on equal opportunities and 'choice' for individual women within existing structures. By the summer of 2018, I was dimly aware that there was some kind of controversy playing out between, I thought, radical feminists and the trans rights movement, but I thought it had nothing to do with me, a long-standing materialist feminist.

That changed in the autumn of 2018, when the then rector of the University of Edinburgh, Ann Henderson, was targeted for retweeting details of a meeting for MPs in London, hosted by Fair Play for Women and other groups. Ann had been the campus trade unions' candidate as rector, and was well known and respected for her campaigning record. When I put it to our UCU branch, of which I was a local officer at the time, that we should support Ann, I was astonished and dismayed at the response. According to other UCU committee members, Ann deserved not support but censure. I was firmly told that 'trans women are women', there is no conflict of rights, and that these were unassailable truths, beyond challenge or debate.

At that point, all the klaxons sounded for me. I hadn't realised that we were supposed to believe that men who want to 'live as' women literally are women: I could see straight away the many conflicts of rights to which such a reorientation of social reality would give rise. I had long thought that there should be sensible and sensitive accommodation for individuals who need to present as far as possible as the opposite sex, but what I now realised was being demanded was something of a different order. Having worked for women's rights within the labour and trade union movement, I knew how crucial it is to have a stable definition of the category 'woman', so that inequalities and disadvantage can be accurately identified, and the effect of measures designed to reduce inequalities can be properly implemented, calibrated and evaluated.

But perhaps what troubled me most was the assertion that 'there is no debate'. I was coming to realise that sex and gender was a topical and controversial social issue: changes to law and policy on the basis that self-declared gender identity – a relatively new and unscientific belief – should replace biological sex everywhere and for all purposes had already taken place, and further changes were proposed. A university should be a place where arguments and evidence for such full-scale social change can be set out, their wider implications for everyone critically examined, and fully discussed. The slogan 'there is no debate' has no place in a university. Or so I thought.

Large universities such as Edinburgh typically host hundreds of public engagement events each year, including open lectures, seminars, panel discussions, film screenings and conferences. As I started to pay attention early in 2019, it became apparent to me that public engagement events uncritically platforming gender identity theory were taking place on the University of Edinburgh campus but, as far as I was aware, no public platform had been given to any critical examination of the proposed changes in law and policy.

I was aware I still had much to learn about the particularities of the storm that I now knew to be swirling around me. What I could do, I thought, was organise a public panel discussion on women's sex-based rights, platforming some of the women in academia and policy who were arguing for the ongoing relevance of sex in law, policy, language and cultural life. The event was arranged for early June 2019. I knew it would be controversial, but I was unprepared for the attempts to stop the event from happening: the mass emails to colleagues making unfounded and untrue accusations to which I was not allowed right of reply, the bogus bookings, the social media attacks beforehand and the intimidating protests on the evening itself. After putting in place heavy security, the event went ahead and was well attended, including by several MSPs. But the fallout was shocking. One of the speakers, Julie Bindel, was attacked as she left the campus, and Green MSP Andy Wightman was forced to apologise simply for attending.

Colleagues, some of them in senior positions, privately commended me for standing firm, but said they dared not support me publicly for fear of being tarred as bigots. Support came instead from the growing networks of local women, and broader networks of academics (including a handful at Edinburgh), lesbians and Labour Party women who were organising to defend women's rights. It was, and is, a privilege to know these brave, principled women.

Battle-scarred but, I thought, wiser, I began planning another event. In June 2019 the Scottish Government withdrew its endorsement of the LGBT Youth Scotland (LGBTYS) guidance on supporting 'transgender young people' in schools, and committed to producing guidance of its own. With new guidance on the horizon, I thought it would be helpful to bring together people with diverse experiences and viewpoints to have a respectful, evidence-based discussion about how best to support schools, teachers and pupils. I thought with enough preparatory work, I could prevent any attacks on such a discussion. I attended events run by LGBTYS and Scottish Trans Alliance (STA), where I engaged in good faith and sought to build connections and relationships. I then invited a selection of people and organisations to contribute to a public seminar on supporting transgender-identifying and gender non-conforming pupils in schools. Professor Michele

Moore, an academic known to be critical of gender identity theory, and Stephanie Davies-Arai of Transgender Trend accepted invitations to speak. However, LGBTYS declined my invitation, stating that they wouldn't share a platform with speakers who in their view contested the validity of 'trans identities', and STA never responded at all. The University of Edinburgh's Staff Pride Network (SPN), of which I'm a member, initially engaged in discussion with me, but eventually refused to provide a speaker.

With the support of my then head of school I went ahead and organised the seminar with three speakers – Michele, Stephanie and myself – to be held in December. I am a lecturer in primary education in my day job, and I was now fully conversant with the issues as they applied in schools. The campaign to stop the event was fast and vicious. A blog post by the SPN (publicised to its around 700 members) accused the speakers of transphobia, alleging that our presence on campus would have a 'harmful impact'. Appeals to university managers to allow me the right of reply and to prevent any further escalation of the campaign were unsuccessful. A few days after the publicity went live, the event was 'postponed' on the head of school's advice, and we requested university managers to 'establish appropriate boundaries for protest' so that it could be rescheduled as soon as possible.

Meanwhile, public events promoting gender identity theory continued to go ahead unhindered. My head of school was reluctant to authorise another attempt to platform the seminar. Then Covid-19 came along, putting things on hold for a few months. Once online events became a possibility, I restarted the discussion. There followed many months of meetings and written proposals as different options for platforming the seminar were explored, but obstacle after obstacle was found until eventually, on 13 October 2021, my head of school said that the school could not host it, meaning that it would almost certainly have to be cancelled.

I was despondent. 'There is no debate' was, it seemed, a reality in the very last place where it should be thinkable: a prestigious university. A contentious belief – that an individual's 'gender identity' must overwrite biological sex – was being promoted as an unassailable fact on our campus.

This was something I couldn't live with. In effect, instead of being a place where a new and controversial view of the world would be subjected to robust discussion across all relevant disciplines, my university had become the engine room for the uncritical promulgation of that new, untested view, and debate was supposedly beyond the pale.

Elsewhere in the university, other concerns about the chilling of academic freedom were emerging. A colleague, Neil Thin, was targeted for his criticism of critical race theory in 2021, prompting some academic colleagues to come together to defend him. Relatively small in number, we were unsuccessful in persuading managers to take action, but we had found each other. One of the problems with public attacks is that people self-censor, and nobody knows who they can trust. Now we had an emergent network of academics who were known to care deeply about academic freedom – the pursuit of truth and understanding according to established scholarly conventions – and wanted to defend it.

We decided that we needed to establish a presence online and on campus. Some of us were signatories to a statement produced by the UK-wide organisation Academics for Academic Freedom (AFAF). On 5 March 2022, we asked the AFAF co-ordinator for permission to form our own local branch, which would use the AFAF statement and branding. He greeted the idea with enthusiasm, and later that month Edinburgh Academics for Academic

Freedom (EdAFAF) – the first of what has become many local AFAF branches – was born. We set up a Twitter account, a blog and a mailing list, and organised an inaugural discussion meeting for University of Edinburgh colleagues and students.

EdAFAF was never intended to be a 'gender critical' group. But with sex and gender being the most obvious flashpoint issue on campus, it was fitting that our first public event would be the long-postponed public seminar on sex, gender and schools. Our plans seemed to fly under the radar, and the seminar took place, albeit during the summer vacation period, with a large, appreciative audience and very little in the way of attack or protest. It had taken nearly three years to make the event happen, however, and it came too late to influence the government's work on guidance for schools, which had been issued the summer before.

We subsequently planned a public screening and discussion of *Adult Human Female*, to take place in December 2022. Within days of the publicity going live, UCU Edinburgh published an open letter to management calling on them to cancel the screening, and the SPN emailed their long membership list, accusing the film of containing 'transphobic rhetoric designed to spread misinformation', describing EdAFAF as 'holding . . . outdated, harmful and hateful attitudes' and stating that our screening would create 'an unsafe environment for our trans staff and students'. In a depressingly familiar sequence of events, I tried in vain to get a right of reply in order to defend EdAFAF and the film against smears, slurs and monstering, but neither the SPN committee, nor managers to whom I subsequently appealed, were willing to circulate my response.

One of the effects of these attacks, landing as they did in an already febrile campus climate, was to whip up hostility. Whilst this was unpleasant and intimidating, I wasn't prepared for what happened on the day of the screening. When I arrived at the venue, the head of security informed me that a group of protestors had occupied the lecture theatre, and he could not safely allow our attendees access. There followed a tense couple of hours as security colleagues attempted to find an alternative venue, only to have that blockaded as well. Eventually I was directed to announce to attendees that the screening would not go ahead. In short, a relatively small group of censorious individuals had taken upon themselves the right to decide what could and could not be discussed on campus, and had, on this occasion, prevailed.

I naively thought this would be the wake-up call, and that there would be immediate and serious action from university managers. There wasn't. We rescheduled the event for April 2023, and again it was targeted. This time, the SPN announced they would partner with an outside group to host their protest. This group created publicity material, shared online and subsequently circulated by the SPN via its mailing list, which again made hyperbolic claims about the harms that the screening would cause, and used demeaning and dehumanising language to describe both EdAFAF and anyone associated with the film. Again, no action was taken to provide a right of reply or stop the circulation of this material, despite the risk that it would lead to a second sabotage.

And so, the inevitable happened. On the day, a few masked thugs blockaded the entrance to the venue, cheered on by a larger crowd of protestors. Management directed us to cancel the event, which we did. Those attendees who hadn't heard about the cancellation in time arrived at the venue where they were subjected to misogynist and ageist insults, and jeers and taunts, blared out from industrial-strength amplification.

Even this second cancellation wasn't enough to prompt action to address the university's climate for discussion, and its hostile environment for staff and students with gender critical and similar views. Rather than work behind the scenes to improve that environment, and rather than put in place mechanisms to stop or at least address the use of university mailing lists to spread smears and lies, managers instead authorised a major security operation, which would ensure a third attempt to show and discuss the film went ahead, despite, rather than in the absence of, hostile, aggressive protest.

And so, to November 2023. A third attempt to screen and discuss *Adult Human Female* went ahead. Again, it was targeted with mass emails. As attendees arrived, and as they left, they were greeted by banners saying 'Fuck TERFs' and subjected to jeers and chants of 'Shame on you', but this time protestors were safely corralled behind barriers and riot fencing.

University of Edinburgh managers will no doubt claim this as a success. But at what price? When the university climate for discussion of women's rights is such that it takes a major security operation to show a feminist film, something has gone very wrong indeed.

Chapter 19

Women still don't count

Fiona McAnena

On Sunday 5 December 2021, campaign group Fair Play For Women initiates judicial review proceedings against plans to collect data on sex in the census in Scotland on the basis of self-ID

Counting people matters. The national census, which is carried out every ten years, gives policy makers an accurate picture of the United Kingdom. The public also needs to be confident that the process is robust, or else they may not take part.

When the Office for National Statistics (ONS) proposed that respondents to the 2021 census in England and Wales could answer the question, 'What is your sex?' according to documents such as a passport, Fair Play for Women reluctantly took the matter to court.

As you can change the sex marker on any document except a birth certificate without having a Gender Recognition Certificate (GRC), ONS's guidance meant that people whose birth certificate said they were male would be able to say they were female, if they had other documents saying so.

Legal action in the High Court is an expensive and uncertain business. We felt fairly sure the law was on our side, since the Census Act of 1920 predates any notions of self-ID. All the same, it was a massive relief when we won. On 17 March 2021, the High Court ordered that 'What is your sex?' means sex 'as recorded on a birth certificate or Gender Recognition Certificate'. ONS were also told to pay our costs.

We expected that the National Records of Scotland (NRS), responsible for the census in Scotland on behalf of the Scottish Government, would follow suit when it went live a year later in 2022. After all, the Census Act 1920 is UK-wide.

We were somewhat surprised when, in response to a query from us, NRS insisted that not only was it going to ignore the High Court ruling, it was planning guidance that would allow people with a trans identity to explicitly ignore their legally recorded sex. The guidance would say:

> *If you are transgender the answer you give can be different from what is on your birth certificate. You do not need a Gender Recognition Certificate (GRC). If you are non-binary or you are not sure how to answer, you could use the sex registered on your official documents, such as your passport.*

It was nothing less than self-identification. Again we had to launch a legal action and a crowdfunder. As the case had been decided in England on the legal issue of whether ONS was free to deviate from the Census Act, our case in Scotland would focus on this clear point of law.

Nic Williams, the driving force behind Fair Play For Women, has always valued our connections with women in Scotland. They helped us adapt our submission, pointing out where the matter had been debated in the Scottish Parliament. We also needed a King's Counsel to argue our case in Scotland's Inner

Court of Session, and in Roddy Dunlop we found one of the best.

The hearing lasted one day. A week later, on 17 February 2022, the judgment was published. The court ruled that guidance issued alongside the census, which informs transgender people they can register as male or female regardless of their legal status, was lawful. We had lost.

We felt we had no option but to appeal. It seemed barely credible that the census guidance could vary so significantly in different parts of the country. In England and Wales, you had to give your sex as it was recorded on your birth certificate or GRC. In Scotland, the law now said you could just go with your feelings.

Time was of the essence. The census was set to launch on 28 February, a few weeks ahead of the formal census date. Our hearing was granted almost immediately. Watching proceedings unfold was excruciating. The lawyer for NRS argued that 'sex and gender are used interchangeably', and it seemed to us at least that the judge didn't fully grasp the importance of data in policy-making – and the importance of the census within that. The census provides the population baseline against which all other surveys benchmark, and the more you dig into the detail, by area, age, ethnicity and other factors, the more reliable data on sex matters, to understand how the experiences of women and men compare.

The census is an important, almost sacred, public document – it is an offence to knowingly give false information when completing it. Our counsel argued that NRS's advice to allow people to self-identify their sex was unlawful because it 'sanctioned' the unlawful act of providing a 'false' answer. In other words, it was leading ordinary Scots to break the law.

But his argument fell on deaf ears. The need to allow trans-identifying people to be 'true to themselves' seemed more appealing to the judge. The looming census deadline meant we got the ruling only two days later on 24 February 2022. We lost. Again.

It was like a punch in the gut. The judge, Lady Dorrian, had just dismissed reality. She said that the Scottish government advice was not unlawful because 'an answer provided in good faith and on reasonable grounds would not be a false answer'. In effect, she ruled that if a man says he is a woman, and believes it, it can be true, even in the eyes of the law.

A careful reading of the judgment did reveal some positive assertions about sex-based rights. It said, 'There are some contexts in which a rigid definition based on biological sex must be adopted', and went on to say that, 'There are other circumstances in which matters affecting status, or important rights, in particular the rights of others, may demand a rigid definition to be applied to the term "sex" of the kind proposed by [Fair Play For Women] . . . The point which these examples all have in common is that they concern status or important rights.'

But, as we recognised at the time, the Scottish census ruling was a setback in the fight to protect women and girls. We had always known it would be a long haul. This was just one skirmish in a long fight and we were not deterred. We knew public opinion was with us.

The winning side had three months to claim its costs. As the deadline approached, our solicitor had still not heard anything, and we began to hope that they would not pursue us. But on the very last day they could, the Scottish Government lodged a claim. After negotiation, we had to pay them £74,000. A bitter pill.

SECTION 4

The parliamentary battle over self-ID: Holyrood under the spotlight

Chapter 20

Women's voices in the Parliament

Pam Gosal MBE MSP and Rachael Hamilton MSP

On Tuesday 15 March 2022 the Equalities, Human Rights and Civil Justice Committee begins its detailed scrutiny (Stage 1) of the bill

In May 2021, I made history and shattered the glass ceiling when I was elected to the Scottish Parliament as the first Indian female, first Sikh Member of the Scottish Parliament (MSP) and one of the first two women of colour elected, both in 2021.

So, from the outset, I've been aware that Holyrood is not as diverse as some parties like to pretend. We often hear lofty claims from politicians, particularly those from the SNP, that the Scottish Parliament is inclusive of all faiths and customs.

But the truth is, it is not a very welcoming place at the best of times, unless you happen to agree with every word that comes from Bute House. I can say this with both sincerity and disappointment.

During committee deliberations and the Stage 3 proceedings for the Gender Recognition Reform (Scotland) Bill (GRR Bill), my eyes were opened wider to just how poorly the Scottish Parliament represents people from backgrounds like mine, as well as women and girls more generally.

If you come from outside the Holyrood bubble, your views are not taken seriously. They are shouted down. Sometimes, as happened during this process, they are shut out entirely.

I'm not only referring to the views of people from Asian backgrounds. I mean people of all minorities and, indeed, anybody who holds views that don't chime with the prevailing consensus within the corridors of power in Scotland.

When it came down to it, in the heat of the law-making process, the Scottish Parliament demonstrated how poor it is at representing diverse views. It doesn't strike a balance. It railroads through rights for some at the direct expense of rights for others.

The words of politicians who proclaim themselves to be progressive were proven to be hollow when it comes to a difficult issue such as gender recognition reform. Suddenly, some so-called liberals were exposed as being illiberal. Some who claim to be feminists trampled on women's rights. Some who claim to value unity became the proponents of division.

As a member of the Equalities, Human Rights and Civil Justice Committee which scrutinised the bill, I had a front-row seat to how insular, narrow-minded and browbeating the Scottish Parliament can be at its worst. And, make no mistake, this bill was our Parliament at its worst.

From day one, the intention of bitterly ideological politicians was clear. Attempts to invite speakers from a wide spectrum of society were limited. Evidence from outside a hand-picked list of experts was dismissed. We were told those views could be heard later. Sometimes, there supposedly wasn't time to continue questioning or call another guest.

The committee stacked up the evidence it wanted to include, and almost everything and everyone who didn't fit with the government view was limited using any means possible. In many cases, conclusions were reached before evidence had been heard. As a member of the committee, I came to my judgement cautiously. Even when I instinctively disagreed, I listened carefully. I wish everyone had done the same.

But the process seemed to be an exercise in rubber-stamping the flawed bill before us, no matter the practical flaws it contained or the destructive way that it could strike at the heart of fundamental issues of faith and conscience.

Evidence was taken from a selective, hand-picked group of organisations. The whole parliamentary process was rushed through without fully considering all viewpoints. In May 2022, I wrote a letter to the committee noting how the witness list is 'overwhelmingly skewed' toward those in support of the general principles of the bill. I attached a document with a potential list of witnesses to give evidence, including Sharron Davies MBE. It had been put forward by my colleague in March 2022, when he was still a member of the committee.

There were also several potential witnesses who were simply too scared to give their views. As a sitting member I can sympathise with that. I was labelled a 'transphobe' for merely questioning whether a piece of legislation – however well intentioned – might erode the rights of women and their representation in public life.

The committee itself had an unfriendly atmosphere. Away from the public eye, my colleague Rachael Hamilton and I were repeatedly shut down when we raised concerns about the scrutiny of this legislation. I began to grow extremely concerned when women's groups, particularly those representing women of faith, were too frightened to speak out due to fears for their safety or credibility.

The beauty of living in a democracy is the freedoms we enjoy, such as free speech and freedom of thought. But when that is no longer enjoyed by some, we ought to be alarmed. And this undoubtedly affected the scrutiny of this bill.

Irrespective of the unbalanced list of witnesses, it was abundantly clear that the parties pushing the bill refused to take the proper depth and breadth of relevant information from key stakeholders. The legislative process was skewed by powerful activists for ideological reasons.

When we heard evidence from the former Cabinet Secretary for Social Justice, Housing and Local Government she waved away any concerns as if they were completely invalid. We would raise justified objections to government evidence, only for some patchwork counterpoint to be quickly arranged to try and discredit our position.

The case of United Nations Special Rapporteur on Violence Against Women and Girls, Dr Reem Alsalem, was the worst and clearest example of the way that any dissenting view was sidelined. She had written to the UK government on 29 November 2022 expressing her concerns about the impact of the GRR Bill. I was delighted to speak with Ms Alsalem at length to hear her expertise and use that information to inform the law-making process, which is what every MSP should have done. She spoke eloquently about her fears that sexual predators could exploit the bill to gain access to women's single-sex spaces, and services such as domestic abuse shelters or women-only prisons. Yet, despite her obvious expertise, it took my colleague Rachael Hamilton MSP, writing to the committee, followed by further pressure from myself, for this meeting even to be set up.

They refused at first, even though they had readily heard from another UN expert. Eventually, they relented for an online meeting – but only on the day before the final stage of the bill began, at the last possible moment, so her views could not possibly be fully considered by the committee.

As if that were not enough of an attempt to quiet her concerns, the committee also hastily invited the UN Independent Expert on Protection against Violence and Discrimination based on Sexual Orientation and Gender Identity, Victor Madrigal-Borloz to give evidence for the second time, right after Dr Alsalem. This was a clear attempt to discredit her work.

When we objected to the committee's approach, we were shouted down. We were outvoted without any meaningful debate. Rachael Hamilton and I, the two Scottish Conservative MSPs on the committee, had no choice but to submit a minority opinion report, so we could at least have it on record that not everybody agreed. This is not a typical practice in the Parliament. It is reserved for occasions when committee members cannot find any middle ground.

At times, it was a lonely and depressing experience. I was often left searching for answers, asking why? Why is our Parliament so afraid of debate? Why can't it cope with opposing views? Why is this bill being pushed through in this flawed form? This went beyond politics for me. As a woman and as a minority ethnic woman, I felt unheard.

Throughout the process, I was heartened by the cross-party support from outside the chamber. People came up to me when I was out shopping, thanking me. Many of these individuals wouldn't typically vote for me. However, matters concerning women's rights are beyond politics.

Women who typically vote Labour, Liberal Democrat and even SNP would get in touch with me to offer praise and thanks. That kept me going when it got really difficult. They made me feel part of a movement. I knew the cause we were fighting for was worth it. Their strength of feeling gave me the strength to keep speaking up. Their passion was a daily inspiration.

But I have to say, the cross-party support that I received outside Holyrood was simply not there within the Scottish Parliament. There, politicians from Labour and the Liberal Democrats were far too quick to jump on the bandwagon, to agree with the government view, refuse to provide serious scrutiny and, in some cases, even to help the gender identity ideologues to shut down debate. They did not reflect the best of their party.

This exposed a rift between Holyrood and the real world that came to symbolise the entire passing of the bill. No matter what political background people came from, if they were outside of the Scottish Parliament and the political circles of civic society, they seemed to grasp the dangers of this legislation. I was often surprised by people on the street who would come up to me and seemed to know the finer points of clauses within the bill better than some MSPs.

Then came the three days of hell in the chamber. I hardly slept as my amendments were not read until late into the night. I was tired. My focus was waning. As midnight grew closer, I'm certain members of the public would have tuned out of the debate. That is no way to pass legislation.

As expected, common-sense Scottish Conservative amendments were defeated, including my own amendments. The changes I submitted were straightforward and sensible. They only sought to give women and girls assurances that they would be safe, particularly in single-sex spaces and at single-sex services, and to protect the rights of religious people, especially from BAME (Black, Asian and Minority Ethnic) communities.

My amendments would have protected single-sex spaces from abuse and ensured that dangerous criminals could not fraudulently exploit single-sex services. But the SNP voted them down.

On the bill's final reading, I knew I would have to water down my amendments, even if that meant just minimal reassurances for women. Other changes I proposed looked at monitoring the impact of the bill on Scottish Government funding for specialist single-sex services, given that so few currently exist.

Perhaps the most shocking amendment to be defeated was the one put forward by my colleague Russell Findlay, which sought to prevent sex offenders from being able to change gender in the eyes of the law. When I speak to local people about this, they think it's mad that anyone would allow abusers to change gender in this way. These dangerous criminals will exploit any loophole they can to attack victims, especially women.

The Scottish Conservatives brought forward amendments that would have stopped heinous individuals abusing the new process. But the SNP voted against those amendments and, despite a rebellion from within their own ranks, the bill passed with the help of Labour and the Liberal Democrats.

In the end, a dangerously flawed bill was passed which undoubtedly put women at greater risk, dismissed the religious views of Sikh, Muslim and Orthodox Jewish women as irrelevant, and created more problems than it solved.

The only positive to come from the bill was the political awakening of thousands of women across Scotland, who came together during this process to stand up for their beliefs, their safety, and their rights. The groups For Women Scotland (FWS) and Keep Prisons Single Sex established a forum where we could express our anxieties and show support for one another.

During one of the biggest protests outside the Scottish Parliament, I recall feeling empowered and wondering why women's rights were not being honoured by politicians on all sides of the aisle. Rather, it fell on deaf ears.

Around that time, I read so many letters, cards and emails. One that really stuck out was a card I received from an eight-year-old that read, 'mummy says you are keeping us safe, and I want to thank you'. That one short sentence made it all worth it for me.

At the time of writing, the Gender Recognition Reform (Scotland) Bill has been stopped in its tracks by the UK government. But should it return to Holyrood, we must keep in mind that although legislation is written in Parliament, its effects are felt well beyond the confines of Holyrood. I will do my utmost to ensure the voices of women and girls are not ignored by the Scottish Government again.

Pam Gosal MBE MSP

> Thank you to the women protesting the SNP's Gender Recognition Reform (Scotland) Bill. It is a real risk to women's safety and threatens our rights. A majority of Scotland is against the bill. I hope MSPs will listen and vote against it
>
> *Rachael Hamilton MSP, Wednesday 21 December 2022*

Christmas is usually a time where we all come together, forget our differences and be kind to one another.

Even in the Scottish Parliament, where there are seismic differences of opinion on policy and a gulf between unionists and nationalists on the very future of the country, the debates around Christmas tend to have a little more goodwill and cheer than they normally would.

The 2022 festive period was the polar opposite, for one reason and one reason only – the SNP's Gender Recognition Reform (Scotland) Bill (GRR Bill). It was truly, and I don't mean to make light of the situation at all, a nightmare before Christmas.

I've never heard the word 'toxic' bandied about so often and so openly as I did during the passage of the bill. But personally, when I think back to that time, one word stands out above the rest – scary.

It might seem like an overreaction to some people, but in the midst of the debate around that bill, I was often afraid. Sometimes I felt fear for my own safety because of the threats and abuse that were flying around. At moments, I felt real alarm at the divisions the debate was causing. And throughout, I was genuinely frightened to witness the government carelessly put fundamental rights at risk.

When I felt overwhelmed, what kept me going was the unbelievable support from women outside of Parliament, women of all parties and none, women who bravely stood up for their rights.

I can't overstate how important it was to be urged on by the many inspirational women who gave up their time and chose to protest the bill. Many had been members of political parties and played an active role in women's rights groups such as For Women Scotland (FWS). But many were ordinary, typically apolitical women who were simply concerned about the impact of the bill. Some just wanted their questions to be answered by the government without feeling like pariahs.

Any time the debate felt too dark and unwinnable, the enthusiasm and warmth of those women was instrumental in keeping me and other MSPs in my party going. To those women, I want to say thank you.

I owe them my gratitude because there were many, many moments where it felt like I was fighting a lost cause. It often appeared that the government had stacked the odds so firmly in their favour, often through dubious tactics, that nothing could be said or done to prevent flawed proposals from becoming law.

From the very beginning, as a member of the Scottish Parliament committee scrutinising the bill, it was apparent the extraordinary lengths that the proponents of this legislation were prepared to go to, so they could achieve their aim of imposing a strict gender identity ideology on all aspects of Scottish life.

At the committee stage, we were assured evidence would be taken from every available expert. Words like 'inclusive' and 'open' were regularly used. But all of that was just a smoke-screen. In reality, the committee was hellbent on shutting down any scrutiny and calling a very selective list of witnesses who would say the right things and dismiss any criticism as unfounded.

Many people have asked me how this was allowed to happen. The sad truth is that other than my party, nobody else in Parliament was willing to stand up and speak out. Outside of Parliament, women of all parties would make their concerns and feelings known to me. A small number of women from the SNP and Labour would write to me and come up to me to say, 'Well done, keep going.'

But inside Holyrood, especially in the earlier stages, before the bill reached final votes on the floor of Parliament, it is regrettable that so many Labour, Liberal Democrat and SNP MSPs were silent. Or, even worse, actively helping supporters of the bill to limit debate. Not all of them – some MSPs in the SNP were particularly vocal and helpful – but most were unfortunately unwilling to even question the government.

The consequence was that the evidence we heard at committee was allowed to be stacked in one direction. The process was dictated firmly, designed to limit the amount of time for dissenting voices. A litany of lobby groups with a very one-sided agenda were allowed to shape and mould the bill however they saw fit.

Pam Gosal MSP and I, as the Scottish Conservative members of the committee, decided to submit a minority report on the evidence we had heard. That was the situation we found ourselves forced into, not because of an unwillingness to compromise ourselves, but as a result of a downright refusal of the supporters of the legislation to even countenance any meaningful changes to the government's proposals.

I couldn't help but think at regular intervals throughout the process that this was not what the founders of Holyrood intended. Holyrood was supposed to be a Parliament that accounts for the voices of everyone. It was meant to be a more consensual and cooperative way of doing politics. It was supposed to bring people together.

But the commitment by many MSPs to rigid, unbending, immovable gender identity ideology had broken down any semblance of give and take. By the time the bill reached the final phase of voting, Stage 3, both compromise and Christmas at Holyrood had been cancelled. Even when my colleague Russell Findlay MSP submitted a common-sense amendment to prevent biological males standing trial for a sex offence from being able to force a victim to call their attacker 'she', the government refused to give any ground.

I say the government, but in reality it was mostly Nicola Sturgeon herself. It was evident very early on that this law was being pushed aggressively from the top down. From the minute the then First Minister Nicola Sturgeon dismissed justified concerns as 'not valid', it was blindingly obvious who was driving forward this bill.

But contrary to Nicola Sturgeon's boasts, the bill was not landmark legislation for trans rights. It was a landmark blow for women's rights, inflicted by our own government. That over-mighty government acted with arrogance and contempt for opposing views. It refused to engage in good faith on serious issues.

Even when it became clear that passing this seismic law responsibly before Christmas was not possible, and the inevitable result was going to be another rushed and flawed piece of legislation, like the Named Persons (Scotland) Act or Hate Crime and Public Order (Scotland) Act, they carried on with gusto.

We appealed as reasonably as we could, basically pleaded with the government to just pause and take a breath to hear more evidence from experts, such as the UN Special Rapporteur on Violence Against Women, Reem Alsalem. By that stage, we knew the bill would pass with a majority of SNP, Green, Labour and Liberal Democrat MSPs backing it. But we still tried to open a small window of time for calm and cooler heads to prevail.

All our requests were in vain because Nicola Sturgeon was not for listening. The breadth and depth of opposition she brought together might be the real legacy of this bill. The people raising concerns about gender recognition reform were not unionist or nationalist, right- or left-wing. The GRR Bill brought together women, and many men too, from all parties and none.

That is the only unity that Nicola Sturgeon achieved with this legislation. She divided the country – but united thousands of women against her dangerous plans.

Rachael Hamilton MSP

Chapter 21

The women the committee would not see

Anonymous and Ms M

On Tuesday 7 June 2022, Reverend Karen Hendry, speaking as convener of the Church of Scotland's Faith Impact Forum, tells the committee, 'We are concerned that the voices of survivors are being used in a way that risks confusing vulnerable women and demonising another vulnerable group.' She later apologises

I have experienced sexual and physical male violence as a teenager and young woman from boyfriends and a supposed friend. Decades on, I am still fearful around men.

When one perpetrator turned up in my town, I wanted to contact Rape Crisis. I then saw that Rape Crisis was not a female-only survivor service and they actually had a trans-identifying man running one of their centres.

I couldn't believe it, and was further horrified to find that our female prisons, hospital wards, toilets, changing areas and Women's Aid services all permitted trans-identifying men. I self-excluded from Rape Crisis but knew that women in prison were trapped. I felt totally alone but eventually, through social media, found like-minded women.

I contacted my MSP but was ignored. My new MSP agreed with me – but voted for self-ID anyway; Rape Crisis Scotland told me that the trans-identifying man running Edinburgh Rape Crisis Centre was a woman. I contacted my employer regarding female hospital wards and, to my alarm, the Hate Crime Bill was mentioned; I met with civil servants who advised me none of our conversations would be passed on to the minister. I spoke to a journalist. I spoke at the Women's Scottish Trades Union Congress (STUC) to ask unions to support women's rights to single-sex services and was called 'transphobic'. A trans-identifying man was at that conference, making it difficult for women to speak freely. One topic was male violence against women and girls, yet women voted against single-sex services – it was like watching turkeys voting for Christmas.

One of the lowest points was watching my government debate whether to allow women the right to request a female forensic rape examiner. Rape Crisis Scotland grotesquely betrayed survivors by not supporting Johann Lamont's 'six words' amendment.

Having tried to get my voice heard over and over again, I decided to attend the Scottish Women's Convention Conference on Male Violence Against Women and Girls (MVAWG). I asked the panel why we had no female-only MVAWG services in Scotland and was told it was not the right place to discuss it. I was raging by this point and stated this was exactly the right place to discuss the issue. I asked at least three times where the right place was to discuss female-only services if not at this meeting. I asked the chair to name a time and place to discuss our services but she wouldn't. It is terrifying to be ignored by every decision maker.

By this time, I'd had enough. I can't exactly remember what I said but I did comment on the person running Edinburgh Rape Crisis Centre and how if that person was there then it wasn't a female-only service. Sandy Brindley, head of Rape Crisis Scotland, who had been muttering under her breath and shaking her head, stopped to inform me this person was a woman. She then, wrongly, accused me of pointing at her. This situation would have been hilarious if it wasn't so grim. I walked out mid-conference. Going down Byres Road, I began to worry that I would be reported under the sneaky guise of committing the dreadful hate crime of 'misgendering'.

None of the violent men I have known were ever held accountable, yet asking for female-only services left me anxious about the consequences. As a single parent I had to ask someone to be available to watch my children that night in case I got a police visit. I wrote to the Scottish Women's Convention with my story, explaining why I was so angry at the meeting, and was invited to a round-table event. Fortunately, following this they wrote a report advising that women do in fact need single-sex services.

Following this meeting, Murray Blackburn Mackenzie (MBM) asked me if I would be willing to speak to the parliamentary committee responsible for gender recognition reform. I agreed, but by this point it was clear that the government had decided the outcome in advance. They clearly had no intention of considering evidence given by women who would not submit to the misogyny that is transgender ideology.

In my view the committee was pro-trans/anti-women, and the contributors they called were cherry-picked to provide biased evidence. They even managed to find a Church of Scotland minister, Reverend Karen Hendry, to declare that women like me were being used to 'justify arguments against reform'. Witnesses who opposed the government narrative were treated with hostility and disrespect. The questioning style and wearing of rainbow lanyards signalled that, rather than considering evidence, they were manipulating it to arrive at their predetermined outcome. My views, needs and fears had been ignored and slandered by my government and their captured organisations, Rape Crisis Scotland, Engender and Scottish Women's Aid. Those organisations took government money and sold women and girls out. I didn't expect the committee to hear my evidence and was proved right. In some ways it was a relief, as I knew it would have had no impact on the outcome. Being asked to submit my evidence in writing to the committee was the final insult.

Many things have to align for survivors to speak. We have to be healed enough, find the confidence and drive and the platforms to speak, become knowledgeable, use the right language and tone, be ready to tell our stories and be confident we will be heard. I was prepared to share my story, yet my government refused to hear my evidence and my first minister called me, and women like me, 'transphobic', 'bigoted' and 'right-wing'. It was shameful. Women and girls deserved better.

Anonymous

On Tuesday 20 December 2022, one of the women the committee had refused to see is threatened with arrest in the Scottish Parliament during the Stage 3 proceedings of the bill

While I am just one of many Scottish women who has experienced male violence, I am specifically one of the five women the Equalities, Human Rights and Civil Justice Committee examining the Gender Recognition Reform (Scotland) Bill (GRR Bill) refused to meet.

In June 2022, I volunteered my time to speak to the committee about how self-ID has, and will continue to, negatively impact upon me as a survivor. It was not an easy offer to make, not least because, in June 2022, I was also due in the sheriff court to face my rapist, already a convicted sex offender.

I knew it would be difficult and add an extra layer of stress at an already stressful time, but I wanted to share my experiences with the committee to help ensure MSPs had considered female survivors of male violence.

I spent June waiting on a date to appear before both the court and the committee. My court case came and went, but the invitation to attend the committee never arrived. Instead I was invited to submit a written piece. Incidentally, my perpetrator didn't show up to court either; in that respect, he and the Equalities Committee have a lot in common – both confident they're the good guys, yet neither can bear to look me in the eye.

When I obtained tickets to attend the Scottish Parliament's final debate on the GRR Bill in December 2022, I recognised that, as a survivor of rape, sexual assault and domestic abuse, it was likely I would hear things I would find upsetting, distressing and frustrating.

I had a think about how keep myself psychologically safe. Aside from a few women I'd met a couple of times at events, I would be alone. I decided if it got too much for my grounding exercises to cope, then I would leave. Part of my safety plan involved staying at accommodation within walking distance of the Parliament.

Five hours into Stage 3 proceedings, at around seven p.m. on Tuesday 20 December, the majority of our MSPs voted to allow registered sex offenders, and those awaiting trial, to change their identification by self-ID.

A woman stood to leave, shouting 'shame on you' in protest. The presiding officer's knee-jerk response was to clear everyone from the public gallery. I began to dutifully shuffle along the row towards the exit, but it was blocked by a group of women and Scottish Parliament officials having a discussion about whether we should leave.

I could feel and hear my heartbeat ringing in my ears. I felt completely overwhelmed: by the vote I had just witnessed; by the Scottish Parliament's heavy-handed response to women's outrage at that vote; by the contempt shown to survivors. All MSP eyes appeared to be looking up at us.

As the group began to swell, so did my feelings of panic. Slipping into autopilot, I sat down, looked straight ahead and took some deep breaths. I was looking out over the chamber. It didn't seem real, I felt as if I was looking into the scene through a window. I don't know what was being said because it all sounded as if I was underwater. I felt tiny, as I tried to breathe.

I'd taken a few deep breaths and focused on the feeling of my feet touching the floor, wiggling my toes, when I heard a woman behind me, who I assume worked there, speak. She said, 'Can I ask you to leave?' and I replied, 'Yes, you can.' She asked, 'Will you leave?' and I replied 'No.' She told me that the police might arrest me.

Despite my best efforts, my window of tolerance was pretty non-existent by this point. I jumped to my feet and shouted at my Parliament that I had come to listen quietly, that I was being put out due to the actions of another woman and now I was being threatened with arrest.

Police Scotland wouldn't arrest my rapist, I told them, but they will threaten to arrest me and women like me for sitting quietly. I think I also pointed out what should be obvious to anyone – that sex offenders lie, manipulate, and can't be relied upon to do the right thing.

At some point a bottle of Coke fell from my pocket and I picked it up as I continued talking. The female security officer was now to my right and telling me that waving the bottle made me look aggressive. At some point, she grasped my forearm, presumably to lead me out. I pulled away and reminded her she had no right to touch me, and I left of my own volition.

I sat in the foyer and cried into a cup of tea at the frustration and injustice of it all. I felt ashamed for my outburst. I had not intended to disclose my rape and I worried who within the chamber had heard me speak of my rape and if they would use it against me.

Mridul Wadhwa, the male CEO of Edinburgh Rape Crisis Centre, walked past, looking directly at me. It occurred to me, not for the first time, that perhaps I'd have more robust coping mechanisms around my trauma if I had had the option to access single-sex women's services.

While gathering myself, several women approached me to provide comfort and some well-received hugs. They reassured me I'd not spoken out of turn, and I had articulated some of their own thoughts and concerns.

To be surrounded by women was exactly what I needed, and we sat in disbelief before the Parliament announced they were allowing all visitors to re-enter the viewing gallery. We filed back in and I left around thirty minutes later, exhausted by the day's events.

Ms M
This contribution was previously published in the blog #Women VotingWithOurFeet.

Chapter 22

Watching the Parliament

Lorna Irvine

———

On Tuesday 28 June 2022, Shona Robison told the committee that, 'There is no evidence that predatory men feel the need to try and obtain a Gender Recognition Certificate (GRC) in order to be predatory and abusive.'

I'm ashamed to say that I came to the gender wars as a bit of a political naive. In my upbringing, tea-table politics was infra dig – tantamount to discussing bowel movements with the minister. But an unseasonal accusation – 'You're a TERF' – by a young woman, at my own Christmas table in 2019, set me bolt upright and accelerated a political education that'll stay with me for the rest of my life.

When the opportunity arose to witness the Gender Recognition Reform (Scotland) Bill (GRR Bill) evidence sessions in the Scottish Parliament, my expectations were high. Of dignity. Of gravitas. Of seriousness of purpose, and of forensic, evidenced, fair and open debate.

I expected a firm foundation, a clear definition of terms. But even at the very last session, Shona Robison, when pressed to define precisely what she meant by 'living in one's acquired gender' made a telling pause before underdelivering: a name on a utility bill, an email sign-off, and what your mates call you. It was all just so insubstantial.

And I expected to hear evidence: substantial, substantiated. I was astounded at how little was presented. One witness, called as an expert on data, qualified in theatre, film and TV, and the author of a book on 'queer data', jazz-handed the very concept of evidence as an 'obscuring and stalling mechanism', a cover for 'abstract concern'. From other 'expert' witnesses, there was back-slapping, bouncy theatricality and wistful personal anecdote.

I'll never forget the car-crash submission of Irish Senator Regina Doherty, who confessed to reliance on her own teens and their equivalent fridge-door postings for her understanding of 'gender' and 'trans'. Monikered ever-after 'Regina of the Nine – "Currently there are seven – it may be even nine" – Genders', she unwittingly confirmed that Irish gender recognition reform 'really felt as though it went under the radar', that there was no related data to speak of and, as a final flourish, proudly explained her current project, to strip out Irish maternity policy of all words relating to women and motherhood.

UN independent expert Victor Madrigal-Borloz, uniquely privileged in his double opportunity to address the committee, offered GRCs as the global panacea to LGBT discrimination and violence. He too, airily deflected and systematically dismissed, with no evidence, every concern women have ever expressed about self-ID.

But the most galling 'evidential' indignity came from the Justice Secretary herself, with her 'reminder'. At the bill's first debate she had offered – haltingly – that, 'There is no evidence that predatory and abusive men have ever had to pretend to be anything else to carry out abusive and predatory behaviour.' This time she delivered her refined version without pause.

So, this, my first-ever experience of witnessing the Scottish Parliament at work, was a crushing disappointment. I'd not expected slews of witnesses who relied on the self-same thought-stopping, mealy-mouthed, Twitter/TikTok mantra. Or reliance on magical thinking to wave away pressing, legitimate, heartfelt – and evidenced – concerns. Or nebulous, contested 'best international practice' framed as fact.

All through this committee process, we women, we 51 per cent, were ignored, sidelined, dismissed, naysayed, denigrated, lied to and gaslit. On our way in, we were subjected to the indignity of frisking, huckling into cupboards to remove clothing, confiscation of personal belongings and physical ejection for the temerity of quietly wearing our dissent in suffragette colours, amidst a forest of rainbow lanyards.

Our elected representatives, from whom I'd expected truth, and the ability to bear it with dignity, offered nothing that inspired me to believe that these people had my, your, any woman's best interests at heart.

Chapter 23

A minister resigns

Ash Regan MSP

———

On Thursday 27 October 2022, the Scottish Parliament considers whether to allow the Gender Recognition Reform (Scotland) Bill (GRR Bill) to proceed to its next stage

I'd met with Colin McAllister, the most senior adviser to the first minister (FM), back in March 2022 when he'd finally been sent by Nicola to find out 'What are you thinking on the GRR?' I was prepared, as I knew that meeting would eventually come. It was forty minutes long and in it I laid out all the weaknesses in the legislation and the questions that the government would need to answer.

I told him I would not be voting for the GRR Bill unless the Scottish government could answer the questions on women's safety to my satisfaction. I felt in so saying that I had left the door open, but in reality I knew I had probably painted a target on my back. I confided in a senior trusted journalist, telling her about the meeting. I felt that it was some kind of insurance policy – should the first minister sack me for some other reason in the next few months, at least one journalist would know the truth.

Tuesday 25 October 2022: Group meeting

The government did not answer my questions and I did not see Colin again, until two days before the Stage 1 vote. He was agitated; he again said he was there 'on behalf of the FM'. I reiterated that it was a 'red line' for me and that I could not vote for it – an important distinction. I said, there are three options: 1) The leadership gives the SNP group a free vote; 2) I am away and do not vote; or 3) I resign and vote against.

'You'll *resign?*' Colin said, aghast. 'Yes,' I said. He immediately began backing out of my office door, saying, 'Don't do anything – I'll speak to the first minister.'

Later that day, the SNP group meeting took place. My colleagues spoke both for and against the bill. A number of us, myself included, argued for it to be a free vote which, according to the standing orders of the group, should be 'a group decision'. We argued that it most definitely fitted the profile for a moral decision or a vote of conscience.

It was a heated discussion. Shona Robison began to lose control of the meeting and John Swinney had to step in to stop it going to a vote, which we probably would have lost anyway. He fudged it, saying, 'If you can't vote for it, go and see your whip.' Now I knew that I wasn't alone in the group, and at least a few others were planning to vote against the bill at Stage 1.

Up until this point, I had been hoping that we would be granted a free vote, or that I would be given a pass. I knew there were downsides to those options. I would still attract media criticism. I wouldn't be able to join the debate, or indeed say anything publicly, and it would be difficult to explain to constituents.

I was scared. I was pretty sure I didn't want to become the SNP poster child for this issue at Holyrood. I was also worried about the implications. Would my constituency office be targeted? My sons? My address released online? My political career over? Would it affect my future job prospects? So, I waited. That night I received a text message from Colin. 'The FM is aware of your position.'

I waited.

Nothing for two days.

Thursday 27 October: Stage 1

The day of the Stage 1 vote dawns and I am booked to do a ministerial visit to a school on fireworks safety. Lots of media are in attendance, hoping I'll say how I'll be voting later. I give a talk to the pupils about firework misuse and then I do a round of interviews about fireworks and pose for photos in front of the fire engine. A senior communications official from the Scottish Government is with me and I tell him that these interviews may be superseded. 'I might be resigning,' I say. The official looks pained.

It's raining. I run across the road to the waiting ministerial car. Once inside, I check my phone. I have a text – it's a couple of hours old. 'Turn up and vote with the government.' I sit, staring at the message. Knowing that this is it. That I will not turn up or vote with the government.

I explain to Roger, the driver, and ask him to take me home. I figure if I go in, I have a good chance of being shouted at by angry special advisers, being doorstepped by the media and being turfed out of my ministerial office. It's a scene I don't fancy.

Once home I decide I will write a resignation email and send it at around four p.m. – an hour before the vote – then vote online against the bill and keep my head down.

I speak to a former senior SNP MSP. He says I should keep trying to negotiate. 'They'll fold if you wait it out.' But by this point I'm sure. I don't want a fudge, I want to control it. I want to be able to explain my reasons to my constituents. I want to add my voice to the debate. I want to do what I can to raise the profile of the issue.

I'm pacing around at home, my anxiety rising. I am starting to feel as if I'm having an out-of-body experience. I decide I can't wait until four p.m. I want it to be done, over.

I press send on the email. The reply comes back from Nicola. It is mean, petty and inaccurate.

I phone my mum to tell her, and she says it's already on Twitter. 'Oh,' I say, 'they must have given it to the media.' They begin briefing the media that I hadn't told Nicola my views. This, of course, was rubbish, and Twitter knew it.

The vote is called and I vote against. There are nine SNP rebels.

I'm informed that someone is packing up my office. My ministerial career is officially over. Many ministers are forced to resign but very few choose to do so over a point of policy; I am the only minister since 2007 to do that.

I'm lauded for my principles and bravery online and in emails. It feels surreal.

It is a big story in the weekend media. A few days later I call a press conference and give a short statement in which I explain that I would never vote for something which would endanger women.

Bouquets of flowers arrive at my new office, and cards – lots and lots of cards – from women all over Scotland thanking me for my courage.

I'm now on the outside of my political party. Disloyal. Untrustworthy. Attention-seeking. Uppity. Difficult. Rebellious.

Many of my colleagues stop talking to me. I lose friendships.

I spend the next two months trying in vain to stop the bill from passing at Stage 3. It passes on 22 December 2022, after an intense parliamentary debate lasting into the small hours. I seethe as people repeat stultifying mantras, 'There is no evidence of any harms.' I feel they will come to regret those claims.

Eventually, in October 2023, I change political party to one where women's rights are important.

I don't regret my decision one bit. I'd do it all again. I can sleep at night knowing that I did all I could and I voted for what I believed in – protecting women's sex-based rights.

Chapter 24

A very seditious scarf

@Obsolesence

————

On Tuesday 15 November 2022, the Equalities, Human Rights and Civil Justice Committee holds its first meeting to consider detailed amendments to the Gender Recognition Reform (Scotland) Bill (GRR Bill) – Stage 2 of the bill's passage through Parliament. A middle-aged, professional woman sits down in the public gallery to watch the committee proceedings. She is wearing a striped wool scarf in green, white and purple

---

Obsolesence
@Obsolesence

I have just been asked to remove my new scarf. I refused because its lovely & inoffensive. Apparently@ScotParl believes these colours are unacceptable while several MSPs wear rainbow lanyards. @ScotParl is now policing clothing colours.

#WomenWontWheesht

> **Obsolesence @Obsolesence • 15 Nov 2022**
> Replying to @XXXXX and @ScotParl
>
> The clerk, who was very polite, said she had been asked to ask me to remove it. Other women in the room have also been asked to remove their much subtler scarves that vaguely look radical and womanly.

Obsolesence @Obsolesence • 15 Nov 2022
Replying to @Obsolesence

When asked why multiple MSPs & staff were then allowed to wear rainbow lanyards (since they are one of the THE political statements de jour), the Security Manager squirmed and said he understood the point I was making. Now waiting for call from Security Manager's Manager

Obsolesence
@Obsolesence • 15 Nov 2022

Update: just spoken to Security Manager. Apparently our wicked coloured **scarves** were spotted on the TV coverage of the committee hearing & the Security Manager's manager decided they were political & should not be displayed.

Obsolesence
@Obsolesence • 15 Nov 2022

Let's not let a row over a **scarf** (& the implications of politicising women's clothing) overshadow the reality of why women were in attendance in Holyrood. Very serious amendments were voted down by @S~EHRCJ and we should be bloody raging about it.

#NoToSelfID

****
@********** • 15 Nov 2022

Did the Security Manager explain what political statement they thought the scarves were making?

Obsolesence
@Obsolesence • 6:04 pm • 15 Nov 2022

Oh no. "Associated with the women's movement" was all I got. And no, not sure which movement, which women, but clearly a *very bad thing*

At two p.m., the presiding officer of the Scottish Parliament, Alison Johnstone, said: 'The action was an error and I would like to apologise on behalf of the Parliament. The wearing of a scarf in these colours does not, in itself, breach the visitor code of conduct. The Parliament wishes people to engage with the democratic process, including observing elected representatives debate and make the laws of the country.'

Chapter 25

A hard day's night: the bill is passed

Lucy Hunter Blackburn

On Tuesday 20 December 2022, the bill returns to the main chamber of the Scottish Parliament for its final Stage 3 consideration

It is 20 December 2023. I am sitting in the public gallery of the Scottish Parliament with around a dozen other women, watching Social Justice Secretary Shirley-Anne Somerville confirm that the Scottish Government will not appeal Lady Haldane's recent decision to uphold the UK government's block on the Gender Recognition Reform (Scotland) Bill (GRR Bill). The court will have the last word, for now.

A year ago, I sat in the same seats, surrounded by many of the same women, watching a Parliament descend into something akin to madness.

Tuesday 20 December 2022 was the first day of the last chance to amend the bill. Normally the final stages of a bill are completed in a single afternoon, sometimes two, even when there is opposition. These Stage 3 proceedings, however, will

237

require a parliamentary marathon in the last week before MSPs break for Christmas. Oher planned business will be abandoned to push the bill through. The Parliament's distinctive family-friendly late afternoon clocking-off time, carefully observed since 1999, will be dramatically and chaotically abandoned.

Mid-evening on the first day we will learn that the annual carol service has been cancelled. In normal times, the service brings together MSPs, their staff and other Scottish Parliament workers, with local people. For this first performance post-Covid-19, a local Ukrainian choir was to be joined by child refugees from the war, housed temporarily in a cruise ship in Leith, Edinburgh. But someone, somewhere, will decide that the Parliament cannot break, even for a little while, to fit in this event.

We hear rumours that the timetable is to manage nervousness among SNP backbenchers, who have allegedly been told that if they vote it through quickly, the fuss will die down over the holiday so that they can return to their desks in January, the controversy forgotten.

We wonder if this might appeal also to the Liberal Democrats, who support the bill, despite opinion polling showing that their voters are among the least keen on self-ID. Labour too. Its leadership has spent months precariously balanced on the fence, and late in the day decided to whip their MSPs in support of the bill, even if some of their attempts to amend it fail. As they will do. Only the Conservatives publicly argue for letting the process run past Christmas and into the new year.

This government's crude display of political strength is consistent with the handling of the bill at committee stage over the preceding months. Public witness sessions started within twelve hours of the deadline for sending in written submissions. There was never any sign that the record number of consultation responses – around 11,000, with 60 per cent opposed to the bill – had been digested by the committee or used to influence its inquiry. When individual submissions were published, defamatory statements about some prominent women opposed to the bill had not been redacted, and it took days to get these removed.

The committee chose twenty-five organisations or individuals who supported reform, and just nine that did not, as witnesses for its public sessions. It also held four panels in private involving seventeen individuals who identify as transgender. It took three months to decline a bid to give evidence from a group of women survivors of sexual abuse. Six of the witnesses were members of the Scottish Parliament's Cross-Party Group on LGBTI+, whose minutes recorded it as wishing to 'increase activity as a pressure group within the parliament', including in relation to this bill.

The committee's convener, Joe FitzPatrick MSP, and two of the remaining six committee members, were also members of this parliamentary caucus. No committee member or witness ever declared their connection to the group. The committee's deputy convenor, Green MSP Maggie Chapman, one of the most zealous advocates of self-ID, had come into politics direct from a senior role at the Edinburgh Rape Crisis Centre. She was sanctioned later by Holyrood's standards committee for failing to mention this when the committee took evidence from Sandy Brindley of Rape Crisis Scotland, in a session where the concerns of survivors were dismissed.

The government did not lose a single vote in committee. It did enthusiastically welcome an amendment proposed by Labour MSP Pam Duncan-Glancy, which it had helped to write. This pointlessly declared that the bill did not amend the Equality Act – a simple statement of observable fact – when we had spent months painstakingly explaining to anyone who would listen that the problem was if a GRC affects the way a person is defined under the Equality Act, as Lady Haldane would later determine that it did. Listening, it seemed, was in short supply, and not only on the government side.

At Stage 3, bills return to the main chamber for debate. For the GRR Bill, over 150 amendments are initially tabled. Just over twenty come from the government, or backbenchers working with it, around half the rest are from the Conservatives, and the remainder from Labour and from SNP backbenchers. The evening before Stage 3 starts, the minister in charge, Shona Robison, writes to three MSPs saying they should withdraw certain amendments, as the government has decided they may put the bill outside the Parliament's powers. The MSPs concerned decline, and suggest the place to make this argument is in the debating chamber. When the debate eventually reaches that point, Robison refuses to spell out the reason for her request, beyond speaking vaguely about legal advice. The amendments will be voted down, anyway.

On this first day, an SNP MSP, Michelle Thomson, who has talked about her history as a survivor of serious sexual assault, speaks to an amendment that would pause applications for a Gender Recognition Certificate (GRC) from anyone charged with a sexual offence. She says, 'The impact of trauma falls hardest on the weakest, the poor and the disenfranchised. I have a voice; they do not. In the past six years, who has spoken for them?' Voting on her amendment is a tie. The deputy presiding officer uses his casting vote to defeat the amendment, citing long-standing convention.

In the early evening, MSPs reject an amendment from Conservative MSP Russell Findlay that would block access to GRCs for those on the sex offenders' register. Two women in the public gallery shout out 'shame'. Security staff are instructed to empty the whole of the public gallery. The women who protested tell me outside that it was a spontaneous response: 'We watched MSPs put the feelings of rapists before victims.'

We find ourselves in the Parliament's foyer. The public café has closed for the night, but staff have laid out hot drinks and biscuits, thoughtfully prepared for a planned evening break. Upstairs, supporters and critics of the bill were mainly seated in different parts of the public gallery. Down here, we mix a little. The director of the Equality Network, Tim Hopkins, provides a backdrop to this awkward assembly, in the form of a three-foot-high moving image, part of the 'A Parliament for the People' exhibition that has greeted visitors since 2016. Outside, a Women Won't Wheesht candle-lit vigil is taking place.

Going back in, I note on Twitter, 'All the people in the public seats are now seated together in one block of seats, with 4 security staff stationed round watching us. This is the closest in 6 years that we have had to govt or parliament bringing people with conflicting views together in one place.'

Maggie Chapman claims trans people are being wrongly treated as a threat or risk to others. SNP backbencher Ruth Maguire swiftly intervenes, to say Chapman is the only person in the chamber conflating being transgender with being a risk.

The process is unrelenting. Running votes on amendments mean that the chamber is always busy, even into the small hours, with legislators who have no experience of late-night law-making. We watch them wilting in front of us. One does faint, late on the next day.

Around eleven-thirty p.m., an end time of two in the morning is rumoured. Twenty minutes later, Conservative MSP Jeremy Balfour, who is disabled, requests clarity on the finishing time, as he needs to inform his carers waiting for his return. We are sitting a few feet away, apparently invisible and irrelevant, from a group of government MSPs hunting in a pack, who barrack and jeer him. I tweet, 'Distressingly dismissive reaction from govt benches.' It is a horrible atmosphere.

His fellow Conservative Meghan Gallacher, participating by remote link, has spent the evening managing her childcare on the hoof. She adds her concerns, noting that MSPs have now been here for ten hours. Labour's deputy leader, Jackie Baillie, suggests it is not good to be making major decisions like this, with important issues still scheduled for discussion before MSPs get to go home. At first, attempts to pause proceedings fail. The presiding officer defers to what party business managers have already agreed. I tweet, 'I'm horrified by what I'm seeing here . . . A serious blot on Holyrood. There is no urgency here beyond government desire to press on.' I am told by staff that the Parliament has never sat this late before, not since it was established twenty-three years ago.

Then First Minister Nicola Sturgeon gets up to speak to her business manager, George Adam, who in turn stands up and says he is willing to meet with the other parties to discuss the timetable again. Proceedings are suspended so the parties can talk. I tweet, 'Hard not to feel we're watching govt controlling the Parliament at every turn.'

Just before midnight, while we wait to hear the outcome of discussions, we are warned that the lights in the chamber will black out briefly as they are on an automatic setting that no one can change. I tweet, 'Take a hint.' Right on cue, the lights dim and a comedy 'ooooh' goes up from around the chamber, a moment of shared humour in an otherwise grim few days.

Just after midnight, the sitting ends. Government back-benchers barrack Douglas Ross, the Conservative Party leader, for criticising the timetabling. As the presiding officer thanks staff who have stayed late, I note that the government backbenches are 'noisy'.

At nine o'clock the next morning a blog is published by someone we've never heard of – a legal academic, Michael Foran. He describes a part of the Scotland Act none of us recognise – Section 35. His article also supports an argument we have been making for some time. In the judicial review brought by For Women Scotland (FWS), Lady Haldane had decreed, exactly a week earlier, that a GRC changes a person's sex under the Equality Act. Foran argues that that while a GRC may not confer an absolute right of access to single-sex services and spaces, it at least makes it more complicated to exclude someone from them. It looks important. Today will be the last chance to iron out any problems, or to decide to take a bit longer sorting them. We share the blog with a few MSPs we hope might be interested.

Around lunchtime, FWS hold a 'Say No to Self-ID' rally outside Holyrood. It had to be moved forward half an hour at very short notice, so that MSPs Ash Regan, Pam Gosal and Rachael Hamilton can still speak, and be back in the chamber for the earlier restart time agreed late last night. The rally draws a large crowd, into the hundreds. At the end, they sing a reworking of 'Auld Lang Syne' I had hastily written a couple of days before, for FWS to use. The repeated chorus is:

'For women's rights are human rights, we won't let you forget
For women's rights are human rights, this isn't over yet.'

I miss the singing because I want to be sure of being seated for the start of the debate. 'Back again?' asks a cheerful policeman.

Rachael Hamilton seeks an emergency debate on the implications for the bill of Lady Haldane's judgment. Business is suspended while the presiding officer considers this, with input from the other parties. After a break of almost an hour, she returns and says she will not allow it. The request has come too late, she decides.

Absurdly, Shona Robison then refuses to offer MSPs even a factual summary of the case the government argued in court, and won. She refuses on the grounds that the case is 'live', and that there is the possibility of an appeal. Robison also talks about the 'responsibility to make competent law'. I tweet, 'Outbreak of theatrical coughing in the cheap seats.'

Late in the afternoon, I leave the still busy public gallery for a long-arranged family trip to the Festival Theatre, to see *Snow White and the Seven Dwarfs*. The production includes a sketch where a drag artist plays Nicola Sturgeon. It is a surreal moment, in the circumstances.

Back home, I watch the Parliament's livestream. MSPs are still going. Sometime after midnight, Ash Regan wins a vote, 63 to 62, for a declaratory statement that the bill has no impact on the right to freedom of speech. It is the only government defeat at any point in the entire process, from when the bill was first introduced in March.

After the last amendment is voted on, around one in the morning, the Conservatives again criticise the timetabling. George Adam accuses them of 'disrespect', 'dirty tricks' and 'unnatural ways of working for this Parliament'. Accusing the opposition of 'grandstanding', Adam adds, 'Nobody is watching.' I run a Twitter poll and find around forty other 'nobodies' still tuned in. This, it feels, is Parliament as the private playground of the executive. A government and its allies assuming they are both invisible and invincible.

On day three, there are a fair number of empty seats round about me. Quite a few women who applied for public tickets, as soon as the visitors' office opened, are told none are available. I have a ticket kindly found for me by an MSP. The section of the public gallery in which senior staff from pro-self-ID organisations in Scotland and the rest of the UK have been sitting over the past few days, with their fellow activists, is well-filled.

Before the debate begins, Shona Robison has to make an emergency statement, contradicting an answer she gave the day before on a basic point about the bill's effect. It is extraordinary that any minister could be in a tangle over a fundamental part of her plans, in the last few hours of the process.

Robison makes her closing speech. Oddly, she thanks the presiding officer for letting Conservative MSP Jamie Greene speak. Greene is the convener of the LGBTQI+ cross-party group and he will vote for the bill. Robison's comment suggests the government found a speaking slot for him, in a debate where many of its own backbenchers did not get a chance to contribute.

She is only a little way into her speech when Helen Steel, a long-time feminist activist and famously once half of the McLibel Two, interrupts. She accuses MSPs of not understanding and not listening to women. The sitting is briefly suspended. When it resumes, Robison looks rattled, saying off the cuff that 'as a woman' she knows 'what a woman is and I know the challenges faced by women in our society'. She wraps up her speech surprisingly quickly.

At three p.m., the bill is passed by 86 to 39 votes. Nine SNP MSPs, five women and four men, break the whip, in a rebellion without precedent since the party took office in 2007. Two Labour MSPs, Claire Baker and Carol Mochan, also break their party's whip to vote against. Three members of the unwhipped Conservative group, all men, vote for the bill, giving the Scottish Government the line it will repeat at every opportunity – that it had support from all parties. The Liberal Democrats and the Scottish Greens vote in favour.

Christina McKelvie, the junior minister for Equalities and Older People, stands and turns towards the gallery above, where self-ID activists are sitting, and pointedly applauds them. She is quickly joined by Alex Cole-Hamilton, the Liberal Democrat leader, all the Scottish Greens, and Joe FitzPatrick, convener of the committee that scrutinised the bill. Eventually, around

30 MSPs, including several government ministers, among them future First Minister Humza Yousaf, give the balcony a standing ovation, and receive one in return. Nicola Sturgeon turns and claps, but does not stand. I can't remember seeing anything like it in the Parliament before. The same thing happens when self-ID is approved in Spain a few months later.

Lisa and I scan the Labour group, immediately across the chamber from us. A few are clapping the gallery from their seats; most look as if they simply want it all over. We start to pack up. Then to my right, Elaine Miller interrupts in furious protest. To my left, other women unroll a banner hand-painted with the words 'Privacy. Dignity. Safety'. Cries of 'Shame on you!' ring round the chamber. Elaine is escorted out. The rest of us continue packing up and leave. We have seen it through to the bitter end.

We go to the pub, shattered. At five p.m., the Secretary of State for Scotland, Alister Jack, issues a statement: 'We will look closely . . . at the ramifications for the 2010 Equality Act and other UK wide legislation, in the coming weeks – up to and including a section 35 order stopping the bill going for royal assent if necessary.'

I have already set off into the night, to catch up on my lost preparations for Christmas. But Jack's surprise intervention means we will not get to clock off quite yet.

A year passes. On 20 December 2023, Social Justice Secretary Shirley-Anne Somerville is about to give a ministerial statement. Once again, this bill highlights the government's casual attitude towards the Parliament. The presiding officer rules Somerville may only give a shortened version of her statement because her colleague, Shona Robison, now the deputy first minister, had revealed the gist of it on television the night before. Opposition parties point out that they only received their advance copies a few minutes earlier, another breach of parliamentary protocol.

The minister's response to Lady Haldane's Section 35 judgment is muted. The bill is now in limbo, but at no point does she concede any fault, and offers no apology. Up in the public gallery, the seats that this week last year were the focus of a standing ovation are all empty. There is no sign of anyone from the organisations that for years have promoted the bill's core aim – self-ID – to MSPs.

On our way out, the dozen or so women who came to hear Somerville stop to take a group picture by the Christmas tree in the main foyer. On impulse, we sing the song written for last year's rally. We get through all three verses, and no one tries to stop us. Finally, in the last days before Christmas 2023, women's voices are freely heard inside Holyrood:

'For women's rights are human rights, we won't let you forget
For women's rights are human rights, this isn't over yet.'

Chapter 26

That merkin moment

Elaine Miller

———

At three p.m., Thursday 22 December 2022, the Scottish Parliament votes to pass the Gender Recognition Reform (Scotland) Bill (GRR Bill)

The GRR Bill taught me that a gradual realisation lands with a thump. I, naturally, believed my Scottish Parliament operated on the principles of the Scottish Enlightenment, with a focus on debate to improve the welfare of our citizens. The Mace, representing authority, is engraved with 'Wisdom, Justice, Compassion and Integrity', and I understood those words to be a commitment from the Parliament to Scotland's people.

I had concerns about the GRR Bill and, like a good girl, I emailed MSPs, signed petitions, submitted evidence and, in November, attended the Stage 2 committee meeting in Holyrood.

I was struck by Shona Robison's behaviour – if the evidence being submitted did not fit with the government position, she slumped and doodled on her notes like a sullen schoolgirl, and if the evidence did fit with the government position she sat bolt upright, as attentive as a meerkat. It appeared that the vote was pre-decided on political grounds, not on evidence, and that realisation landed right on my solar plexus. There was no debate, absolutely no sign of wisdom, compassion, justice or integrity, and harm to women and people with a gender difference was inevitable.

The figures of the Scottish Enlightenment actively rejected unjustified authority; perhaps that's why I thought 'C'mon then', and interrupted the meeting.

'Excuse me, Mr Fitzpatrick, in your capacity as chair do you have any power to force my Cabinet Secretary to stop doodling and listen to the evidence? I cannot believe the contempt she is showing the democratic process.'

Society conditions women to endure rather than address injustices. However, women use anger as a tool to build solutions – see any charity attending to women's needs as an example. The majority of my elected representatives were intent on removing my sex-based rights and I wasn't best pleased.

By the time I got to the Parliament café for a cup of tea – one of the few reliable examples of excellence in Holyrood is the shortbread – J.K. Rowling had tweeted, 'You speak for women and girls across Scotland', and there was an online fuss.

That evening two very brave people shared their experience of gender clinics and subsequent detransition with MSPs, most of whom didn't bother to show up. Afterwards I asked a Labour MSP why the SNP was being allowed to ignore anything which didn't fit their manifesto:

> MSP: *'It's just very difficult to get them to listen.'*
>
> Me: *'Isn't it your job, to oppose? Are you leaving that up to the likes of me?'*
>
> MSP: *'What do you mean? What would you do?'*

Me: 'Well, you just told me that democracy is dead in
        Scotland, so I suppose I'll have to organise civil unrest.
        Are there other options?'

His reply was a shrug.

In December at the debates for the GRR Bill, I couldn't decide which was worse – watching people with power and influence behaving like zealots, or watching people with power and influence behaving like cowards, and that was my anger trigger.

Our first minister needed the bill to pass because she relied on the Scottish Greens alliance and the Greens had given up on climate and focused on gender. Ash Regan had resigned, and more rebels could wreak havoc in her party. The MSPs could hear the women's sighs, gasps and mutterings in the public gallery, and this clearly irritated Nicola Sturgeon, who, at all times, kept her chair turned away from us.

Our first minister had only met with the 'right' women, who were paid to have the 'right' opinions and say the 'right' things and said that concerns like mine were 'not valid', and now she refused to even look at us?

If due process had been followed, I would have accepted, if not liked, the bill passing. Being denied and dismissed, though? 'OhdyabloodyTHINKso?'

I decided to do two things: make Nicola Sturgeon look us in our eyes as she stole our rights to privacy, safety and dignity, and pinch her photo of victory.

Anasyrma, the exposure of one's naked genitals, was named by Ancient Greeks. It is a global form of female protest. It is intended to shock. A man lifting his kilt is practically obligatory at Murrayfield, but for women to do it? Some of us agreed to mark the passing of this shameful bill with me.

I wanted protest, not indecent exposure, so I made a dozen merkins from craft box scraps. Pubic wigs were used in the 1400s, probably to control pubic lice, and are now usually limited to Hollywood special FX. Fake fannies seemed fitting for Holyrood.

I tucked *Dangerous Coats*, a poem about women's clothing not having pockets to prevent us from spreading sedition, into a pocket on the back of a merkin. I was amused by the prospect of 'Exhibit A' being held aloft with a stern, 'Is this yours, Mrs Miller?' 'I don't know, Your Honour, does it have a pocket?' I cackled myself to sleep thinking that if the world *was* watching TERF Island we'd give them a show.

The debate dragged on, and the presiding officer agreed to another day. Most of the 'Faux Flash Mob' could therefore not attend – even hardcore feminists cannot always escape the wife-work and emotional load of Christmas. As far as I know a manila envelope with a dozen fur triangles and safety pins remains tucked behind the sanitary bin in Holyrood's women's toilet to this day.

Sadly, the beautifully embroidered merkin of the only other 'muffragette' fell off, so it was down to me and an oversized, un-hemmed, off-centre nylon minge.

I am ashamed that the seat of the Scottish Enlightenment became the seat of the Scottish Entitlement. Eighty-six MSPs voted for the GRR Bill, opening the way for rapists being held in prison to get a bit of paper from the state saying they are women, on their own say-so, and David Hume, the Scottish Enlightenment philosopher, turned in his grave.

When the cheering and jeering from the trans activists in the public gallery and chamber died down, I grabbed my chance. Fury made me loud: 'If this Parliament will not respect the rights of women, then you have no decency, and if you will not be decent towards women who are being raped right now in jails that you're in charge of . . . if you will not be decent then I will be indecent!'

I lifted my skirt and a bit of Glasgow vernacular slipped out. 'Get it right up yas, you terrible, terrible people.'

I did not know that an MSP would record me on his phone, or that the video would have upwards of 150 million views on social media. Christmas in my house was a bit awkward as my family tried to figure out whether they were horrified by my behaviour, concerned that I had lost my mind, or both.

I knew David Hume was a sceptic and when I passed his statue on the Royal Mile, with streetlamps twinkling on his tourist-polished toe, I realised that I was too. I had been radicalised by Shona Robison, Nicola Sturgeon, and eighty-four other MSPs who wilfully ignored the words on Parliament's Mace.

I achieved my objectives. The enduring image of the passage of the GRR Bill is one of female anger, and I will never forget the expression on Nicola Sturgeon's face when, at long last, she turned her head and looked at the pubic gallery.

Section 5
Reflections

Chapter 27

The unthinkable happens

Caroline McAllister

———

In the end, Nicola Sturgeon's resignation on 15 February 2023, unthinkable only a few months before, did not come as a surprise. Her car-crash interview with ITV's Peter Smith on 30 January, after double rapist Adam Graham/Isla Bryson had been initially sent to a women's prison, was excruciating to watch. She tied herself in knots as she was held to account for her long-time claim that 'trans women are women':

Sturgeon:	*That is not the point that we are dealing with here . . .*
Smith:	*That is the question I am asking.*
Sturgeon:	*Trans women are women, but in the present context there is no automatic right for a trans woman—*
Smith:	*So there are contexts where a trans woman is not a woman?*
Sturgeon:	*No, there [are] circumstances when a trans woman will be housed in the male prison estate . . .*
Smith:	*Is there any context in which a woman born as a woman will be housed in the male estate?*
Sturgeon	*Look, we're talking here about trans women—*
Smith:	*And I'm now asking about women born as women.*

Sturgeon: I don't think there are circumstances there, but—
Smith: So it's different for trans women?
Sturgeon: Well, yes . . .

And she found herself tongue-tied again a few days later when, at a press conference on 6 February, she referred to the double rapist as 'her'. 'She regards herself as a woman,' she added in a desperate attempt to backtrack.

But the damage had been done. The merest scrutiny of her position in the wake of Graham/Bryson's conviction left Sturgeon a laughing stock. When the nation is laughing at you, there's nowhere to hide. On 15 February 2023, she resigned as first minister.

Watching her rapid and very public downfall offered some vindication to the women within – and outwith – the SNP who had, over recent years, raised valid concerns about the unintended consequences of her gender recognition reforms, only to be ignored, traduced and harassed.

Her stubborn adherence to the self-ID policy exposed a lack of intellectual rigour that stunned her previously loyal supporters. And by ignoring every tenet of safeguarding, she managed to contradict her government's rhetoric around male violence against women and girls.

Women watched in horror as she ignored the pleas of female survivors of male violence who had begged her to rethink. Instead, she sent the very clear message that – despite our concerns – she was going to prioritise male desires over female needs. Years of learning and experience on safeguarding were tossed in the bin, ignored during the passage of the Gender Recognition Reform (Scotland) Bill (GRR Bill). None of it made sense.

Looking back at the six months I spent as the SNP's women's convenor, until I resigned in March 2021, reminded me how strange Sturgeon's stubborn adherence to gender identity ideology had been. She had refused to even listen to dissenting voices.

Late in 2020, frustrated female party members, many of whom were survivors of male violence, approached the Equalities convener Lynne Anderson and me, and asked us to co-ordinate an open letter to Sturgeon. We agreed, and in a time-consuming exercise, collated and verified over 260 signatures. The number would have been significantly more; however, after two weeks we decided to close the letter due to the lengthy process of validating each signature.

Still a party loyalist, I had mixed feelings about the letter being open rather than sent directly to her; however, I was reminded of the times when women, me included, had previously written to the party on this issue and had been ignored.

Several years previously, when gender recognition reform was in its infancy, I had written to the National Executive Committee (NEC) on behalf of women who had shared their worries about self-ID with me. We wanted to highlight the potential impact on survivors. At the time, I naively believed the first minister, our party leader, wouldn't ignore a large group of female members raising real and valid concerns. Yet she did. Repeatedly.

Perhaps one of the most bizarre incidents of her leadership was what became known as the emergency 'broom cupboard' broadcast, made during the height of the Covid-19 pandemic. Party members watched in horror as she broadcast an 'unscripted' video message 'from the heart', characterising the debate around gender recognition reform as 'transphobic'.

She did not mention the needs of women, nor acknowledge the toxic abuse female members of her party had endured. A competent leader would have acknowledged the hurt on both sides, and at least attempted to calm the waters. Instead, the first minister added to the toxicity of the situation and gave the green light to misogynistic bullies to continue with their campaign of the vilification of women.

It was a sobering moment. It felt very much as if those who controlled the party, from Sturgeon down, were intent on ignoring us, no matter how committed, reliable and hardworking we had been in the past, and continued to be, despite everything.

Another example of the leadership's disdain for those of us who did not agree with their approach was when the NEC agreed to review the definitions of misogyny, lesbophobia, bi-phobia and transphobia. Neither Lynne Anderson, the Equalities convener nor I, as the women's convenor, were involved in this work, despite us being the only two NEC members who held mandates from the wider membership. I wrote several times to the business convener, Kirsten Oswald MP, expressing our concerns. She eventually replied, but only to dismiss our fears out of hand.

When I discovered that only the definition of transphobia was to be presented to the NEC for discussion, I and others objected. But again, our views were dismissed without explanation. It was becoming clear that the NEC was in thrall to a powerful clique around Sturgeon, unafraid to ignore the party's constitution.

Their hypocrisy knew no bounds. I remember an occasion when the business convener expressed her disdain about leaks from the NEC. Under normal circumstances I would have wholeheartedly agreed with her. However, when Nicola Sturgeon made her 'broom cupboard' video, she leaked internal party business. And Keith Brown MSP and Kirsten Oswald MP had discussed confidential party business on Twitter. It was becoming increasingly difficult to maintain respect for those people in high office who indulged in low standards of behaviour, while berating others for doing what they did.

Two hugely respected, senior women members, Joan McAlpine MSP and Joanna Cherry MP, both vocal critics of gender recognition reform, were the most high-profile victims of this hypocrisy.

On 31 January 2021, as candidates were about to be picked for the Scottish Parliament elections in May, the NEC voted on a new 'equality mechanism' for the selection process. If passed this would allow 'reserved places' on four of the eight regional lists of prospective MSPs, giving priority to BAME (Black and Asian Minority Ethnic) and disabled candidates, who were allowed to self-declare their disability.

The national secretary ruled that those members of the NEC likely to benefit from the new rule could vote, insisting there was no conflict of interest. Moreover, in my opinion, the motion itself should not have been accepted as competent, as the party had received independent legal advice, confirming it was potentially unlawful. However, it was pushed through, and it secured what I suspect was the outcome most desired by the party leadership: the end of Joan McAlpine's parliamentary career.

She had won the party ballot to be top of the South of Scotland regional list, with the overwhelming support of party members. However, party chiefs placed aspiring MSP Emma Harper at the head of the list as she had declared she was disabled – she is diabetic. Joan was pushed further down and her new placing meant she was not re-elected in May. It was a truly shameful moment in the SNP's history.

As well as manipulating party rules to get their way, the behaviour of some members of the governing body reminded me of playground bullies. Those of us who were identified as troublemakers were commonly referred to as the 'enemy within', and were left in no doubt that our presence was not welcome, despite holding mandates from members. Some of the affiliate groups not mandated by all members, such as Out for Indy, were particularly hostile.

Joanna Cherry was clearly a target from her first meeting as an NEC member. Her contributions were frequently met with hostility and contempt. Nicola Sturgeon's callous disregard towards Joanna when she reported the death and rape threats she had received was difficult to witness.

And it seemed that anyone associated with Joanna was also a valid target. Equalities convenor Lynne Anderson was later disgracefully smeared by party members, and accusations of impropriety splashed on the front page of a national newspaper. She went through months of hell and great expense to clear her name.

I was particularly shocked by an aggressive and co-ordinated attack on a female member during the NEC meeting in March 2021. Alison Graham, of the SNP's Finance and Audit Committee, was berated after she had read out a resignation statement from her and two other members. They were standing down because they could not gain access to the party's books and were concerned about the party's governance and transparency. A video leaked two years later shows Nicola Sturgeon lashing out at the three members. She said:

> The party has never been in a stronger financial position than it is right now and that's a reflection of our strength and our membership.
>
> I'm not going to get into the details . . . but, you know, just be very careful about suggestions that there are problems with the party's finances, because we depend on donors to donate.
>
> There are no reasons for people to be concerned about the party's finances, and all of us need to be careful about not suggesting that there is.

We've got to be careful we don't reap what we sow, if we have leaks from this body it limits the ability for open free and frank discussion.

At the time of writing, Police Scotland are still investigating the SNP's finances. Operation Branchform, one of Scotland's biggest ever police inquiries, was launched in July 2021 to find out what happened to £667,000 donated to the SNP. Peter Murrell, Nicola Sturgeon's husband and the party's CEO, who resigned amid a row over membership numbers a month after his wife had stood down as party leader, was arrested in April 2023 and their family home searched over two days. Sturgeon was arrested in June 2023. Both were released without charge, pending further inquiries.

I had never worked in an environment where such naked intimidation was tolerated or, it could be argued, encouraged. Yet here was the governing body of the SNP behaving as though this was normal and acceptable.

'The process is the punishment,' as Lisa Mackenzie of Murray Blackburn Mackenzie (MBM) wrote of her experience at the Royal College of Nursing, when she was investigated for co-authoring an article on the impact of self-ID on the census. She was right. I watched in horror as women who had given their all during the independence campaign quit politics because of how badly the SNP treated women. Complaints were ignored and the disingenuous statement that 'both sides were as bad as each other' was used to justify the ongoing dismissal of women's concerns. The atmosphere was toxic.

My health began to suffer, and I wasn't sleeping. My mood was low. I had sat on several boards and committees over the years, yet had never witnessed such unprofessional conduct. I knew I had to address its impact upon me. I was in turmoil. Many members had bought a not-inexpensive conference pass in order to give me their vote the year before, and I felt a great weight of responsibility not to let them down. And my family were increasingly worried about my health and well-being.

I had to act, to protect my many commitments. As councillor for the Leven ward, I had a responsibility to my constituents, and I was deputy leader of West Dunbartonshire Council. I also had a job, and I was looking after my increasingly fragile and dependent mum.

Something had to give, yet I felt I couldn't think clearly or make an informed decision, not a position I'd ever experienced before, nor one I would want to experience again.

Then, out of the blue, I was asked if I was interested in joining the recently formed Alba Party, set up by former SNP leader and first minister Alex Salmond in February 2021.

Without thinking it through, I grasped what I saw as an unexpected lifebuoy in stormy waters. It was the right decision for me to leave the SNP in March 2021, but I should have taken more time to recover from my experience. I am no longer a member of any political party.

Looking back at my last few years as an SNP member, and my continued involvement with the women's rights campaign, I am reminded of how fortunate I am to have a network of funny, strong and intelligent women around me. Some were SNP party members, others from the opposite side of the constitutional debate on independence, as well as many with no political affiliation.

The last five years taught me that when all around you feels cold and dark, seek out seditious women, for the sisterhood will light up the road ahead while helping you carry the load. The women who now form the Women Won't Wheesht campaign group, Glasgow Tactical Feminists and Alloa Women, and the support from the Women's Rights Network (WRN) and Sole Sisters, among others, lifted me up when I felt deflated and defeated. They spurred me on when everything looked hopeless, and they reminded me that my voice was not in vain. They supported me even during those terrible times when felt I was banging my head against a concrete wall of abject stupidity and extreme arrogance. They remain good friends and I will always be grateful for their wit and warmth.

Reflecting on the politics of the last five years has been tough. As a supporter of independence, it is still inconceivable that the party of independence chose to focus on such an unpopular and divisive piece of legislation – effectively throwing women and gay people under a bus and causing a huge split in the movement.

And I believe that Nicola Sturgeon's biggest mistake was to underestimate Scottish women, our sense of justice and our determination to protect our hard-won rights for future generations. The more she ignored us, the stronger we became.

As a self-declared 'feminist to my fingertips', she shamefully turned her back on grassroots women's groups, including those from within the independence movement, who were organising and collaborating. We were taking to the streets across Scotland. We ran stalls, delivered leaflets, funded litigation, put on events and went on the streets to alert the public to the gender recognition reform proposals that would render safeguarding almost meaningless – nothing but a tick-box exercise.

As we grew in numbers, our voices became louder. It became increasingly difficult to ignore us. Public opinion moved in our favour as people grasped what was being put in law. And still Sturgeon ignored us.

The irony of needing Westminster to intervene with a Section 35 order and veto the GRR Bill was not lost on me, or many other independence-supporting women. But we warmly welcomed the Scottish Secretary's intervention and the subsequent court ruling that upheld Alister Jack's decision to stop the bill becoming law because of its impact on UK-wide equalities legislation. An argument that Nicola Sturgeon sneeringly dismissed when put forward by women's rights campaigners like me.

The SNP government under Nicola Sturgeon, and latterly supported by their coalition partners, the Scottish Greens, repeatedly demonstrated they did care not for women, lesbians and gay men, despite their rhetoric on violence against women and faux concern about discrimination against LGB people. By outsourcing their critical thinking to lobby groups, and replacing serious policy development with soundbites, all while seeking their next selfie, our elected representatives let us all down. Not just women.

And the damage wrought to the independence movement by Sturgeon and her allies has not yet been fully understood. Once trust and confidence in a party is lost, its governance vandalised, it's all but impossible to recover. The election of Humza Yousaf, Sturgeon's anointed continuity candidate, as leader and first minister, certainly didn't help. If we persist in electing clowns, our politics will continue to be performative. And it's the people of Scotland who will suffer.

Chapter 28

The human cost

Susan Dalgety

———

Amid the roar of the women's rights campaign, quiet voices have begun making themselves heard. Broken-hearted parents. Angry child-development experts. Detransitioners. All desperately trying to get the Scottish Government, the Scottish Parliament, teaching unions, mental health services – anyone – to listen to their concerns about the way in which gender identity ideology has taken root in many schools across Scotland and risks long-term damage to the physical and emotional health of vulnerable adolescents.

Esther is one such parent. The mother of three girls, her family's life has been dominated by gender identity for nearly five years. Her eldest, Lily, now seventeen, believes she is a man, trapped in a woman's body, having gone through a period of being non-binary. Her younger sister, Rachel, is fifteen. She has tried binding her breasts and taking testosterone supplements bought online, believing she can change her sex. Both have been affirmed by teachers at their secondary school, against their parents' wishes, but in accordance with the Scottish Government's guidance issued to schools in 2021.

The non-statutory guidance, published by the then-Education Secretary, Shirley-Anne Somerville, is the subject of much controversy – it is used in state and private schools. One of the first parents to highlight its impact was @rogdmum, whose child attended George Watson's College, a popular private school in Edinburgh.

In her foreword to the seventy-page document, Somerville insists that the guidance will help schools deliver a learning environment, 'where privacy, safety, dignity and respect is afforded to every pupil so they can each achieve their full potential'.

Campaign groups like Safeguarding Our Schools Scotland (SOS Scotland) want it withdrawn, arguing in a 2023 petition to the Scottish Parliament that it:

> Encourages teachers to affirm the social transition of children who say they are trans, to use their chosen pronouns and to avoid misgendering, alongside changing pupils' names and their sex on official school records.
>
> We are concerned about this affirmation first approach and the risks it poses to vulnerable children. Emerging evidence advises against this approach and recommends 'watchful waiting'.

The petition was rejected by the Public Petitions Committee on 6 December 2023. The chair of the committee, Jackson Carlaw MSP, was one of only three Conservative MSPs who voted for the Gender Recognition Reform (Scotland) Bill (GRR Bill).

Educational psychologist Carolyn Brown, who has forty years of experience working with children and adolescents, agrees with the petitioners. She says:

> Safeguarding children and teenagers has always been incumbent on parents and education professionals. But the complexities of

safeguarding have increased significantly in the last two decades as a result of social media and postmodernist academic theories advising that some children are 'trans'. We know from extensive research that children and teenagers are highly suggestible and easily influenced but social media's promotion of gender identity ideology is really testing parents in new and unexpected ways. This makes the Scottish Government's guidelines, and the teaching resource Relationships, Sexual Health and Parenthood (RSHP) all the more shocking in their insistent promotion of gender identity ideology as fact. There is abundant evidence clarifying the ideology has no basis in reality. There is no evidence to prove that children are born 'trans' and there is no clear definition of what is meant by the term 'trans'. There is good evidence that the idea of the 'trans child' is a 21st century invention.

Children's emotional wellbeing in education depends on schools not providing leading material or using resources which state that children and teenagers can be something that is not physically or biologically possible. Why is it that LGBTQ materials use fairytale-like terminology with colourful avatars and cartoons? Children are being sold a fantasy which infantilises and appeases. How is this facilitating the development of an informed and healthy mind?

Esther, frustrated by years of trying to support her children as they struggle with their mental health, has a simple message for Nicola Sturgeon and her ministers who promoted gender identity in schools. 'What were you thinking? Why would you impose an adult agenda on children? There is no such thing as a "trans brain". Don't you realise what you have done?'

Esther, and her husband Chris, are exhausted by their family's ordeal. Writing in her blog *Suddenly Trans* she describes how gender identity ideology has 'completely derailed' her family's teenage years.

I grieve for the actual teenage years my kids could have had.

I grieve for the years taken up having to learn EXACTLY what it means for my children and our family and how we as their parents should parent.

I think along with their dead name, their dead teenage years would have been way more interesting in a fun way and we would have parented them, as we always had, in an attachment parenting way, with gentle supportive guidance.

We didn't know then what was happening.

We couldn't see it, for being loving and supportive parents that we were just always being. Don't get me wrong, it started off fun and interesting. Pride marches, badges, posters, music and flags. So many flags . . .

Sitting in her cosy sitting room, she recalls how pleased she and Chris had been at first that Lily had made friends. 'She is on the autism spectrum and finds making friends difficult. She didn't have any friends when she started secondary school. She spotted the rainbow flag at an open day at school – it was the flag that attracted her, she didn't know what it meant. It was the Pride club, and she was quickly signed up. She had found a "tribe".'

Esther describes how Lily become obsessed by gender identity. 'It was a non-stop discussion about gender and sexuality. At one point she talked about ninety-six different genders. Ninety-six. She was looking for a reaction, we think.

'We talked about it endlessly, at every family meal. And her younger sister became interested too. We tried to be as supportive as you can be as parents. They wanted flags, badges, all the paraphernalia, and we supported them. After all, what's a badge. It is just a badge.'

Then came Covid-19, and like almost every teenager across the country, Lily and her sister Rachel disappeared online. 'At the start of lockdown, we did lots of things together as a family, going for walks together, that kind of thing, but it wasn't a normal society. The girls starting spending most of their time on their computers. At the time, we didn't know that gender identity ideology is all over TikTok and YouTube, and of course the algorithms sucked them in deeper and deeper.'

Esther and Chris agreed to the school's advice that the girls be known by their new names at school, having previously changed their pronouns at school without their parents' knowledge. Esther explains, 'The transgender guidance promotes the affirmation model, so we reluctantly went along with it.' Desperate, they sought help from Child and Adolescent Mental Health Services (CAMHS), only to find themselves reported to social work for 'unintentional emotional abuse' because they refused to affirm their daughter's change of identity by using her chosen pronouns at home. Esther describes her sense of betrayal in her blog:

> We started family therapy with the view to creating a space for us all to be able to communicate and live with our differing opinions within the family home, but again, little did we know. Ideology has truly taken a stronghold at CAMHS and before we knew it, we were slammed into a social services wall. We were expecting support and wisdom, instead we got personal unprofessionalism after being lured into a trusting therapeutic bond.

After a seven-month wait, social work decided Esther and Chris had no case to answer, and suggested that the family be referred to CAMHS for support. 'I laughed,' says Esther.

Five years after their oldest daughter started exploring her gender identity, followed by her sister, Esther says she and her husband are now taking a 'watchful waiting approach'. She says, 'We have spent time trying to reconnect with them, to get our family unit back together. I occasionally share articles with them, but I don't want to overload them,' she says. 'It is important to stay close to them. But they are thoroughly entrenched in the ideology they see online, which only presents a positive picture and none of the reality or risk.

'They are an idealistic generation; they don't want to have a male–female divide. Anyone can be anything. As J.K. Rowling said in her tweet, 'dress however you please . . .' but this is different. By telling kids it is possible to change sex, it has confused everyone, and it is damaging. I see the whole world affirming my children – school, doctors, opticians, everywhere they go, all in the guise of "be kind". It's a dystopian nightmare. And if we speak out, as parents, we get lambasted, or sent to social services. But everyone is affirming a delusion.'

Esther says her only hope now is time. 'If we can keep them as far away as possible from testosterone and surgery as their brain matures, we hope by the time they reach the 'magical' age of twenty-five, they will be comfortable in their bodies.'

Some of the most vulnerable children in Scotland are most at risk from gender identity ideology, according to Maggie Mellon, who has forty-five years' experience in social work. She set up the Evidence-Based Social Work Alliance (EBSWA) to 'gather and consider evidence on crucial questions of sex and gender identity in order to inform professional discussion'. She and many other child-protection workers believes that there is insufficient knowledge to support the implementation of policies and practices such as the transgender guidance for schools.

She has been immersed in the issue for five years, as she explains: 'I first became alarmed about gender identity ideology in 2018 and began to write and speak publicly about the potential risks and harms to children. But I did not foresee the rapid capture of social work, along with education and health, of beliefs that children could be born "trans" and should be affirmed and transitioned as the opposite to their actual sex.

'But capture is not the right word because there was no opposition, no obvious dissent by senior figures in social work. In 2018, I would not have believed that the Children's Hearing System, the Care Inspectorate, councils' children's services, and all the major children's charities would, by 2023, promote "gender identity" and the existence of "trans" children as a fact.

'Nor would I have believed that these agencies would be actively complicit in socially and medically transitioning children in their care without allowing any open discussion or challenge.'

She is particularly perturbed by the Scottish Care Inspectorate's publication of its official guidance last year, which advises care services that they should promote gender identity and affirm and socially transition children as the opposite sex.

Maggie points out that the guidance suggests young people be allowed to use the sleeping and bathroom accommodation for their 'gender identity' rather than their sex. 'It leaves no safe place for children who do not believe and who object, and exposes staff to the risk of disciplinary action and even sacking for refusing to follow,' she says. And she stresses how vulnerable young people in care are to gender identity ideology.

'Despite the rhetoric of empowerment and rights, they have little or no control over their lives. Choosing a "gender identity" can offer them an illusion of control and a possible explanation for feelings of distress and difference. They can choose a new name, a new identity. They can be given special attention and feel noticed and rewarded and singled out from other children. Of all the things that these children need to have adults listen to them about, it is not this illusion of care.'

Maggie says all children and young people are at risk from the official adoption of unevidenced beliefs, and gender identity falls into this category. She stresses that some children are at much more risk of significant harm than others. 'Many of those at-risk children are known to social work. We know from the evidence gathered and published in the interim Cass Report that children who are looked after in care, who are separated from parents, and siblings; children with autism, and children who have been abused, are particularly vulnerable to becoming convinced that they are in the wrong body.'

The Cass Review, an independent review of Gender Identity Development Services (GIDS) for children and young people, commissioned by the UK government, has no locus in Scotland. Campaigners have called for a similar approach to examine not only the Sandyford GIDS and the wider NHS, but the impact of the schools guidance, as well as the role of LGBT Youth Scotland (LGBTYS) and the Scottish charity Time for Inclusive Education (TIE) in promoting gender identity ideology in schools. The Scottish government has, so far, resisted all demands for a review, but the Social Justice Secretary Shirley-Anne Somerville told Parliament at the end of December 2023 that she was 'watching closely' events in England.

In the wake of the Cass Review's interim report, NHS England developed modules for professionals working with young people, on how best to offer support to those who are 'gender-questioning'. The modules recognise, unlike the Scottish schools guidance, that the involvement of parents or carers is key:

> *Supporting the social transition without the involvement of parents*
> *or carers can create complex difficulties within families and is not*
> *recommended. Secrets between parents or carers and their children*

are problematic and are likely to create further issues in the future. When parents or carers discover that changes have been made without their involvement, this can increase risks and can alienate parents and carers from their children (and vice versa) and/or the education setting.

Maggie Mellon is clear what should happen in Scotland, to best protect all young people. 'If I was the minister responsible for education, children and young people, I would immediately make it clear to everyone involved in children's education and social care that, unless and until there was established evidence to support affirmation and transitioning as in children's best interests, it would not be happening in any school or any regulated children's service in Scotland.

'I would at the same time commission an equivalent to the Cass Review of the health evidence, but for education and for children's social care. I would make it clear that bullying and silencing was at an end, and there was no longer to be any practice based on acceptance of unproven claims about trans identities.'

She is confident that things will improve. 'In Scotland as in England, women have led the opposition and proved yet again that women are formidable when we decide to say no. It is the strength and anger of women, who represent the sensible majority of people, which will win this fight.'

At a private meeting in the Scottish Parliament on 22 November 2022, on the same day that the Equalities Committee ended its consideration of the GRR Bill, a group of MSPs gathered to listen to the testimony of two young people, Ritchie Herron and Sinead Watson.

Both had undergone surgery and hormone treatment in a desperate effort to change their sex. They shared the harrowing, intimate details of the medical procedures that mutilated their bodies and spoke with quiet authority of the struggle to live a normal life after detransition.

Ritchie recalls the meeting: 'Sitting at the foot of the large wooden conference table, I'm surprised at the turnout. More than expected. After the first few speakers, Sinead offers her account to the crowd of about fifty. Passionately she recounts stories of medical negligence, the same themes I hear over and over – a troubled life, addiction, and other issues that are often overlooked. Her story grips the members present.

'Usually, very few politicians listen, many seem to have their mind made up, so I was happy to be given the chance, even if it wasn't in England. However, it was a private clinic in Edinburgh that helped fast-track me onto hormones a decade earlier. It felt somewhat symbolic to be back in the city, giving my one-star review of medical transition.

'After Sinead spoke, it was my turn. Like every other time I've spoken, there was no script, just bare truth. I told them honestly, how I felt back in transition and how I felt now. "I might not be here in five years' time," I told them frankly.

'Not because of the hormones rotting my body, but my resilience isn't always as firm as it appears. I have dips, and whilst they are getting fewer and further between, they are always deep. Once I've fallen in, it's hard to climb out of. That being said, I've taken extraordinary risks with my health in more ways than one, and I wouldn't be surprised if that alone shortened my life.

'The room was stunned. It's not until witnessing the reactions of others, that I realise just how much of a sledgehammer with words I can be. Moments like this, I begin to realise that the life I'm living is far from normal.

'Sinead is upset by my declaration. A more optimistic mode kicks back in and I make a small quiet joke to make her smile.

It works, but the sense of grief is still lingering in the air for the audience who weren't comforted in the same way.

'No one really knows what to say at times like these, and truth be told, neither do I. I'm not quite sure what to tell the younger ones, in their early twenties, who are straying on the edge of suicidality on a daily basis.

'There are no words of comfort or reassurances that can ease the reality of the loss. Especially when the body part is imperative to your health and in many ways, your individuality.

'As the session ended, a few of the MSPs shook my hand and others thanked me for the account. And that was it. I had no doubt in my mind that the bill was going to pass anyway. Despite the fierce campaigning by groups such as For Women Scotland (FWS), there was a notable silence from ministers throughout the process.

'When the bill passed, I felt mostly sorry for the campaigning group of women. Many months later, again, to no surprise but to much relief, the bill was blocked by the UK government.

'With confidence, I can tell you how terrible my experience was, but I cannot confidently speak for everyone. There is a duality that must be recognised, especially when it comes to the medicalisation. Some achieve what they set out to do with surgery, yet many are guided down this path perhaps when they shouldn't be. Either way, that's a hell of an investment to sacrifice body parts. Such a commitment of flesh should be carefully considered and measured, not just by the individual but those who [are] apparently under their care. Long-term, unbiased research is desperately needed to determine the impacts of hormone usage and, most importantly, the efficacy of the surgeries.

'I do worry for our future, not just those who regret undertaking the process, but those who don't. Some of the kindest, most loving souls I've ever met were in transition, and they are not all these demon-esque clichés many would propose them to be.

'Those who pursue this path, all wanted to better ourselves, and some, like me, invested everything, including our healthy bodies. If I had known just how steep the price I was paying was, I wouldn't have done it.

'People deserve to know, transition isn't the liberation we were promised. It's ugly, not beautiful. It's brutal, not easy. No matter what happens in law, who wins, who loses, nothing changes with us. And whether I'm here for five or fifty more years, this is my life. It's for ever.'

Chapter 29

Asking questions

Mandy Rhodes (interviewed by Susan Dalgety)

M andy Rhodes is one of Scotland's most senior journalists, with an enviable reputation for tackling social issues many others will shy away from. She learned her trade on the *Wester Hailes Sentinel* during the 1980s, when the Edinburgh housing estate was plagued by cheap heroin and HIV / AIDS.

She was the social affairs correspondent for *Scotland on Sunday* when it launched in 1988, working on major investigations such as the Orkney child abuse scandal of 1991. She had a long spell in radio and television, in front of the camera and in production, working for STV, the BBC and Channel 4. And since 2004 she has been editor of *Holyrood* magazine, Scotland's highly respected parliamentary and public policy journal.

No one understands Scotland's public sector and civil society better than Mandy, nor the idiosyncrasies of its political class. She counted Nicola Sturgeon as a close and long-standing contact; indeed, considered her something of a friend, occasionally enjoying a glass of wine in Bute House with the first minister, and sharing confidences, personal and political. It was Mandy who broke the story of Sturgeon's miscarriage in 2011, waiting for five years after the tragic event to tell the story, and only after she was sure that Sturgeon was happy for it to be told.

Today, as she sits in her office within shouting distance of the Scottish Parliament, 'my workplace' as she describes it, she recalls the evening her friendship with Scotland's most powerful woman started to fall apart.

'It was October 2019, there was just Nicola and I in Bute House for a catch-up over a glass of wine. During our conversation that covered various things including the upcoming trial of Alex Salmond, I told her that her plans to reform the GRA were going to be bad, really bad for the SNP – that women were in a terrible place concerned about the risks of self-ID and what that could mean for them. She looked at me, in that way that she does that basically shuts down a conversation and says, "Young people are really distressed about it. And that's all there is to it. We need to do something about that." I could just tell there was no point in pursuing this any further. I honestly don't think she put any more thought into it other than that and I guess, given what I was writing about the issues, that is when our relationship started to deteriorate. Obviously there was then a pandemic, but we certainly didn't continue to share the same kind of trusted or warm relationship and I stopped getting regular interviews.'

Writing in March 2023, Mandy recalled how she was frozen out by Sturgeon and her inner circle:

> [I]n one of a series of columns written in and around the gender recognition reforms, the same advisor [Liz Lloyd, Sturgeon's chief of staff] messaged me to suggest it was inappropriate to use the line 'is this a hill the first minister really wants to die on?' when so many transgender people committed suicide. When I responded by asking for her empirical evidence for that, she stopped following me on Twitter. The first minister did the same sometime later. And thus, the tone was being set for the last couple of years.

It was another party leader who first alerted Mandy to the dangers of questioning gender identity orthodoxy. Patrick Harvie, co-leader of the Scottish Greens, is an ardent supporter of self-ID. He stopped speaking to Mandy in 2018, when she first started to, gently, question self-declaration and its impact on women and girls.

But the extent of his contempt didn't become clear until August 2021 when, in response to a request for an article for an upcoming review of the political year, he submitted a piece that described *Holyrood* as being part of the 'transphobic agenda'. It was an astonishing attack and, as the magazine's lawyers warned, defamatory. It was even more astonishing given that, when he submitted it on 12 August 2021, Patrick Harvie almost certainly knew that he was about to become a government minister. Eight days later, the Scottish Greens and the SNP announced the Bute House agreement, where they agreed to form a coalition government. Self-ID was, according to the Scottish Greens, 'a crucial part' of the deal.

Harvie's article was not published. But it was almost a breaking point for Mandy. Sitting in her office on the evening she received it, she started crying. 'That was the one time when I really felt under the cosh. It was there in black and white. He [Patrick Harvie] thinks I am a transphobe. This is affecting me. It is affecting business.

'Since then, I have passed Patrick Harvie in the street, and said "Hi". He snubs me. I know he does that to other women in the Parliament and that is uncomfortable for us all. Certainly not grown-up. That's my place of work as well, not just his. I got to the point of getting really panicked at the thought of going in. I still don't like it.'

So why did she persist in writing about the subject? Could she not simply have spiked it, as many other media outlets did, particularly in the early days of the debate? Mandy is very clear she was simply doing her job as a journalist. 'I approached the whole debate around sex and gender in the same way as I would any other issue that had sparked my journalistic interest, and where I could see a divergence of opinion on what was becoming a major policy issue. I looked at the evidence, I followed the debate and I attempted to speak to all interested parties to come to some kind of informed point of view.

'I looked at the influence Stonewall had had on this debate and went back to interview founding members of Stonewall like Simon Fanshawe, who had become very critical of the way it worked as a lobbying organisation. I was continually criticised for only taking his side, no matter what I did. I invited groups of transgender women into the office to meet with my journalists and was criticised for speaking to the 'wrong kind of transgender people'. I carried articles written by Debbie Hayton, a transsexual who believes that you can't change sex, and I countered that with an article written by a transgender woman, Katy Montgomerie, whose view is very different from Debbie's. None of it was ever enough or satisfied the trans activists. What was fascinating about the piece from Katy Montgomerie was that when I received it, it still had all the tracked changes on it and the name of who had made them, and some edits had been made by an SNP MP's staffer which was, to say the least, interesting in terms of the personal connections this revealed. I also interviewed a twenty-something-year-old drag queen who finished up by telling me my feminism was a very old-fashioned view of feminism. I guess, I came to the opinion that this was such a polarised debate that there was literally nothing you could bring to the table in terms of fact, evidence or even truth, that would help bring any clarity or consensus and, instead, I would just be personally attacked.

'I always faced opposition when I was breaking taboos and people didn't like what was being said, but my integrity as a journalist was never questioned in the way it has been over this issue.'

She has thought long and hard about why gender identity has proven so controversial. 'In some respects, this whole issue has reminded me of when I was first involved in breaking stories around child sexual abuse. On that subject, people didn't want to hear or believe the levels of abuse or listen to what some human beings were prepared to do to others. They would rather just close their ears to it or get defensive.

'On this issue people didn't even want you to ask questions or present them with fundamental facts about science or biology. I remember saying to Patrick Harvie at the very start of this that even on the basis of a sharp spike in young, autistic girls presenting at gender clinics, that that should surely pique interest in why that was happening. He simply said, it's because there are more trans people now able to come out. I didn't buy that, and I still don't.'

Nor could she understand the criticisms levelled at then-MSP Joan McAlpine when, as chair of the Scottish Parliament's culture committee, she questioned the government's plans to conflate sex and gender in the 2022 census. 'A census is a record for the future, as well as an aid to present policy-making, and the government was proposing to distort reality to suit a particular agenda. That seemed wrong to me.'

The controversy over the census and the collection of data touched a nerve with Mandy, whose father had died in late 2017: 'I remember my mother being so upset that Dad's death certificate recorded that he had been suffering from depression, when that wasn't true. At the time we were all so sad that we weren't up for the fight of changing that medical account, but it was wrong and will be wrong should anyone look at that in the future. Data matters and data being recorded accurately to reflect facts matters.'

As she started to research more about the issue, she says the risks to women of self-ID became obvious. 'They were so clear to me that I couldn't believe that politicians like Nicola Sturgeon didn't see that. She just dismissed any of the concerns raised. She certainly didn't ever engage with the arguments or bother herself with facts, and that did change my opinion of her as a woman who I believed to be driven by a sharp intellect and I thought cared about the safety of women and girls. That was just beyond disappointing.'

Not surprisingly, for a journalist whose career has been rooted in social justice, long before it became a mantra for self-proclaimed progressives, Mandy became increasingly concerned about the protection of children. 'My concern was centred on young, vulnerable mixed-up kids, girls in the main, who were being sold a lie that they could change their sex and that that would solve any issues that they might have around their identity.

'As someone who has written extensively on child abuse, I couldn't believe we were condoning young people taking experimental drugs to apparently pause puberty when we had no idea of the risks of using these drugs for that purpose. We were also, it seemed, willing to lead them down a lifelong medical pathway, even offering surgery to remove their breasts. All in the name of gender identity ideology, which is based on a feeling of who you might be, nothing more.

'I remember a conversation I had with the MP Mhairi Black early in the debate. She told me that puberty blockers were completely reversible and there were no adverse consequences and I asked her how she knew that. She had no answer, and as it turned out that conversation was enough to end what had been, until then, a very good relationship. It wasn't as if anyone ever said, "I am cutting all ties with you now", but the coolness was clear.

'But I simply I could not grasp the logic to be your "true self" you needed to chop bits of yourself off or take drugs. It made no sense and still doesn't. I think there is a medical scandal waiting to happen and I don't ever want to be accused of being complicit in that.'

Words have always mattered to Mandy. It is why she went into journalism. 'I was being steered towards social work at university – I even did a social work placement in my final year. But I was also involved in the university newspaper, and I knew I wanted to use my words to speak out for people without a voice.'

When she found herself being coerced into using the language of gender identity ideology, she balked. 'I was presented with a demand by lobby groups that I comply with the mantra that "trans women are women". I just couldn't go along with that because it isn't true but, for that, I was vilified.

'I remember speaking to a Scottish trans activist who was instrumental in lobbying for self-ID, and he told me that using that rhetoric was deliberate, because if you got people to buy into the idea that trans women are in fact the same as any other women, then the arguments for self-ID would follow on more easily. Again, I was struck by consequences for biological women if the media bought into that lie without questioning it.'

And she grew increasingly frustrated by Scotland's political classes or the lobby to take the issue seriously. 'Veteran politicians would just tell me that they didn't want to "go there", and many hoped they would be out of the Parliament before it came round as a live debate. Most male journalists didn't want to think about it, let alone write about it, with the exception of Alex Massie [of *The Times*] and eventually a couple of others, but what was so frustrating was that having taken so long to write about it, the men always got more attention on this than women journalists and certainly not the same level of abuse for doing so.

'I remember speaking to a number of male editors about the way we were reporting court cases and going along with the whole preferred pronouns thing, even in cases of sexual assault. No one had any answers; they were just going along with it for fear of being attacked. That's bizarre for people who have gone into a profession which is all about exposing the truth. I couldn't believe that, even in rape cases, the feelings of the rapist could possibly be put above those of a woman who had been assaulted. Madness.

'My journalism was always about exposing the truth, no matter how messy that might be. Yet on this issue, it felt like we were all meant to suspend our mental faculties and ignore the truth, ignore facts, ignore evidence. Stop asking questions.'

Mandy says her starting point on the issue, as with any other, was a desire to be fair, to let people be how they want to be. 'But you can't allow that to blind you to other issues of harm', she says, and she was never in doubt that self-ID would have a negative impact on women, particularly those most vulnerable. 'I could clearly see that spaces that were deemed single-sex, such as in refuges, hospital wards, changing rooms, toilets, had evolved into places that weren't single-sex at all. Yet women had never been consulted about losing our rights; they had basically been taken from us, almost by stealth, and we were made to feel it was impolite to ask for them back.'

She was perplexed by the lack of curiosity among Scotland's political class. 'Politicians who previously had a lot to say about many other subjects, just didn't want to be bothered by thoughts that might provoke uncomfortable questions or answers in their own heads. I found that deeply disturbing. I could feel the barriers go up with politicians who had previously been close contacts, who had known me for years and would have previously seen me as someone who stood up for the rights of any marginalised group, and yet on this one subject, their view of me did a 180-degree turn.'

As time has gone on, Mandy says her views on gender identity have hardened. 'I have become more hard line about it. While I can respect people thinking they believe they are another sex to the one they were born as, it's a lie to say that is true, yet as journalists, we have, in the main, gone along with that.'

Holyrood magazine celebrates its twenty-fifth birthday in 2024, as does the Scottish Parliament. What has been the impact of the debate around gender and self-ID on Scottish politics? 'It's most definitely one of the most divisive debates of the last twenty-five years. And it's ironic given that identity is at the heart of all our politics that it was actual identity politics that destroyed Nicola. I do think it destroyed her; if this whole debate hadn't happened, if those pictures of Isla Bryson hadn't driven a coach and horses through the idea that there were no risks around self-ID, she could still be around. And from the outside looking in, it makes us look ridiculously small. So, yes, I do think it has changed us. And yes, it's changed me. I feel a bit broken, damaged, by it all.'

The ferociousness of the debate, played out in public, almost stopped her from applying for a role that she had long coveted, as a member of the Scottish Committee of the Equality and Human Rights Commission (EHRC). 'There were vacancies advertised a couple of years back and, while I had thought my experience could be put to good use, I decided not to apply because it was at the height of all the arguments around the Gender Recognition Reform (Scotland) Bill (GRR Bill).

'There had already been concerted attempts by people and organisations to get me sacked from my job and I didn't want to humiliate myself by even putting myself forward, given how I was being painted on social media. But this year [2023],

I was encouraged to think about applying by a number of women whose motivation has only ever been about advancing equality, and I decided that, on a point of principle, I shouldn't be afraid to put myself forward for a role that I was eminently qualified for and felt I could bring value to.

'I went through the application and interview process, always being very open and honest about the whole sex and gender debate and how I had been portrayed and how that might reflect on the organisation. I am extremely glad that the EHRC felt my background and profile offered them something useful, and I look forward to being able to contribute on matters pertaining to equality for all groups. We have all been very focused on one particular protected characteristic, and meanwhile people with disabilities have been largely ignored in the media and they are some of the most marginalised people in our society and they deserve a lot more of our attention.'

Looking back on the five years from 2018, when Patrick Harvie first shut her down for asking a straightforward question about sex and gender, does Mandy regret speaking out?

'I have watched colleagues ignore what is front of them, not ask questions, ignore the consequence of this to women, to children, and to the truth. That is deeply worrying for my profession. People will tell me that I have been very brave, but I don't feel very brave, all I've done is write, and I just don't know what else I could have done and still felt I had been true to myself or to my profession.'

Chapter 30

Watching Scotland

Kathleen Stock

———

In 2017, three years into her first ministership, Nicola Sturgeon was in the news for the wrong sort of reason. Prime Minister Theresa May had flown to Glasgow to discuss Brexit, and a photo was taken of the pair of female leaders sitting carefully posed for the camera, each dressed in her usual attire of tailored jacket, skirt and heels. 'Never mind Brexit, who won Legs-it!' thundered the front page of the English edition of the *Daily Mail*, immediately unleashing a torrent of righteous condemnation from commentators on nearly all sides. A spokesman for the first minister seized the opportunity to score a point: 'Brexit may risk taking Britain back to the early 1970s, but there is no need for coverage of events to lead the way.'

As it happens, I was one of those critics expressing outrage – for this event also marked my first nervous foray into the realm of media commentary. Based on some academic essays on sexual objectification I had previously written, I was wheeled out by my university to talk to several local radio stations about 'Legs-it' in back-to-back interviews. From Bristol to Glasgow to Cardiff and beyond, I could be heard across the airwaves roundly deploring the reduction of two capable women to a sexually objectified stereotype. It was particularly galling that they had done this to Nicola Sturgeon, I thought – after all, she was such a well-known feminist!

It's all quite funny now I think about it. For back in 2017 – though I had yet to fully catch on, or to say anything critical in public about the matter – Sturgeon's government was already drawing up plans to make it easier for males to legally identify as women, based on little more than a preference for skirts and stockings over trouser suits. Equally, for three years already, the very same government had been ignoring the availability of single-sex exemptions in the Equality Act and quietly allowing violent male offenders into women's prisons on similarly hackneyed grounds. And for even longer, clinicians at the Sandyford Gender Dysphoria Service for Young People in Glasgow had been doling out experimental puberty blockers and cross-sex hormones to children and teenagers – many of them depressed or autistic – based on their young patients' strong distress at not conforming to feminine or masculine ideals. All in all, the underlying moral seemed to be that capitulation to sexist stereotypes was perfectly okay in Scottish institutions, and to hell with the consequences – as long as you weren't making jokey remarks about the first minister's legs, that is.

Back then, Sturgeon was far from the only political leader pushing for changing the law in favour of gender identity over sex; but still, she stood out as the only one positively doing it under the banner of feminism. Then-Prime Minister Theresa May was also a big fan of self-ID, but as a good vicar's daughter it seemed likely this came more from a felt responsibility to be kindly than from any close acquaintance with the works of Simone de Beauvoir. Labour leader Jeremy Corbyn also pronounced himself in favour of the policy, but was apparently mostly motivated by empathic thoughts of the 'trauma' of being trans. Myopic as both of these party leaders obviously were about the ramifications of such simplistic moralising for women in prisons, rape crisis centres, changing rooms, or sports teams, at least neither May nor Corbyn had the brass neck to mention feminism in the same breath.

But Sturgeon was different. A flavour of her rampant doublethink can be gained by considering a speech she gave on International Women's Day in 2019. Full of her trademark teacherly vim, she said it was important to recognise 'how much progress has been made' and that 'women today have opportunities today that our mothers and grandmothers could only have dreamed of'. But she also lamented how far Scotland still had to go. Politics, she said, was 'still predominantly male'; 'a world where male culture still dominates, a world where the treatment that is dished out to women on a daily basis, the criteria that we are judged by, leads to a very different experience for women, than the experience for men'. She lamented the fact that men outnumbered women in politics and business and pronounced herself determined to 'reduce Scotland's gender pay gap'. She finished her speech by exhorting her listeners to 're-dedicate ourselves to that role of ending gender inequality'.

Yet even as she spoke these rousing words, her government was preparing to loosen existing restrictions on who could get a Gender Recognition Certificate (GRC) and so be counted legally as the opposite sex. Equally, in June of the same year, it was announced that the forthcoming Scottish census – normally a crucial source of data about contemporary socioeconomic life in Scotland, including about differences between males and females – would officially allow respondents to answer the question about their biological sex with information about their inner feelings of gender identity. In effect, this would altogether remove the female and male categories from the survey as robustly tracked variables, and hamstring any future researchers wishing to use the data to establish sex-based patterns of inequality.

By then, Sturgeon was starting to look like she had accidentally become a character in a satire: a passionate feminist intent on reducing inequality between the sexes by making it easier for men to count as women. No doubt partly motivated by a desire to drive another wedge between Holyrood and Westminster, she appeared obsessed with conjuring an image to the wider world of Scots people as maximally 'inclusive', leaving her incapable of admitting to the existence of any possible downsides.

Watching the first minister as she tut-tutted impatiently, rolled her eyes, and patronised the life out of the few people brave enough to criticise her government's policies, I began to see her as emblematic of a certain kind of professional feminist also prevalent across the modern women's sector. This was someone good at making the right faces and mouthing the right mantras, but whose commitment otherwise to the cause of women, when detached from any political kudos for herself, was about as deep as a mountain snow patch during a hot summer. And almost as bad, Sturgeon appeared to leave the female critics of her policies within the SNP to face monstrous bullying from hostile MPs, trans activists, and members of the public, sometimes even appearing to fan the flames by putting out lofty statements abhorring 'transphobia' in the party. Certainly, there seemed to be no concerted attempt to put the fire out.

Eventually, as was well publicised, in January 2023 Sturgeon's personal take on feminism met with a reckoning of sorts. This came in the form of convicted rapist Adam Graham/Isla Bryson – a physically intact male without any GRC who was initially remanded to the female estate, in line with established Scottish prisons policy, after he suddenly discovered his inner womanhood on the way to his court case. The usually adept Sturgeon stumbled her way through journalists' questions, and tried to square the impossible circle of why, if this really was a 'woman' – as Sturgeon refused to deny – then the right destination should not be a female prison after all. The message to onlooking politicians on both sides of the border was clear. Whatever you do about the humongous ongoing row caused by trans activist attempts to redefine womanhood, make sure you don't end up doing a Nicola.

Indeed, only months after this debacle, Labour MPs were suddenly rediscovering the lessons of GCSE biology after years of pretending to journalists that the nature of womanhood was far too complicated for them to hazard a guess. By March, Wes Streeting was bravely venturing that 'men have penises and women have vaginas'. By April, Scottish Labour leader Anas Sarwar was gnomically saying 'you can't argue with biology'. And by July, leader Keir Starmer had finally gained the confidence to assert in public that 'a woman is an adult human female', after many earlier prevarications.

Also, that month, UK Labour indicated that it was now prepared to recognise a distinction between biological sex and social gender and announced that it was dropping its ambitions to get rid of medical gatekeeping for GRCs. One can't help suspecting that senior members of the party had learnt a lot by watching the fiasco up North, perhaps now realising that there is a limit, after all, to how much contradictory and performative bullshit left-wing voters are prepared to put up with in the supposed name of moral progress.

And there are a couple of further lessons for politicians watching from Westminster to digest here too. Effectively, over many years the Scottish Government used taxpayer money to set up an echo chamber for itself, giving hundreds of thousands of pounds to external campaigning organisations like Stonewall, Scottish Trans Alliance (STA), and the Equality Network, and then letting these bodies more or less dictate the development of Scottish equality policy. The highly ideological nature of these groups meant that their activist emissaries spent little time explaining to MSPs what the law actually is, and much more time imagining what they would like it to be – and then lobbying hard for it. Though a version of this also happened in Westminster, mainly thanks to the influence of Stonewall, in Scotland it took on a particularly intensified form – perhaps due to the relatively small numbers of people involved, comparatively speaking, and the proportionately large amounts of funding on offer.

Those who work for these campaigning organisations tend to have scant understanding of why rational people might oppose their proposals. Instead, they will put nearly all of it down to intolerance and bigotry towards trans people, in a manner reminiscent of the way cult leaders tend to dismiss all critics as 'haters'. Over time, this simplified way of thinking appears to soften the brain. Dependence on such bodies for advice, and the cosy relationships that were apparently built with them, has left some MSPs quite exposed, apparently unaware of how the slogans and rhetoric they have ingested from contact with activists comes across in public, and sometimes doing reputationally risky things as a result.

It is not clear what else could explain the flawed framing of the census, or the clearly inhumane prison policy – inhumane, that is, to female prisoners. Nor indeed, the government's commitment of taxpayers' money in 2023 to a 'Non-Binary Equality Action Plan', yet without it being able to clearly state what special social problems non-binary people are supposed to face. There have also been unfortunate recent events like the photos of four grinning SNP politicians at a protest, standing immediately in front of a sign saying 'Decapitate TERFs', apparently without noticing. Humza Yousaf's decision, in one of his first actions as new party leader, to test the UK government's blocking of Scottish gender recognition reform in the Court of Sessions was also unwise, eventually resulting in a thorough-going dismissal of the Scottish government's case. With more neutral, less ideological advice, all of this embarrassment might have been avoided. Useful intelligence, then, for Westminster politicians still tempted to farm out their brains to activist groups and put them in charge of national LGBT policy-making.

A second interesting facet of the trans activist capture of the Scottish Government is the way that a relatively superficial focus on LGBTQ+ policy issues has been used by politicians to distract voters' attention from more difficult and intractable social problems they cannot seem to fix. Again, this too happens elsewhere in the UK, but seems particularly prevalent in Scotland. As the gap between rich and poor increases, public health worsens, NHS waiting lists lengthen, wages stagnate, and the education system falters, the Scottish Government's approach has often seemed to be to stick a rainbow on something, somewhere, and hope for the best. It doesn't really work, though. Once they see past the near-impenetrable jargon and heavy-handed guilt-tripping from trans activists, voters can tell that policies around the redefinition of sex are not, after all, hermetically sealed from negative consequences for other people – far from it, in fact – even if certain rainbow-bedazzled politicians cannot.

As I write this in 2023, not enough has changed in official government policy to be confident that key figures have learnt much from their own mistakes. The new Scottish prison policy, due to be implemented in early 2024, still defends the possibility of a violent male being put in the female estate, in principle, as a way of 'supporting their gender identity' – as if the female prisoners around him were mere props in the service of his way of life. References to diverse gender identities, and to the expectation that women's services and spaces should be 'inclusive' of males who say that they too are women, are both now thoroughly embedded in many facets of Scottish policy-making. Whether the topic is changing rooms, hospital wards, schools, rape crisis centres, domestic violence shelters, data collection agencies, universities, media organisations, or sports teams, a reference to gender identity is in there, often at the expense of biological sex.

Perhaps, then, the final lesson for those in Westminster to learn from looking at Scotland – if, that is, they don't already know it from their own sorry experiments in the field – is how fiendishly hard it is to roll back gender identity ideology from one's national institutions, once it has got a firm grip there.

Chapter 31

Sisters across the water

Iseult White

———

On 21 March 2023, Leo Varadkar, Ireland's Taoiseach, had his Nicola Sturgeon moment. Staring down the barrel of a newspaper camera, he chose to fight another day. Like other world leaders he must have followed Nicola Sturgeon's fall from grace in the storm of negative publicity around her much-vaunted gender recognition reform.

The journalist Ben Scallan described how 'Barbie Kardashian, a violent biological male with a penis, an individual who threatened to rape, kill and torture a woman' is housed in a women's prison. He then asked the Taoiseach, 'In principle, do you believe that violent biological males should be put into women's prisons?' Varadkar answered, 'No I don't.'

He went on to suggest that after the Scottish situation, Ireland might need to change the law to ensure that women are protected. Out of the other side of his mouth he claimed that he personally had no knowledge of violent men being housed in women's prisons. It is hard not to be sceptical about his protestations. His party colleague, Regina Doherty, formerly Ireland's minister for Social Protection, had only months earlier forewarned the Scottish Parliament's Equalities, Human Rights and Civil Justice Committee about the issues of trans-identified males in women's prisons.

Doherty was invited to testify at a special sitting of the committee. Many of the submissions to the committee held Ireland up as a shining example of how gender self-ID is an uncontroversial good in society and claimed that Ireland had implemented its legislation effortlessly and without adverse consequences. It seemed like the committee wanted to rubber-stamp the Scottish Gender Recognition Reform Bill (GRR Bill) with an informal seal of Irish approval.

Those of us watching Doherty's testimony wondered if she was a stealth gender critical double agent. She explained to the committee that there were several prisoners housed in female prisons in Ireland who had identified as women after they had been arrested and charged, and highlighted that it is important to assess if a male has done this so that he can gain access to women in prison. Unfortunately for Nicola Sturgeon, the committee did not pay much heed to the concerns she raised. Some rather bizarre anomalies in her testimony may offer a clue as to why. She expounded sincerely that in Ireland 'there are seven recognised genders – there may even be nine'. Ireland, in fact, recognises only two genders: woman and man.

The Irish Gender Recognition Bill was enacted in 2015 in the halo afterglow of Ireland's referendum on marriage equality. We are the first country in the world to approve same-sex marriage by popular vote. As a nation we were jubilant. Leo Varadkar said the overwhelming YES vote made Ireland a 'beacon of light' for the rest of the world. Hillary Clinton tweeted 'Well done Ireland', and Joe Biden chimed in too. The country had been rocked by horrifying stories of clerical child sexual abuse, and the inhumane treatment of women and infants in mother and baby homes. The marriage referendum was Ireland's chance at a do-over, remodelling ourselves as a bright, shiny, progressive nation. We were finally out from under the shadow of the Catholic Church.

At the time of the marriage equality referendum, the Irish government was in the final stage of enacting a bill similar to the UK's 2004 Gender Recognition Act (GRA). The proposed legislation required two years' living in the newly acquired gender, along with a medical diagnosis of gender identity disorder. Three weeks after the marriage equality referendum, the government suddenly changed tack, and granted full self-ID with no requirement for medical diagnosis or waiting period. With these two pieces of legislation, Ireland leapfrogged into top position on the global leader board for human rights for gender and sexual minorities. The self-congratulation continues to this day.

The word on the street is that LGBTQI organisations had asked Transgender Equality Network Ireland (TENI) to take a back seat during the marriage equality referendum so as not to tax the public's consciousness with complex conundrums about gender and sexuality. In return they promised to quietly push for full self-ID once the marriage referendum passed. This is confirmed in a report by legal firm Dentons for IGLYO, the world's largest member-based organisation for LGBTQI young people. The report suggests that tying the campaign for gender recognition 'to more popular reform', such as same-sex marriage, provides 'a veil of protection', as gender identity 'is a more difficult issue to win public support for'. It goes on to say, 'The legislation went under the radar in Ireland because marriage equality was gaining the most focus . . . this was helpful according to the activists, because it meant that they were able to focus on persuading politicians that the change was necessary.'

In 2015 I fully supported the GRA. As a same-sex-attracted woman living in genderqueer communities, I had seen first-hand the distress that trans people suffer through pathologising medicalisation and gatekeeping. I hold my hand up and admit that I was naive. I had not anticipated that self-ID would be used to ride roughshod over the hard-earned rights of women. I imagined, like most reasonable people, that the government had done an impact assessment for all groups affected. I was very wrong about that. At no time before or since the passing of the GRA has the Irish government assessed the impact of the legislation on protections afforded to women under Irish equality law, nor have they assessed the impact on services offered to vulnerable women, such as victims of homelessness, rape or domestic violence, or incarcerated women. The lack of impact assessment allows the government to claim that there are no known adverse impacts on women. Lack of evidence of harm, however, is not evidence of lack of harm.

During the years after the passing of the GRA, I had started to question the collision of rights between women and trans people and take note of the vilification of any women who raised concerns. Then in November 2020, Colm O'Gorman, executive director of Amnesty Ireland, signed an open letter titled 'A Call for Irish Solidarity' published by TENI. It was co-signed by twenty-five Irish nongovernmental organisations (NGOs) including, lamentably, the National Women's Council of Ireland (NWCI). They called on 'media and politicians to no longer provide legitimate representation' for people who believe that sex is material in law and in life. It was a badly written, melodramatic screed, demanding censorship, and punishment for anyone who challenged their gender orthodoxy.

I quickly learned the letter was in response to a nascent, but tiny, gender critical voice that had emerged in Ireland. In the summer of 2020, groups such as Radicailín, Women's Space Ireland and The Countess had sprung up on Twitter. Radicailín are a women's liberation group, made up of Irish and migrant women who recognise that women's oppression is based on the material reality of biological sex. They came together to counter misogynistic narratives and practices and hold an abolitionist position on all forms of violence against women and girls. Women's Space Ireland is a website that documents in forensic detail the issues with the GRA. The Countess was established to focus attention on the resulting conflict of rights and child safeguarding issues.

After three days of watching Colm O'Gorman on Twitter patronisingly dismissing Irish women who challenged the letter, I felt compelled to speak up. I had no choice. I was raised to believe the right of freedom of expression is a fundamental safeguard in democracy. My family had learned that through bitter experience. My grandfather, Sean MacBride, founded Amnesty to protect the rights of political prisoners, people who exercised the human right of freedom of expression to challenge authoritarian governments. His concern for prisoners of conscience was founded directly on his own experiences as a political prisoner, and from fighting at the age of fourteen for the release of his mother, Maud Gonne, from an English prison.

On a Sunday evening I sat staring at the tweet I was about to post. My heart was racing. I knew there would be repercussions for speaking up. But I had no idea how life-changing a single tweet could be. I did not emerge unscathed. In the following weeks I was embattled and beleaguered. I received non-stop fake calls, silent hang-ups, and bizarre and unusual requests for psychotherapy from suspicious email accounts. My computer was hacked. The Gardaí clearly didn't know what to do with a middle-class feminist reporting a cybercrime down the local station, and were unable to offer any recourse. I packed up my freaked-out daughters and sent them to their gay dad's house while I rebuilt my Wi-Fi network and computers from the ground up.

The morning after my first tweet, I started fielding messages from a variety of Irish and UK women. The Irish women told me tales of online harassment and real-life doxing by trans activists. Friends and colleagues asked me if I was sure I wanted to get involved, suggesting I back down gracefully and go back to life as normal. I felt fearful. The psychotherapist in me was actively working to quell an unsettling paranoia. But once I started speaking up, I could not stop. My family fought too hard and lost too much in the struggle for a democratic Republic of Ireland. I live with the scars of that intergenerational trauma. If my family could face house raids, imprisonment, and execution by firing squad, without wanting to a be a drama queen about it, I could face down a tranche of tech-savvy and potentially unhinged trans activists. They took the fight to me. I was not for backing down.

Among the maelstrom of messages there was one thoughtful email that stood out. It came from Scotland and opened with the line 'Please forgive an email out of the blue'. Lucy Hunter Blackburn of Murray Blackburn Mackenzie (MBM) was politely, but quite determinedly, requesting that I make a submission to the Scottish Parliament's Justice Committee concerning the Hate Crime and Public Order (Scotland) Bill. And, by the way, could I please submit before the end of the week because 'the whole thing here is running to a very tight timetable'. She had seen my Twitter thread about the letter signed by Amnesty and urged me to send a copy of the letter, with an explanation about how government-funded NGOs were using the construct of hate to demand government and media muzzling of women who raised issues about gender identity. That was my first, but far from my last, engagement with my courageous Scottish sisters.

Other connections between Scotland and Ireland have flourished since. It has been a spontaneous, loosely coupled and creative cross-pollination. We have picked each other's brains, shared resources, and offered each other emotional support. In Ireland we were inspired by the courage of Johann Lamont, Joan McAlpine and Joanna Cherry, while simultaneously mourning the lack of established Irish female parliamentarians who are willing to take a stand publicly. In the summer of 2022, The Countess ran a successful campaign under the hashtag #TheseWordsBelongToUs to fight the removal of the word woman from employment legislation. The Irish government had put forward legislative amendments changing language from 'pregnant women' to 'pregnant people'. While not directly related to Johann Lamont's #sixwords campaign, which enshrined the right of female rape victims to same-sex forensic examiners, it would be impossible not to notice the influences.

It has never been lost on me that I had an uncomfortable reaction when I realised that my submission to the Scottish Parliament's Justice Committee involved me writing to a Conservative MSP, Adam Tomkins, the committee's convenor. It crystallised my awareness how deeply engrained it is in the Irish nationalist psyche to react negatively to the English. We see all Tories, no matter their actual nationality, as fundamentally Sassenach. I mention this because it helps me understand the disdain I see in Irish NGOs, politicians, media and the Dublin twitterati about any gains made by British women. I believe the Irish and Scottish governments and NGO complex share the same fundamental reactions to Westminster.

Just as there are loose connections and sharing of resources among Irish and Scottish women, the Irish NGOs look to the work of the Scottish NGOs. At a recent public meeting about the progress of a bill to ban conversion therapy, activists from a number of Irish NGOs told me how they respected the work being done by NGOs in Scotland. They complained about how slow the Irish government was to bring in promised legislation, while commending the progressive programme of the Scottish government. Our small nations build our identity around opposing the English. Both are working to a similar legislative agenda, one which will unassailably enshrine gender identity in law, placing the whim of men who would be women above the dignity, safety and needs of women and children.

Despite Leo Varadkar's forced public acknowledgement of the problems inherent in housing violent male rapists in women's prisons, the landscape for women in Ireland remains bleak. The programme for government is committed to amending Irish equality law to protect gender identity. This change will remove existing legal anomalies between sex and gender that currently await challenge and interpretation through the courts. The Irish government is determined to enact a hate crime bill that is more draconian than Scotland's. We expect that one day an Irish woman who will not wheesht will face the same fate as Christina Ellingsen and Tonje Gjevjon of Norway. Both were threatened with three years in prison under Norwegian hate speech law for pointing out that men cannot be women, girls, mothers or lesbians. Ultimately the investigations did not lead to prosecution, but we know that the process itself is the punishment. We watched what happened to Marion Millar in horror.

The Irish government is aware that they have a growing gender problem. A government report on a public consultation on Irish equality law reported that the issue of gender is 'contentious', with many respondents concerned about the erosion of sex-based equality protections. Gender is one of ten equality grounds in Irish law, yet 84 per cent of the submissions to the public consultation pertained to gender. Despite recommendations by a citizens' assembly, the government has decided not to amend the constitution to explicitly refer to gender equality for fears that a referendum 'could spark a nasty culture war'. This is political speak indicating that the government parties know there is growing public concern about the erosion of women's and children's rights. The clearest indication of all is that several months after Leo Varadkar claimed not to know anything about men in women's prisons, Kardashian, the 'violent biological male with a penis', was quietly moved to a men's prison. Irish politicians don't want to create opportunities for a Nicola Sturgeon-style conflagration.

Groups like Radicailín and The Countess continue to chip away at the gender edifice. A new group of young same-sex-attracted adults calling themselves Not All Gays is doing impressive advocacy work. Nonetheless, the government and the opposition parties remain staunchly supportive of gender self-ID. There are a small number of independent or retiring TDs and senators who have spoken up. But no Irish politician with an eye on their career is prepared to challenge the gender orthodoxy in public. The failure of legacy media to report the issues leaves the debate consigned to an ever more fractious and polarised war of words on social media, one that will be promptly shut down once the hate crime bill is enacted.

I will continue to speak up. I speak up for my daughters and my granddaughters. I speak up for women and children who should not be coerced into contact with abusive men through a wilful cultural amnesia about the role of safeguarding in preventing sexual assault. I speak up for the distressed young people who are sold a promise that gender medicalisation is the answer to their problems. They deserve a thoughtful and caring response to their distress rather than an immediate prescription for life-limiting medication and surgery. I speak up for young same-sex-attracted women who have a right to be told that their exclusive attraction to women is natural, beautiful, and to be celebrated. I speak up for the butch lesbian I love because I am determined to challenge an insidiously regressive cultural narrative that shames young women into becoming ersatz men instead of celebrating all women in our glorious diversity.

Just like my inspirational Scottish sisters, I have no plans to wheesht any day soon.

Chapter 32

A poet finds her voice again

Magi Gibson

―――――

I often look back over the past few years and wonder – how did it all get so crazily out of control? My husband, novelist Ian Macpherson, had written *The Book of Blaise* in 2015, essentially a comic take on our lives. How stress-free it all was! And how unsuspecting we were of what was coming next.

Over 30+ years I'd built up a solid reputation as a respected writer; I was a popular tutor travelling all over Scotland. I'd become the go-to person for creative writing projects with the most marginalised in society.

I'd started my own writing in an all-women group, and had created the highly popular Wild Women Writing Workshops. I'd been Reader in Residence with Glasgow Women's Library.

But when I spoke up in 2016 about the potential impacts on women's sex-based rights of proposed legislation on self-identification of gender; when I argued that it was necessary to protect the word 'woman' and associated language, both my career trajectory and my personal life changed drastically. Invites to read at events, to lead workshops, all but disappeared.

On occasions when I did venture out to a poetry reading, I never knew if I'd be welcomed or harassed. Especially hurtful was when a poet I'd taught, who'd previously publicly praised the impact of my workshops on her writing, pointedly shunned me.

An unevidenced complaint that my husband and I were transphobic and should be banned from events for making people feel 'unsafe' was sent to the Federation of Writers (Scotland). By a fellow writer, 'Anonymous'. On investigation the accusation was found to be groundless. The process was very distressing.

Spurious complaints were made to other organisations, such as my previous workplace, Glasgow Women's Library, who then asked me to remove from my social media that I'd ever been their Reader in Residence.

My six poetry collections mysteriously disappeared from a display of work by Scottish Makars in the Scottish Poetry Library (SPL). It was suggested that I should be uninvited from the launch event as I – a woman in my late sixties – would make the space 'unsafe'. My collection *Wild Women of a Certain Age* was marked online as available to buy in a major Glasgow bookshop, but when a visiting Irish poet could not find it on the shelves, she was met with obfuscation. Only because she was insistent and persistent was it reluctantly fetched from the back store.

My publisher was contacted and told he should cease working with me as I was such a hateful individual. There were nasty and completely untrue tweets online – sometimes from other writers – accusing me of bigotry and transphobia. Always unevidenced. There were sustained attempts to hack into my Twitter account. There was anonymous hate mail via my website. Emails which had been sent to me, and which contained sensitive information, were somehow deleted from my online email archive, and I had to get the police involved.

In 2020, I was co-opted onto the board of the SPL, which was in need of knowledgeable and experienced women members. When it became clear that the fury of poetry trans activists at my appointment might cause serious damage to the library's continued existence, I made the decision to voluntarily stand down.

The sense of social ostracisation, exacerbated by a lack of support from a writing community I'd done so much to develop over decades, was extremely damaging to my sense of self. Moreover, organisations and festivals were hardly likely to invite a writer whose presence might incur complaints, even protests, when they could simply invite someone else.

All this deeply affected my creativity, my ability to write, my sense of who I was, of what my life's work had been about. Unsurprisingly, I ended up in need of mental health intervention. The NHS stepped up quickly and, over the course of eighteen months and many, many hours of one-to-one therapy, I recovered.

And when, in 2022, the Scottish Book Trust sent out a new Code of Conduct for authors to sign to remain on the Live Literature Funding Register, I objected that its terms endangered freedom of speech, and by extension the health of literature in Scotland. The Scottish Book Trust denied these dangers, dangers also highlighted shortly after as a 'Culture of Censure' by author Chimamanda Ngozi Adichie in her Reith Lecture on Freedom of Speech.

As both my husband and I refused to sign the code, which was unnecessarily over-authoritarian and especially chilling for gender critical authors, we instantly lost access to grant-funding, making us even less attractive to event organisers.

Yet through all this, I've never backtracked or deleted one tweet or comment. Why? Because I've never said anything during these turbulent years I cannot fully stand by. And I'm not about to change now.

THE WOMEN WHO WOULDN'T WHEESHT

Even in the darkness and the depths we sang

We were the songbirds, so bright, so full of life.
We learned our tunes from our mothers' mothers,

our voices clear, carrying on swiftly shifting winds.
We were the sensitive sixth sense ones. The seventh

daughters of seventh daughters, in harmony
with the rhythms of the heartbeat of the earth,

darting about our small towns, our teeming cities,
our far-flung villages. We were the ones who

shivered at tiny changes in the atmosphere, who
quivered when storm clouds darkened the horizon

(while others laughed and played). We were the ones
who sang out early warnings when discord roiled the air,

who sang of hidden dangers, coming threats,
the need to be alert, to be prepared.

Some labelled us hysterics, hate-filled harridans.
Some tried to drown our voices with their noise.

And though we feared their power
(even as they claimed *they* were the powerless ones)

we sang our woman truth. On high cliff edges we sang,
in thickening mists of confusion, we sang. We sang

of unintended consequences, of risks of harm.
We refused their commands for silence, their furious

demands for acquiescence, their threats of punishment
and violence. We patiently unpicked the tangled wires

of their distortions. We deftly snipped through nets of lies
they tried to trap us with, endured their stinging pellets

of denial and derision. We sang our song of womanhood,
we sang, golden-voiced canaries, deep in the hearts

of our communities. We sang at the gates
of power, we took our song to Holyrood.

We rejected their insults of cow and bitch,
embraced it when they called us terf and witch.

For like Cassandra millennia before, we knew
it was our fate, even in the face of ridicule and hate

to warn of dangers others had unleashed
to tell our truths, to never haud our wheesht.

Magi Gibson

Chapter 33

Finding my sisterhood

Nina Welsch

———

As I write this, I am on the train back to Edinburgh, having just left the FiLiA 2023 conference in Glasgow. Over the three days I've attended, I've heard harrowing, unspeakably moving panel talks delivered by courageous women who have escaped the sex trade, I have attended workshops on the misogynistic as well as deeply racist escort industry in Canada, I have listened to speeches from campaigners across the globe fighting to end female genital mutilation (FGM), the caste system in India, honour killings.

I have reflected on my own traumatic experiences with men and been made to imagine and acknowledge injustice far worse than I have endured. I have left with a visceral sense of connection with every other woman there – all 1,500 of them – regardless of age, race, religion, nationality and sexuality. She could have been me, had my life, and I could have had hers, were it not for accident of birthplace and bloodline. I am both thankful and resentful at the terrible wonder of being born female.

This might sound sentimental, as though I'm trying to paint a saccharine, picturesque image of sisterhood. To be honest, I've always balked at the idea of all women as a sisterhood.

Individual women, yes, I feel sisterly affinity with and love them as family, but to extend that emotion to 51 per cent of Earth's population, including mean girls I went to high school with, is a bit much. I'm only human. The deep care for all suffering women across the globe that I felt at FiLiA, as profound as it was, was acknowledging the simple material reality of femaleness. The inescapability of our predicament that no deconstruction of language or utopian ideology can change.

As a baby millennial, I've been weaned on liberal feminism: a feminism that is not exclusively women-focused but for 'all genders'; a feminism that reframes prostitution and sexual exploitation of women as sex work – empowering provided it's 'consensual'. A feminism that, whether its crusaders realise this or not, believes that for all of us to be truly liberated, we have to be liberated from our bodies and biology. This utopian endeavour, while highly appealing at a glance, falls apart with very little scrutiny. Its dependence on truth denial is harmful to us all, including men, but it's especially disastrous for women.

Long before I could articulate my objections this way, I felt discomfited by liberal feminism's values, even while gaslighting myself into championing them as a proud intersectional feminist at university. The women's rights activism that always spoke to me is materialist: male violence, sexual abuse, exploitation and objectification of our bodies. Children's rights too, which I see as intrinsically linked to women's rights. Safety, dignity and equal opportunities, as opposed to the nebulous concept of empowerment. I've no desire to disclose personal experiences in detail, but certain traumatic life experiences mean I've never had the privilege of pretending males and females do not have massive physical differences and some crucial psychological ones too, and that, because of this, women need special protections. It's been a depressing and sobering discovery just how many progressive, feminist-identifying women fail to register the ability to go through life with little concern for these differences as a privilege.

The Gender Recognition Reform Bill (GRR Bill) in Scotland was as detached from the material reality of women and children's vulnerability to men as a piece of legislation could be. It was a bill that, as eloquently expressed and explained by countless critics, created massive safeguarding loopholes and placed absurd and censorious restrictions on speech. Most people waving it through might have had good intentions, but the road to hell is – as the saying goes – paved with exactly that.

For almost two years, I had been in hell, silently screaming at the treatment of a woman who dared to point out the consequences of gender identity overriding sex as a protected characteristic, namely Professor Kathleen Stock. Her views were so excruciatingly sensible, it near-disturbed me to see academics, writers and friends I'd respected, wilfully mis-understanding and denouncing her. Unable or unwilling to even consider the ideology they had blindly championed as 'the right side of history' might have some serious logical and practical shortcomings. A cult mindset. As I'd later describe to other young women like me: 'I felt like the last unbitten person in a zombie apocalypse film.'

I'm not alone as a young woman though. Far from it. But I didn't know that then. Ironically, what kept me silent for two years was the same thing that made me crack and officially join the fight against the GRR Bill: how familiar the intimidation tactics were. As a survivor, I recognised the gaslighting used to (try and) terrorise women into submission. The excusing of death and rape threats against cunts hags bitches witches TERFs. The idea that words were somehow worse than violence. It was all a regurgitation of: 'Look what you made me do', 'If she had just shut up . . .' When female survivors call out these parallels we are accused of weaponising our trauma, the #bekind translation of 'She's playing the victim.'

And then there were those who didn't openly jeer or threaten, but who chose, like the neighbour who hears scream-ing but doesn't want the hassle of getting involved, to turn out the light and ignore it. When they had the power to stop it.

A cowardice I saw personified in our former first minister, Nicola Sturgeon.

In October 2022, a significant protest was taking place outside of Holyrood against the GRR Bill. At that time, I was too afraid to show my face publicly, but I wanted to add my voice. I decided I'd publish an open letter to the first minister on Twitter. Writing is my forte more than improvised speech. I'd be stronger, more fearless on the page. And so, in stolen moments at my then-job, I furiously typed a 2,300-word plea for courage from the country's supposed leader.

It was too long and rushed. It was slightly eccentric in places. Now, I'd probably remove the throwaway reference to *2001: A Space Odyssey*, where I compared Sturgeon to HAL 9000. I spelled authoritarianism wrong. But the letter did what I hoped, which was struck a chord with many people in Scotland watching in incredulity at the conduct of the Scottish Government over this farcical piece of legislation. And connected me with other young women who felt they too, had to hide their faces and silence their voices. As the engagements hit the thousands, I cheekily – and with no expectations – tagged J.K. Rowling, Helen Joyce, Julie Bindel, Kathleen Stock and Maya Forstater, asking if they might want to read it. By the end of the night, everyone had shared it, along with Martina Navratilova.

Did Nicola Sturgeon respond? Of course she didn't, I knew she wouldn't. That wasn't the point. The letter wasn't for her, really. It was a personal exercise in courage that I hoped might embolden other young women to find ways of speaking out themselves, however they chose. To not be afraid to call out a naked emperor – or indeed, empress – when they see one.

Over the last year, reflecting at the time of writing this, I have had many moments where I've felt something cross over in me. Confidence and resilience blossoming. Sending that open letter into the Twitter stratosphere was the first major step. I write more fearlessly and unapologetically now. I speak out loud.

I can't understate how hard it is, though, to be treated like a thought criminal for having a materialist outlook on sex. Not by many but by enough. I still have moments, when seeing women's events getting censored or cancelled, or hearing about women getting abused or assaulted at protests, accompanied by the smug silence of high-profile progressive figures, that I'm struck with that dizzying sensation of trying to navigate a zombified, dystopian landscape. I have only lost one friend but it was ugly, and the breathtaking misogyny he espoused towards me left a scar. I have lost respect for and trust in a lot of people I formerly admired, and institutions I once felt so at home in – universities, most of all. Despair is a second-hand emotion to me.

Yet, as mad as it sounds, this last year has probably been the happiest of my life. There is unparalleled relief in living life with integrity and rising above those who try to stop you. I'm part of a young women's feminist network and we will pick up the mantle for our daughters. The main reward has been friendship, though. I thought speaking out would leave me alone in the world but the extreme opposite has happened. I feel like I've found the people – the women – I've been looking for all my life. Brave, principled, fiendishly intelligent and absolutely fucking hilarious. I loathe the circumstances that we met in but I'm inexpressibly thankful we did. My sisterhood.

Chapter 34

Looking to the future

Nicole Jones

———

'If your Nerve, deny you—
Go above your Nerve—'
Emily Dickinson

At the time of writing, I am preparing to graduate from Edinburgh University, which in usual circumstances would be an uncomplicated moment of pride. But we are not living in ordinary times. The week before my graduation, in November 2023, a heavy security presence was needed on Edinburgh University's campus for a screening of the documentary *Adult Human Female* to go ahead, after two previous attempts were sabotaged by protesters. I've attended all three screenings, and it's been a surreal experience to walk through screaming crowds, many of whom are my peers (and superiors) at the university.

In 2015, as a young woman with an interest in feminist theory, I started engaging with what would later come to be known as the gender debate. I could see that a conflict had emerged between sex-based rights and the politics of gender identity that no mainstream feminist organisations seemed willing to address. I began writing under my own name about the topic on my blog, and attending events, and in 2016 I attended a conference organised by Dr Julia Long called 'Thinking Differently: Feminists Questioning Gender Politics', which was one of the first of its kind.

Travelling to London from a small rural town in Cornwall, it was the first time that I had been around such a large group of women, all of whom shared my enthusiasm for political debate. My world opened up – it seemed like anything was possible. I met incredible women at this event that I'm still privileged to know and call friends. I also met Magdalen Berns, who is integral to this story. I still remember the sight of her, at the window in the Bloomsbury flat we had stayed in, smoking a cigarette, and immediately falling for her confidence and composure. I found friendship, solidarity and, ultimately, love.

In Magdalen's final year, 2015–16, she stood for Women's Liberation Officer, and was banned from multiple student groups, including the LGBT and feminist societies, for violations of the Edinburgh University Students' Association (EUSA) safe space policy, which she had pledged to bring in line with the Equality Act as part of her campaign. In 2014, the term 'whorephobia' had been added to this 'zero-tolerance' policy. It was in this stifling context that Magdalen's vocal criticism of Jean Urquhart's 2015 Prostitution Law Reform (Scotland) Bill, and prostitution generally as an exploitative industry, which proposed to 'decriminalise activities associated with the buying and selling of sexual services', led to her being branded a 'whorephobe' in student spaces. The campaign against Magdalen on the basis of her feminist beliefs resulted in an official reprimand on her academic record following a complaint from a trans-identified male student.

In 2018, I received an unconditional offer to study Fine Art at the University of Edinburgh. I was apprehensive. But despite her own experience, Magdalen was proud to graduate with her degree in physics, and encouraged me to take up the offer to study. Shortly after she graduated, she was diagnosed with brain cancer, but continued to set an example of bravery to follow. A month after my freshers' week, however, her prognosis became terminal. She passed away a year later.

In my first year at university, the Scottish Government launched its public consultation on the Gender Recognition Reform (Scotland) Bill (GRR Bill), and – just as Magdalen had experienced when trying to discuss the issue of prostitution – I didn't feel confident that the necessary room for debate had been made before student and staff groups began endorsing the bill.

Indeed, when events were organised – thanks to the efforts of Dr Shereen Benjamin and, from March 2022, Edinburgh Academics for Academic Freedom (EdAFAF) – that challenged the monopoly of gender identity theory on campus, these were condemned as 'transphobic' and aggressively protested by the likes of EUSA, University and College Union (UCU) Edinburgh, Pridesoc and Femsoc. I have attended most of the events promoting gender identity theory on campus, in which I took notes, asked questions, and engaged respectfully – I wish the groups opposing our views would extend the same courtesy.

My academic performance soon began to suffer as a result of my political engagement. I struggled to attend classes and interact with peers in the aftermath of violent protests. My trust in the integrity of my higher-education institution was further eroded with each cancelled academic event. When I wrote to the principal about my experience as a student witnessing these events, including an incident which led to an elected representative of the student union being charged with assault against an event attendee, I received the same brief copy-paste reply that was sent to others outside of the university. It included the following: 'I am very sorry to hear that you have been suffering with anxiety. We are here to help you and our counselling services can support you with your well-being.'

It felt as though, rather than addressing the hostile environment, I was expected instead to privately manage my response to the intimidation. The personal and the political had become hopelessly tangled up. I became withdrawn and guarded as a matter of self-preservation. I felt unable to fully explain to my tutors why I experienced such localised anxiety in academic settings. My art practice consists largely of portraiture, including portraits of women involved in the contemporary women's movement, some of whom feature in the documentary *Adult Human Female*. A sympathetic tutor reassured me, when I alluded to the context surrounding my work, that they were there to support my freedom of expression. But these had been the same words used in the press statements issued by the university after every failed attempt of the screening, and so they felt empty. While I trusted this particular individual, I didn't trust that I had the support of the institution, or that they had the support of their fellow academics, which was what would matter if push came to shove.

Women who are discriminated against on the basis of their gender critical beliefs face an impossible dilemma in which seeking support poses the risk of exposing them to further abuse. It can be easier – for your own sake and for the sake of everyone around you – to disappear quietly. But as the poet Jenny Lindsay wrote in her essay for *The Dark Horse*:

> *The lesson is not to avoid what happened to me by compromising your writing, second-guessing a hounding, nor to avoid writing about sex, gender and feminism in whatever way you want to. It is to write with*

integrity, to stand your ground, to hold your own, and to leave any clique or small forum that makes you feel you are being compromised.

My advice to young women is the same as Jenny's. The war on women is a war on competency. Academics, artists, writers, politicians, etc., who are doing their jobs by exploring ideas, are being pushed out of their professions and replaced by those who hold its values in contempt. As difficult as it may be in the circumstances, women need to continue to act according to our rights, and not as though these rights have already been lost. What we're saying isn't unlawful – it's not even unreasonable. Do not internalise the idea of yourself as being toxic. If you feel you are being compromised, trust that your creative and intellectual freedom will be nurtured elsewhere, and seek to either find or build that space.

I feel proud to have worked alongside many competent women to build these spaces. They have given me friendship and mentorship, something I hope to pass on to the next generation. In 2020, I formed XX, a network to support young women experiencing hostility for their feminist views. The false narrative of a generational divide is partly the product of a censorious climate on campus that denies women the freedom of enquiry, association, and expression needed for them to reach or voice their own conclusions. Despite escalating protests, however, growing numbers of young women are now engaging with feminist politics. I've met countless young women who possess a strength of courage and curiosity that makes me hopeful for the future of feminism.

I will graduate knowing that I have taken the portraits of groups and individuals that I believe make up an important part of women's history. Magdalen features among them. The camaraderie I found in the company of women over half a decade ago has only grown in the years following. With all the women I have met since. The women who wouldn't wheesht.

Afterword

This isn't over

Susan Dalgety and Lucy Hunter Blackburn

E arly in the creation of this book, a highly regarded man in the Scottish literary establishment looked us in the eye and said, 'You will have to tell both sides of the story, you know.' We glanced at each other and as one replied, 'No we won't. That would be a different book – a different take on history. We want to tell the story of the women who wouldn't wheesht, even when no one would listen to them.' He shrugged and changed the subject.

It struck us, not for the first time, that those advocating self-ID have never been expected to present both sides of the argument. The expectation that women with a different viewpoint should have to do so was at the heart of the story we wanted to tell.

Like many people at the centre of Scotland's civic life, he didn't understand why so many women had risked so much to speak out about the impact of gender identity ideology on women's rights, young people and freedom of expression.

He had made the same mistake as many others, including most elected politicians. By considering the Gender Recognition Reform (Scotland) Bill (GRR Bill) in isolation, he had failed to grasp what hundreds, then thousands, of women understood. 'Trans women are women' was no throwaway political slogan, but was now intended as a universal truth, to be taken literally, without exception.

The decades-long project of the Equality Network and other activists to embed the principle of self-declaration (self-ID) into language and policy, and then codify it into law, was on the verge of its ultimate success. Male prisoners were in women's jails. Schools accepted teenage girls when they said they were now boys. Women were othered as 'cervix-havers', or rebranded as 'cis-women', a sub-class of their sex category. Sex was now 'assigned at birth'. The passage of the GRR Bill was to be the state's final seal of approval for the notion that any man must be accepted, without question, as a woman, simply on his say-so. And that 'trans women' were to be treated by definition as more vulnerable, and their requirements given more political priority, compared to 'non-transgender women', in the language of Scottish Prison Service (SPS), whose policies embodied this world view.

What drove women across Scotland was the understanding that they share the experience of being born, growing up and ageing as female – no less and no more. Being a woman is a lifelong material reality, not a mode to slip into, like a costume. The fight for recognition of the equal social, economic and political worth of women, the female half of the population, across class, race and age, starts from there and nowhere else.

Many of the voices in this book are those of women prominent in their chosen careers, but they will be the first to recognise that they fought this battle alongside a legion of unnamed women whose grassroots campaigning exposed the reality of self-ID. Many were the second generation of second wave feminism, who read Germaine Greer rather than Judith

Butler, who had campaigned against section 28 (2A in Scotland) and for Scottish devolution. They included veterans of
peace camps and picket lines, women who took part in Pride
marches before they were fashionable, seasoned campaigners
for social and economic justice. Some had found their political
voice in the YES campaign for Scottish independence in 2014.
Others had never campaigned before.

As Jackie Mearns, a speaker at the 14 February 2018 meeting
in Edinburgh, said: 'If oppressed people – and women are a
class of oppressed people – if we can't define who we are, then
women are unable to determine for themselves and inform
their own struggle. And to change the very meaning of our
words and determine which words we can and cannot use to
describe ourselves and our bodies, and our experience of living
in these bodies under the patriarchy . . . is, in my opinion, a
profound assault on . . . human rights.'

Something magical happened in the five years from St
Valentine's Day 2018. Women from all backgrounds were
united by a single common denominator – their sex. One of
the world's most famous women, J.K. Rowling, pulled on a
campaign T-shirt and placed herself shoulder to shoulder with
women from Scotland's housing schemes. The constitutional
question that had so bitterly divided this small country was set
aside as women fought to protect in law, policy and language
that the material reality of sex matters.

At the same time, connections were also made across the
border, as part of the UK-wide campaign to resist the imposition
of self-ID. When the committee was told by two male witnesses
that there would be no problem in sport, and then refused
to see Sharron Davies MBE and Mara Yamauchi, these two
international medallists came to Edinburgh and held briefings
with the press, and those MSPs willing to meet them. Among
others not already mentioned in earlier chapters, women

from Sex Matters – Rebecca Bull, Naomi Cunningham, Maya Forstater, Helen Joyce and Anya Palmer – all spoke at meetings inside or rallies outside the Scottish Parliament, as did Karen Ingala-Smith, an expert in supporting survivors of male violence. Jane-Clare Jones' *Sex and The Census*, co-authored with Lisa Mackenzie, looked at how self-ID activists had sought to replace data on sex with data on self-declared gender identity in Scotland and in England and Wales. Women travelled across the UK to attend meetings and rallies. Scottish women contributed to crowdfunders for major court cases in England and women in other parts of the UK helped fund cases here. In the run-up to FiLiA holding its international feminist conference in Glasgow in October 2023, chief executive Lisa-Marie Taylor and her team worked with grassroots women's groups across the city to help them develop campaigning skills.

As the pandemic hit, women's voices become stronger and louder, and by the time the GRR Bill was introduced to the Scottish Parliament in March 2022, there was a sprawling, diverse, grassroots women's rights movement in place. The focus of much of the campaign was by necessity Edinburgh, the administrative and political heart of the country, but women were scattered across Scotland, united by social media. The movement's strength lay, not in its access to the corridors of power, nor its financial resources, but in its energy and determination. There was also a shared sense of betrayal that national women's groups, such as Engender – Scotland's 'feminist policy and advocacy' organisation – had abandoned women. In 2022–3 alone, Engender received £450,000 from the Scottish Government, an unimaginable sum for those outside the government tent.

As in the rest of the UK, Scotland's rape crisis movement had grown out of second wave feminism. The Glasgow Rape

Crisis Centre opened its doors in 1976, with the Edinburgh group established two years later. In August 2021, the male chief executive of the Edinburgh Rape Crisis Centre insisted in the *Guilty Feminist* podcast that women who wanted female-only spaces and counselling should address their 'unacceptable beliefs' (on self-ID) first. Mridul Wadhwa said:

> [I]f you bring unacceptable beliefs that are discriminatory in nature, we will begin to work with you on your journey of recovery from trauma. But please also expect to be challenged on your prejudices, because how can you heal from trauma and build a new relationship with your trauma . . . I think that's a very important message that I am often discussing with my colleagues that in various places. Because you know, to me, therapy is political, and it isn't always seen as that.

When one employee challenged ERCC's refusal to guarantee survivors a female-only service, she was subject to a nine-month disciplinary process. As we write, the judgment in Roz Adams' employment tribunal, where she argued constructive dismissal, is still to be decided. Her testimony, however, gave an insight into how the service had been captured. She described how a woman had approached ERCC for help, seeking reassurance that the support provided would be same sex. As Adams recounted, 'she said the tone of the conversation changed and a few days later she got an email saying you're not suitable for our service'. Multiple witnesses for the centre confirmed that as far they were concerned a person's gender identity supplanted their sex, and they expected users to assume the same.

It came as no surprise then that, when the Scottish Secretary of State, Alister Jack, lodged a Section 35 order in January 2023, effectively vetoing the GRR Bill, the government-funded national women's organisations lined up to condemn the move. A statement, issued by among others, Rape Crisis Scotland, Engender and Scottish Women's Aid, said:

> Trans people across Scotland have endured seven years of being dangerously misrepresented in public discourse. We are deeply concerned about the impact of misinformation around what this Bill actually does, and the perception that it creates that women's rights, and the rights of trans people are in conflict. They are not.

The central political figure of the five years from 2018 – both as a unifying force and as a source of deep division – was Nicola Sturgeon, the country's first female first minister. The argument over self-ID and its impact on women's rights was not unique to Scotland, but it played out in a distinctive way under her leadership.

She was anointed first minister in November 2014, after her mentor's resignation in the wake of the referendum defeat; but she was a very different political animal from Alex Salmond. As Magnus Linklater wrote in *The Times* in December 2023, her approach to government was far less collegiate than her predecessor's. He said, 'She insisted on absolute control from the centre and maintained party unity by ensuring critics were side-lined.'

Several contributors in this book who dealt with her in person are blunt about that experience. She moulded Scottish public life to her personality. Dissent was not allowed. Debate discouraged. Opposition dismissed. And the Scottish Parliament, hailed in 1999 as the potent symbol of the reawakening of Scotland's democracy nearly 300 years after the Act of Union, seemed cowed by her. Even after she lost her parliamentary majority in 2016, in the first election she fought as first minister, she and opposition politicians seemed to behave as if she had still commanded one.

One of Alex Salmond's special advisers, Alex Bell, also writing in *The Times* in December 2023, described Holyrood as easily controlled in 'action and message' for the eight years of Sturgeon's reign. 'Our parliament abjectly failed to hold the cabinet to account, or to nurture debates beyond the government agenda. We are a political monoculture, bereft of diversity of thought.'

And by the start of 2024, SNP MP Mhairi Black, who in the past had referred to women opposed to self-ID as 'Jeremy Hunts' in a piece of crude rhyming slang, was tempering her admiration of her former boss by agreeing that the cult of personality around Sturgeon 'always made me quite uncomfortable'.

In Nicola Sturgeon's first speech as first minister in November 2014, she asserted herself as the first among feminists, promising the women of Scotland she was on their side:

> *I hope that my election as first minister does indeed open the gate to greater opportunity for all women. I hope that it sends a strong, positive message to girls and young women, indeed all women, across our land – there should be no limit to your ambition for what you can achieve.*

Why she then went on to embrace self-ID, which reduces being a woman to nothing more than a feeling, thinking it would endear her to women whose lives were shaped, for good or ill, inevitably, or unfairly, by their sex, will forever remain a mystery. Perhaps political editor Mandy Rhodes, who arguably knew her better than any other journalist, and even than many of her backbench MSPs and MPs, came closest to understanding Sturgeon's motivation when she describes in this book a conversation she had with the then first minister, where Sturgeon said, 'Young people are really distressed about it. And that's all there is to it. We need to do something about that.' Then made it clear the subject was closed.

Yet she stubbornly refused to listen to anyone, even deeply concerned parents, who pointed out that gender identity ideology was destroying their children's lives, so determined was she to portray Scotland under her leadership as a modern progressive nation, where the Progress Pride flag flew proudly alongside the Saltire. And for a politician who was failing in her two major commitments – closing the attainment gap between children from the richest and the poorest households, and securing a second independence referendum – self-ID may have seemed an easy win. Having risen to the highest office under the patronage of Alex Salmond, she had no base of her own in the SNP or the wider electorate. One way to secure a new generation of Sturgeonites was to prove her progressive credentials by championing this issue. For a performative politician obsessed by style and messaging, wrapping herself in a rainbow flag proved irresistible.

But by early 2023, and in the wake of the Adam Graham/ Isla Bryson crisis, her stubborn adherence to self-ID weakened her so much that she had little social or political capital left to deal with other major issues, such as the police investigation into the SNP's finances and her failing independence strategy. And so, on 15 February 2023, almost exactly five years to the day after the first public meeting organised in Edinburgh by women to oppose gender reform, she resigned.

Women campaigners found that diversity of thought on gender identity was not encouraged in other spaces either. Scottish Labour – which had prided itself on its 50–50 approach to the selection of women for the first Holyrood elections in 1999 when forty-eight women MSPs were elected (37.8 per cent) – ignored the concerns both of Jenny Marra, from the mainstream of the party, and veteran left-winger Elaine Smith. Its MSPs were whipped to vote for the bill, even after its key amendments fell. The two women who voted against it, Claire Baker and Carol Mochan, were forced to resign their shadow spokesperson positions. Under the leadership of Alex Cole-Hamilton MSP, the Scottish Liberal Democrats gave their unquestioning support to Sturgeon's self-ID project, despite consistent evidence from successive opinion polls that their voters were among the most opposed.

On this issue, it stands out that that pro-self-ID activists in other parties, who were more usually to be found condemning Sturgeon's record in government and her iron grip on Scottish politics, repeated government lines with increasing enthusiasm, happy to be part of Team Wheesht. If, as some politicians and commentators on the centre and left became fond of saying, Scotland was riven by a 'toxic culture war', it was not one of the women's making. And not one in which those politicians showed any practical interest in trying to broker peace, despite repeated attempts by women to engage with them on the issue.

The leadership of Scotland's trade union movement, too, dismissed grassroots female voices. Women are the majority of the membership of Unison Scotland, the country's largest trade union, yet a 2023 briefing paper continued to say there was no conflict between trans rights and those of women, arguing that gender recognition reform did not affect access to single-sex spaces or facilities.

At the same time, those who pushed self-ID should perhaps reflect on how the very existence of the 2004 Gender Recognition Act (GRA) has become controversial in a way it was not in the first decade after it became law. What many women had been inclined to accept as a legal fiction intended for – they assumed – only a very few post-operative transsexuals, has come to be seen as the beginning of fundamental changes in language, policy and law. Changes that end with the complete denial of sex as a material reality, and a Scottish court deciding in 2023 that pregnancy and maternity were nothing to do with being a woman.

Warnings made in 2004 have come to pass, most notably in sport, where the controversy over male athletes who identify as women competing with female ones at professional and amateur levels continues to rage.

It is not to political Scotland's credit, nor its media's, that it was the sight of a double rapist in a cheap blond wig and crotch-hugging leggings that finally forced the government to deal with the truth: that 'trans women' are not women. It was the women's rights campaign that had, over several years, done the work to challenge the campaign slogan and expose its risks.

So, when the downfall of the bill came, it was not as the result of diligent scrutiny at Holyrood. Women campaigners had been ringing the alarm bell about a potential clash with the Equality Act from 2018 and before. All the clues were there that the Scottish Government knew it was playing at the edges of its powers – from the bill's convoluted format to the absurd reluctance of ministers and officials to answer questions on this subject. After all, the Scottish Parliament had agreed in 2004 that a complex interaction with reserved matters meant that the original GRA was best handled in Westminster.

Not even the strong intervention from the Equality and Human Rights Commission (EHRC) at the start of 2022, nor a court judgment at the end of the bill process, was sufficient to make the majority of MSPs, from all parties, notice that this bill had much wider implications than Scottish Government spin asserted.

And women campaigners had no expectation that Westminster would have the appetite to step in, until the moment, only hours after the bill passed, when the Secretary of State for Scotland, Alister Jack, announced he was considering invoking the 1998 Scotland Act to block it. Up to that point women had focused all their efforts on trying to make the Scottish Parliament work.

While Jack deserves credit for having the political courage to use a Section 35 order to act, a source close to Kemi Badenoch, the UK government's minister for Equalities, acknowledged to us that it was grassroots campaigning in Scotland that laid the ground:

> *Seeing how fiercely ordinary women were fighting to be heard – putting everything on the line – made such a difference. Their work challenged – in detail – what the Scottish Government was saying and led to intense media coverage. It helped change things in Whitehall – made people more receptive to the questions Kemi [Badenoch] was asking. Had officials really understood the ramifications of what was proposed, and were we doing enough? Were we truly upholding our role as envisaged in the Scotland Act if we sat back? Fundamentally this wouldn't have happened without women's campaigning. They changed the politics.*

In the twenty-fifth anniversary year of the Scottish Parliament, what does the story of the GRR Bill tell us about the state of politics in Scotland?

It is clear that the episode is a poor reflection on the quality of policy development and law-making here, as this book sets out in detail.

This story shows how easy Scotland's political class and civil society finds it to exclude voices they do not want to hear. Our contributors provide many examples. One group not represented here, but also ignored by the Scottish Parliament and Government, is the partners and families of those who transition in adult life.

Politicians in all parties can be quick to assert that Scotland has superior democratic values to Westminster. Yet this is a political community that took over twenty years and six elections to find space for any women of colour in its Parliament. In these pages, one of those two women, Conservative MSP Pam Gosal, alongside Black radical lesbian writer Claire Heuchan, hold up a challenging mirror to all engaged in Scotland's political life, including women resisting self-ID, from their different perspectives.

It was also striking how often women campaigners identified that self-ID was a class issue. Those women most reliant on the public and voluntary sectors, and those more likely to find themselves homeless or in the criminal justice system, were at the sharp end. The country that prides itself on the tradition of Red Clydeside should have been more willing to hear their voices. The casual ageism of Twitter also seeped into mainstream politics. It was an SNP MP who said that the campaign against self-ID was 'fuelled by fifty-something Karens'.

Where were the men? When those in Scottish public life did speak up, it was more often to tell women challenging self-ID to be quiet. Those who stayed silent justified it by asserting it was not their battle: 'it's the women's fight'. In the early stages, in particular, Scotland's most prominent male voices largely either ignored, or did not understand, how much was at stake.

There were men who supported the campaigning, writing letters, meeting their MSPs, contributing to crowdfunders, and attending meetings and rallies, though to be at these events was to experience being in a predominantly female crowd. Striking images of these gatherings were taken by male photographers who lent their time and skills to observe and record. Andy Wightman was among those who lost his political career.

LGB campaigner Malcolm Clark used his voice to great effect. Some male journalists used their platforms to challenge the government's lines, and male MSPs in several parties were among those who signed parliamentary motions, put down questions and laid amendments to bills. There was private moral and practical support from male family and friends. But this was a movement where the energy and direction came unambiguously from women, and which put women on the frontline to speak. And a political establishment led by women froze them out.

Scotland's grassroots campaign for women's rights is not over. Women, with no access to government funding and excluded from the private discussions where decisions are made, proved that a courageous grassroots campaign still has the power to change the world. Along the way, they exposed the damage that a small cadre of powerful, but mediocre politicians and civil servants, and their ambitious allies in civil society, can do to a small country. The Scottish Nationalist Party and its coalition partners the Scottish Greens may remain in power until May 2026, but they no longer set the political agenda. The GRR Bill, while still on file, seems unlikely to become law. First Minister Humza Yousaf may have urged UK Labour to work with him to amend the blocked legislation. 'We're willing to sit down with the Labour Party – frankly now, let alone if they end up forming the next UK government – to see if they have concerns about the bill,' he said in December 2023, but his words were nothing more than performative. Labour ruled out self-ID months earlier when shadow women and equalities secretary Annaliese Dodds said a medical diagnosis of gender dysphoria upholds 'confidence in the system'.

While Scotland's GRR Bill and self-ID are left indefinitely on the shelf, there are still many battles to fight. Self-ID remains embedded in schools, the NHS and the care system. Keen advocates LGBT Youth Scotland and the Time for Inclusive Education (TIE) charity have significant influence in individual schools and with ministers and civil servants. It is woven through public policy. Despite the public outcry that greeted Adam Graham/Isla Bryson's incarceration in a women's prison, a recent policy review by the SPS decided that some men who declare that they identify as women may still be allowed to serve their sentence in a women's jail, if they are deemed not to present an 'unacceptable risk'.

Scottish government proposals for a bill on conversion therapy, which threaten a ban on talking therapy for children and young people struggling with gender dysphoria, were put out for consultation at the start of 2024. And there has been no review of Scotland's Gender Identity Development Services (GIDS), provided by the Sandyford Clinic in Glasgow, similar to the Cass Review in England and Wales, which led to the closure of the Tavistock Clinic in London. Just as this goes book goes to press, the final Cass Review report has been published and the hate crime legislation passed in 2021 come into effect, and the Scottish Government seems as determined as ever to ignore public concern about both.

Women's rights activists are also turning their attention to other issues affecting their sex, particularly where politicians at Holyrood are potentially susceptible to well-funded lobbies who present their ideas as progressive. This includes challenging another mantra, that 'sex work is work', and arguing against the liberalisation of surrogacy, as proposed by the Law Commissions in Scotland, and England and Wales. On these and other topics they are strengthening their connections with women further afield, not least in Wales, where some familiar dynamics are playing out.

When courage called, women from across Scotland responded. Women, many who had never been politically active before, hung ribbons, organised petitions, lobbied their MSPs and councillors, set up street stalls, hosted public meetings, challenged public officials and used social media to great effect. They won a battle, but it is not over yet because, above all, this is a story of a failure of Scottish politics as devolution approached its quarter-century.

The democratic renewal promised by the establishment of the Scottish Parliament was largely absent as a small but influential group of activists dominated the political process, from civil servants to the first minister, and across the parties.

Women's rights, at the heart of the campaign to secure devolution, were sacrificed in the name of 'progress'. Parliament failed to properly scrutinise poorly conceived legislation. Public opinion was ignored.

The campaign to resist self-ID exposed how distant Holyrood had become from its electors; disdainful, even, of those outside its bubble – the very charge laid against Westminster by those who had campaigned for devolution.

Grassroots campaigning is a vital part of the democratic process, but it should never be the whole story. If the Parliament, and its executive, are to rediscover their democratic purpose and values, they must, once again, learn to make politics work for all the people they represent. And they can start by listening.

A timeline of key events:
February 2018 to February 2023

Date	Event
14 February 2018	WPUK holds first meeting in Edinburgh on plans for gender recognition reform in Scotland
1 March 2018	First Scottish Government consultation on gender recognition reform closes
3 July–22 October 2018	UK government consultation on gender recognition reform
6 December 2018	Professor Rosa Freeman and Susan Smith, For Women Scotland (FWS), give evidence on Census (Amendment) (Scotland) Bill to committee considering the bill
28 February 2019	Joan McAlpine MSP publishes Twitter thread on sex, gender and the census

22 May 2019	Joan McAlpine MSP hosts first meeting in Scottish Parliament questioning self-ID, with guest speaker Meghan Murphy discussing experience in Canada
	Murphy also speaks at FWS meeting in Glasgow on 24 May
5 June 2019	Meeting on women's rights at the University of Edinburgh
20 June 2019	Shirley-Anne Somerville MSP announces delay to gender recognition reform and further consultation
October/November 2019	Launch of SNP Women's Pledge and Labour Women's Declaration
12 December 2019	General election: Conservatives re-elected
17 December 2019– 17 March 2020	Second Scottish consultation on gender recognition reform
19 December 2019	J.K. Rowling's first tweet
7 March 2020	FWS rally at Scottish Parliament
1 April 2020	Announcement that work on the Gender Recognition Reform (Scotland) Bill (GRR Bill) will be delayed due to Covid-19
23 April 2020	Hate Crime and Public Order (Scotland) Bill introduced
22 September 2020	Liz Truss announces that UK government has dropped self-ID

10 December 2020	The Forensic Medical Services (Victims of Sexual Offences) (Scotland) Bill Stage 3 debate
	Johann Lamont moves #sixwords amendment
27 January 2021	Nicola Sturgeon's 'broom cupboard' video
1 February 2021	Joanna Cherry MP sacked from Justice role at Westminster
11 March 2021	Hate Crime and Public Order (Scotland) Bill passes Stage 3
23 March 2021	FWS loses first judicial review in Outer House of Court of Session
26 March 2021	Alex Salmond sets up Alba
April 2021–October 2021	Marion Millar case ongoing
6 May 2021	Scottish Parliament elections – SNP returned as largest party with 64 seats
12 August 2021	Scottish Government issues revised guidance on transgender young people in school
20 August 2021	SNP and Scottish Greens form coalition government
7 September 2021	Programme for Government promises GRR Bill 'within a year'
26 January 2022	Equality and Human Rights Commission (EHRC) writes to Scottish Government calling for more detailed consideration of bill

17 February 2022	Fair Play For Women lose judicial review on census in Outer House of Court of Session
18 February 2022	FWS win appeal in first judicial review in Inner House of Court of Session
24 February 2022	Fair Play For Women lose appeal in judicial review on census in Inner House of Court of Session
3 March 2022	GRR (Scotland) Bill introduced: Shona Robison makes a statement in the Scottish Parliament
10 March 2022	Interim Cass Review on gender identity services for children and young people in England, commissioned by UK government, published
May–June 2022	Equalities, Human Rights and Civil Justice (EHRCJ) Committee holds public evidence sessions on the bill
6 October 2022	FWS Scottish Women's Rally at Holyrood
	Bill committee publishes its report on GRR (Scotland) Bill
27 October 2022	GRR (Scotland) Bill: Stage 1 debate. Bill passes
	Ash Regan MSP resigns her ministerial post

15 and 22 November 2022	Bill committee considers amendments to the bill
29 November 2022	Letter from Reem Alsalem, UN Special Rapporteur on VAWG (violence against women and girls) to UK government
13 December 2022	FWS lose second judicial review in Outer House of Court of Session
	Establishment of Beira's Place sexual violence support service for women, by women, announced
20 and 21 December 2022	Stage 3: Scottish Parliament considers amendments to the bill
21 December 2022	FWS rally at Holyrood
22 December 2022	Stage 3: Final debate and vote on GRR (Scotland) Bill
	UK government's Secretary of State for Scotland Alister Jack MP announces possible use of Section 35 of the Scotland Act 1998 to block the bill from becoming law
17 January 2023	Alister Jack MP makes Section 35 order
24 January 2023	Adam Graham / Isla Bryson found guilty of double rape and sent to Cornton Vale women's prison
26 January 2023	Adam Graham moved from Cornton Vale

2 February 2023	Nicola Sturgeon refuses to say whether Adam Graham is a man or a woman
9 February 2023	FWS No Males in Female Jails demonstration outside the Scottish Parliament
15 February 2023	Nicola Sturgeon resigns

Acknowledgements

We are above all indebted to all the authors in this book. It has been an extraordinary privilege to be trusted with your contributions, and we are grateful too for your readiness to work to such tight deadlines and your patience in dealing with all our queries. We know that revisiting the experiences recounted here has sometimes been hard. We are grateful also to the interviewees in Chapter 28: Carolyn Brown, Esther and Chris, Ritchie Herron, and Maggie Mellon.

Many other women have helped us. Of those happy to be named, for various forms of assistance, we would like to thank: Kate Alexander, Alessandra Asteriti, Trina Budge, Marion Calder, Jenny Dickson, Shonagh Dillon, Alison Dowling, Holly (who knows who she is), Isabelle Kerr MBE, E. M. McKay, M. Kelly, Jenny Lupton, Julie McKee, Adele McVay, Jackie Mearns, Ali Muirhead, Maggie Murphy, Jenny Reilly, Caroline Robinson, Susan Sinclair, Julie Smith, Maren Smith, Helen Stewart, Leya Terra, Victoria Thompson, Tess White MSP and Nic Williams.

The voices of Magdalen Berns and Mary Gordon are missed.

We want to acknowledge the courage of all the women who were willing to meet the committee to discuss their experience as survivors of male violence and abuse, but who were denied that opportunity. We are grateful to all those women who attended committee hearings on the Gender Recognition Reform (Scotland) Bill, to make it clear to MSPs that women were watching: your reactions as newcomers to watching the Parliament at work were one of the inspirations for this book. Every woman who went to a meeting or a demonstration, stood up inside her political party or trade union, wrote a letter, tied a ribbon, paid into a crowdfunder, met their MSP, responded to a consultation, stood on a street stall, created the campaign without which there would be no book. And those men who provided practical help to a campaign led by women deserve acknowledgment, too.

We are immensely grateful to Rory Scarfe at Blair Partners and Andreas Campomar at Little, Brown for their crucial role in helping to make this book a reality. At the beginning of this process, finding a publisher was a daunting task. The support and encouragement they have brought to the project made all the difference. We are also indebted to Holly Blood, our project editor; Penny Isaac, our copy editor; Sophie Ellis for her striking cover and everyone else at Little, Brown who made our idea a material reality. A very special thanks to Rebecca Salt for her wisdom and guidance. And much thanks to the several people who gave their time and professional expertise to review sections of the manuscript. Their insights improved the book immensely.

Finally, not for the first time in recent years, our partners and children are owed thanks for their patient, practical support. Lucy would also like to thank her mother, Pat Hunter, for leaving copies of Spare Rib lying around when she was a teenager, and her sister Liz, for doing so much over the period the book was being written to look after Mum. Susan hopes her granddaughters Iona and Sofia will read this book one day, and be inspired by the voices within.

Profits from this book will go to organisations helping those women and girls elsewhere in the world who are currently among some of most silenced. We would like to be able to name these organisations without causing them problems. The reason we cannot do so is in this book. We look forward to the day we feel we can.

Contributors

Susan Dalgety
A *Scotsman* columnist, author, grandmother. Travels when she can. Adviser to the McConnell International Foundation. Her first book *The Spirit of Malawi* was published in 2021 by Luath Press.

Lucy Hunter Blackburn
Freelance researcher, part of Murray Blackburn Mackenzie policy analysis collective. Interested in how public policy is made and presented; during these years completed a doctorate examining rhetoric and reality in student funding. Recovering former senior civil servant in the Scottish Government.

@Dis_critic
She can be found on X. She is a part-time student and proud mum.

Lisa Mackenzie
An independent policy analyst and co-founder of policy analysis collective Murray Blackburn Mackenzie. She previously worked as a civil servant in the UK government.

Kath Murray
A criminologist, with a background in policing research, and a policy analyst with Murray Blackburn Mackenzie.

Sarah Pedersen
Professor of Media and Communication at Robert Gordon University. Her research focuses on women's use of the media for political purposes.

Susan Smith
A co-director of For Women Scotland, the largest grassroots women's rights organisation in Scotland and a director of Beira's Place, Edinburgh Women's Sexual Assault Support Service. She has served on the boards and committees of various children's charities and organisations and works as a financial analyst.

Joan McAlpine
Columnist, works in heritage, previously MSP for South Scotland from 2011-2016. She has been editor of the *Sunday Times Scotland* and deputy editor of the *Herald*. Always a mother, daughter, sister.

Ann Henderson
She has worked in the rail industry, in community development, in the Scottish Parliament, and in a senior role at the STUC. She is a committed trade unionist, activist in the women's movement, and has played a role in the Abortion Rights campaign, formerly the National, and Scottish, Abortion Campaign, since the 1970s. Served as Women's National Commissioner for Scotland 2008–2010, and as University of Edinburgh Rector 2018–2021.

Sally Wainwright

A longstanding lesbian feminist with a background in political activism. A serial creator of women's and lesbian spaces and co-editor of *Women's Rights, Gender Wrongs: The global impact of gender-identity ideology* (published by Women's Declaration International).

Jenny Lindsay

A poet, performer, essayist and events programmer who was the winner of the inaugural John Byrne Award for Critical Thinking in 2020. Her debut non-fiction book *Hounded: Women, Harms & The Gender Wars* is forthcoming from Polity Books.

Claire L. Heuchan

An author, award-winning essayist, and Black radical feminist who blogged as Sister Outrider. She is founder and chair of Labrys Lit, an international lesbian book group run via Zoom. In January 2023 Claire was appointed FiLiA's Director of Anti-Racism and Lesbian Community Engagement.

Rhona Hotchkiss

She has been a registered nurse and advisor to Scottish Government and spent the last decade of her working life as a governor with the Scottish Prison Service. A trustee of LGB Alliance, chair of North Ayrshire Women's Aid and a director of Beira's Place, she is enjoying the resurgence of women's activism in Scotland.

J.K. Rowling

The author of the globally beloved Harry Potter book series, as well as three stand-alone novels for adults and children, and the Strike crime fiction series written under the pen name Robert Galbraith. She is also a campaigner and philanthropist, having supported a wide range of humanitarian causes with particular emphasis on women and children over the last 25 years through her charitable trust Volant, her international children's charity Lumos, and the founding of Beira's Place, a new sexual violence support service for women in her home city of Edinburgh.

Gillian Philip

She was a successful author and copywriter of Young Adult and middle grade fiction before being fired in June 2020 after a social media mobbing. She lives in the north of Scotland with many animals, and now works in the haulage industry.

Johann Lamont

Former teacher. Former Labour and Cooperative MSP. Still feminist.

Joanna Cherry KC MP

She has been the SNP MP for Edinburgh Southwest since May 2015. She is Chair of the UK Parliament's Joint Committee on Human Rights. She was the SNP's spokesperson on justice and home affairs from 2015 to 2021

Shereen Benjamin

A senior lecturer in primary education at the University of Edinburgh. She has a long history of trade union activism, and of campaigning for peace, justice and human rights.

Fiona McAnena

She grew up in Northern Ireland, read natural sciences at the University of Cambridge and has a rowing blue. She worked in brand management and marketing for thirty years, before joining Fair Play For Women in January 2019, moving recently to work at Sex Matters.

Pam Gosal MBE MSP
A Scottish Conservative MSP for the West Scotland region. She previously sat on the Equalities, Human Rights and Civil Justice Committee that was responsible for scrutinising the Gender Recognition Reform (Scotland) Bill.

Rachael Hamilton MSP
MSP for Ettrick, Roxburgh and Berwickshire from 2017. Shadow Cabinet Secretary for Rural Affairs and Islands in the Scottish Parliament. Previously an agronomist.

Anonymous
I was born in the seventies. I'm a mum of girls, a healthcare professional and like many women, a survivor of male violence.

Ms M
A Scottish woman who has been let down by the criminal justice system, the Scottish Government and the funded women's organisations who should have supported her. She has found support from her sisters within Scotland's grass-roots feminist movement. She will not wheesht.

Lorna Irvine
Woman. Former creative arts teacher. Who by the mixed blessing of ageing, succeeded in swerving, in a joyful working life, earlier stirrings of identity politics and gender ideology. But who, as the mother of a fine young woman, entered and will remain in this fray so that we, she, and all our daughters, may enjoy the hard-won rights for which our foremothers fought.

Ash Regan MSP
A Member of the Scottish Parliament for Edinburgh Eastern since 2016, leader of the Alba Party in Holyrood and former minister for Community Safety.

@Obsolesence
An engineer who lives in Edinburgh.

Elaine Miller
A Fellow of the Chartered Society of Physiotherapy, award-winning stand-up comedian, middle-aged woman who has no regrets.

Caroline McAllister
A woman who wouldn't wheesht because to do so would've betrayed women who were denied a voice.

Mandy Rhodes
A campaigning journalist for almost 40 years and the editor of Scotland's award-winning political magazine, *Holyrood*, for more than twenty years. She has an unrivalled insight into Scotland's body politic and an enviable contacts book.

Kathleen Stock
A contributing writer at Unherd, a co-director of The Lesbian Project, and the author of *Material Girls: Why Reality Matters for Feminism* (Little, Brown 2021). Until October 2021, she was a professor of philosophy at University of Sussex in the UK.

Iseult White
An author, psychotherapist, and computer scientist. She fights the chilling effect on our lives when governments criminalise speech.

Magi Gibson

Poet and writer, has held three Scottish Arts Council Fellowships, one Royal Literary Fund Fellowship, has been writer in residence with the Gallery of Modern Art, Glasgow and Glasgow Women's Library and was the first Makar of Stirling in 500 years. She has had six poetry collections published and in 2023 edited and published *Unbridled*, a landmark poetry anthology featuring women who will not be silenced.

Nina Welsch

A writer and campaigner. Her work can be found in 'The Critic' and her Substack 'It's My Room'.

Nicole Jones

An artist based in Edinburgh. Her work, primarily in portraiture, focuses on documenting the contemporary women's movement.

Resources

In the course of our research we used many sources of information, mostly online. This list is not exhaustive, but does show the websites and publications we found most useful. We hope our readers will too.

Adult Human Female
https://www.youtube.com/watch?v=94HFMSm-JBo&t=4s

Audacious Women
https://audaciouswomen.scot

The Cass Review
https://cass.independent-review.uk

Edinburgh Academics for Academic Freedom
https://blogs.ed.ac.uk/edinburghafaf/2022/03/09/
hello-world/

Engender
https://www.engender.org.uk

Equalities and Human Rights Commission
https://www.equalityhumanrights.com

The Equality Network
https://www.equality-network.org

Fair Play For Women
https://fairplayforwomen.com

For Women Scotland
https://forwomen.scot

Frontline Feminists Scotland
https://www.frontlinefeministsscotland.com

Gender is not a spectrum (Rebecca Reilly-Cooper)
https://aeon.co/essays/
the-idea-that-gender-is-a-spectrum-is-a-new-gender-prison

Holyrood magazine
https://www.holyrood.com

Keep Prisons Single Sex
https://kpssinfo.org

Labour Women's Declaration
https://labourwomensdeclaration.org.uk

Legislation.gov
https://www.legislation.gov.uk

LGB Alliance
https://lgballiance.org.uk

LGBT Youth Scotland
https://www.lgbtyouth.org.uk

Losing sight of women's rights: the unregulated introduction of gender self-identification as a case study of policy capture in Scotland (Lucy Hunter Blackburn, Lisa Mackenzie and Kath Murray)
https://www.euppublishing.com/doi/full/10.3366/scot. 2019. 0284

Mumsnet
https://www.mumsnet.com

Murray Blackburn Mackenzie
https://murrayblackburnmackenzie.org

The Political Erasure of Sex (Jane Clare Jones and Lisa Mackenzie)
https://history.web.ox.ac.uk/files/political-erasure-sexfull-reportpdf

Rape Crisis Scotland
https://www.rapecrisisscotland.org.uk

Scottish Feminist Network
https://scottishfeministnetwork.co.uk

Scottish National Party
https://www.snp.org/

Scottish Trans
https://www.scottishtrans.org

Sex Matters
https://sex-matters.org

Sole Sisters
https://womenvotingwithourfeet.wordpress.com

SOS Scotland
https://sosscotland.com

Stonewall Scotland
https://www.stonewallscotland.org.uk/node/192

The Scottish Government
https://www.gov.scot

The Scottish Parliament
https://www.parliament.scot

Scottish Women
https://scottish-women.com

Suddenly Trans blog
http://www.suddenlytrans.co.uk

TIE
https://tie.scot

Transgender Trend
https://www.transgendertrend.com

Women and Girls in Scotland
Archived at: https://web.archive.org/
web/20230403050936/https:/wgscotland.org.uk/about/

Women's Rights Network
https://www.womensrights.network

Women Speak Scotland
https://womenspeakscotland.com

Woman's Place UK
https://womansplaceuk.org

X/Twitter
https://twitter.com/home

Burns, C. (2018) *Trans Britain*. Unbound.

Joyce, H. (2021) *Trans: When Ideology Meets Reality*. Oneworld Publications.

Stock, Kathleen. (2021) *Material Girls: Why reality matters for Feminism*. Fleet.

Glossary

AFAF – Academics for Academic Freedom

AIDS – Acquired Immune Deficiency Syndrome

BAME – Black, Asian and Minority Ethnic

BLOGS – Edinburgh University Lesbian and Gay Society

CAMHS – Child and Adolescent Mental Health Services

EBSWA – Evidence-Based Social Work Alliance

ECHR – European Convention on Human Rights

EdAFAF – Edinburgh Academics for Academic Freedom

EHRC – Equality and Human Rights Commission

EUSA – Edinburgh University Students' Association

FGM – female genital mutilation

FM – first minister

FOI – Freedom of Information

FWS – For Women Scotland

GIDS – Gender Identity Development Services

GRA – Gender Recognition Act

GRC – Gender Recognition Certificate

GRPBA – Gender Representation on Public Boards Act

GRR Bill – Gender Recognition Reform (Scotland) Bill

HIS – Health Improvement Scotland

HIV – Human Immunodeficiency Virus

LGB – Lesbian, Gay and Bisexual

LGBT – Lesbian, Gay, Bisexual and Transgender

LGBTQI – Lesbian, Gay, Bisexual, Transgender, Queer/ Questioning and Intersex

LGBTQ+ – Lesbian, Gay, Bisexual, Transgender, Queer/ Questioning and more

LGBTYS – LGBT Youth Scotland

LWD – Labour Women's Declaration

MBM – Murray Blackburn Mackenzie

MSPs – members of the Scottish Parliament

MVAWG – male violence against women and girls

NEC – National Executive Committee

NGOs – nongovernmental organisations

NHS – National Health Service

NRS – National Records of Scotland

NWCI – National Women's Council of Ireland

ONS – Office for National Statistics

self-ID – self-identification/self-declaration

SNP – Scottish National Party

SOS Scotland – Safeguarding Our Schools Scotland

SPICe – Scottish Parliament Information Service

SPL – Scottish Poetry Library

SPN – Staff Pride Network (University of Edinburgh)

SPS – Scottish Prison Service

STA – Scottish Trans Alliance

STUC – Scottish Trades Union Congress

TENI – Transgender Equality Network Ireland

TERFs – term often used as an insult against women, derived from 'trans-exclusionary radical feminists'

TIE – Time for Inclusive Education

UCU – University and College Union

WDI – Women's Declaration International

WGS – Women and Girls in Scotland

WPATH – World Professional Association for Transgender Health

WPUK – Woman's Place UK

WSiS – Women's Spaces in Scotland